Asia in
Soviet Global Strategy

Asia in Soviet Global Strategy

edited by
**Ray S. Cline,
James Arnold Miller,
and Roger E. Kanet**

LONDON AND NEW YORK

The views expressed in these chapters are those of the authors and not necessarily those of the participating institutions. This report on Asia and Soviet global strategy was prepared by the U.S. Global Strategy Council.

Chairman: Dr. Ray S. Cline
President: Dr. Michael A. Daniels
Executive Director: Dr. James Arnold Miller

Project editor: Marjorie W. Cline
Assistant to the project editor: Christopher S. Carver

First publishing 1987 by Westview Press, Inc.

Published 2018 by Routledge
52 Vanderbilt Avenue, New York, NY 10017
2 Park Square, Milton Park, Abingdon, Oxon OX14 4RN

Routledge is an imprint of the Taylor & Francis Group, an informa business

Copyright © 1987 by Taylor & Francis

All rights reserved. No part of this book may be reprinted or reproduced or utilised in any form or by any electronic, mechanical, or other means, now known or hereafter invented, including photocopying and recording, or in any information storage or retrieval system, without permission in writing from the publishers.

Notice:
Product or corporate names may be trademarks or registered trademarks, and are used only for identification and explanation without intent to infringe.

Library of Congress Cataloging-in-Publication Data
Asia in Soviet global strategy/edited by Ray S. Cline, James
Arnold Miller, Roger E. Kanet.
    p.   cm.—(Westview special studies on the Soviet Union and
Eastern Europe)
    Includes index.
    ISBN 0-8133-7481-2
    1. Soviet Union—National security.   2. Soviet Union—Military
relations—Asia.   3. Soviet Union—Military relations—Pacific Area.
4. Asia—Military relations—Soviet Union.   5. Pacific Area—
Military relations—Soviet Union.   6. Communist strategy.
I. Cline, Ray S.   II. Miller, James A. (James Arnold)   III. Kanet,
Roger E., 1936-   .   IV. Series.
UA770.S6616   1987
355'.335'47—dc19   87-22477
                                                                                CIP

ISBN 13: 978-0-367-01426-1 (hbk)

ISBN 13: 978-0-367-16413-3 (pbk)

CONTENTS

Preface   vii

1   Introduction to Basic Soviet Geopolitics, Ray S. Cline   1

2   Nature of Soviet Global Strategy, William Schneider, Jr.   11

3   Awakening of Soviet Interest in Asia, James R. Blaker   17

4   Soviet Collective Security Pacts, Osamu Miyoshi   23

5   Growth of Soviet Military Power in Asia, John T. Berbrich   33

6   Buildup of Soviet Naval Power in Asia, S.R. Foley, Jr.   41

7   Increase of Soviet Economic Relations in Asia, Takehiro Togo   45

8   Soviet Military Strategy in East Asia, Kenichi Kitamura   51

9   Political Aspect of Soviet Strategy in East Asia, Hayao Shimizu   61

vi

10	**Basic Soviet Strategy Toward Japan,** Osamu Miyoshi	71
11	**Japan's Defense of Home Islands and Waters,** Ray S. Cline and James Arnold Miller	77
12	**Soviet Strategic Objectives on the Korean Peninsula,** Kim Yu-Nam	85
13	**Development of Strategy in Sino-Soviet Relations,** Shinkichi Eto	95
14	**Soviet Strategic Concerns in Southeast Asia,** William R. Kintner	101
15	**Assessment of Soviet Priorities in Australia, New Zealand, and Oceania,** Paul Dibb	113
16	**Growing Soviet Interest in South Asia,** Stephen P. Cohen	131
17	**Soviet Inroads to Persian Gulf States,** Roger E. Kanet and Sumit Ganguly	143
18	**Outlook for the Pacific Basin**	

Part I: The American View,
Richard M. Fairbanks, III 155

Part II: The Japanese View,
Comments by Members of the Japanese Diet:

Soichiro Ito	159
Eiichi Nakao	163
Eiichi Nagasue	166
Masao Horie	170
Kazuo Tanikawa	171

Contributors 173

Index 177

PREFACE

The Soviet Union has an integrated global strategy aimed at eventual domination of all the peoples and nations of the world. Since Lenin proclaimed a dictatorship of the proletariat and established a socialist state, Soviet strategy has not deviated from its goals. They are two-fold: first, strengthening Marxist-Leninist one-party dictatorships wherever possible, and second, undermining the stability of other types of society with a view of ultimately controlling them.

In Asia at the present time, the Soviet Union attempts to gain influence in a stalwart grouping of ten nations that are closely associated with the United States -- the USSR's major target of hostility because it is the most powerful capitalist state and the coalition leader of countries with representative governments and comparatively open societies. At the same time, the Soviet Union struggles to build political, economic, and military instruments of national power in the five Asian states controlled by communist regimes. Pursuing this dual track of maximizing Soviet power is the essence of Moscow's strategy in Asia.

In this volume, Asian and American scholars describe the USSR's basic approach to the many states in Asia and the Pacific Basin, including nations stretching from Japan to Australia. It is our belief that, taken together, the papers which we have selected for inclusion comprise a useful backdrop for assessing current Soviet interests and activities in Asia. They develop basic Soviet doctrine as it is applied to Asia and recall how the Kremlin leaders trumpet notions of "peace" as Soviet military forces continue their buildup.

The scholars presented papers for this volume under the auspices of the Soviet Global Strategy Project, an undertaking of 1983-1985 by Interaction Systems Incorporated of McLean, Virginia, and the World Strategy Network, which is now associated with the United States Global Strategy Council of Washington, D.C. The Asian aspect of the project included the holding of three viii

conferences in Tokyo, on March 14, May 29 and 30, and November 20 and 21, 1984. These conferences were co-sponsored by the Tokyo-based World Strategy Council of Japan.

The planning, research, and presentation of the papers were funded by the Office of Policy Support, Office of the U.S. Secretary of Defense. The papers do not, however, necessarily reflect the policies and positions of the Department of Defense.

This project has been continued as an important activity of the United States Global Strategy Council, a recently organized non-profit research institution dedicated to studying strategic issues as they apply not only to the United States but also to the Free World.

It is with great pride that we present, on behalf of all the parties associated with this effort, this volume of the final report of the Soviet Global Strategy Project.

Ray S. Cline
James Arnold Miller
Roger E. Kanet

Chapter 1

INTRODUCTION TO BASIC SOVIET GEOPOLITICS

Ray S. Cline

Soviet strategic thinking reflects a consistent code of international conduct designed to advance the interests of the Soviet Union worldwide. Specific international moves depend upon the assessment made by the Communist Party of the Soviet Union (CPSU) at the time of the evolving world situation called the "correlation of forces." All political, economic, military, psychological, and moral energies linked within a nation's actions enter into this calculation of relative strengths and weaknesses. The final conclusion in Moscow about these subjects determines what the Soviet Union will do in any particular case.

The military factor inevitably is a major element in making this kind of calculation. The Soviet Union has always given special emphasis to using military force, when the correlation of forces favors such use, to push forward, occupy, control, or at least dominate countries outside the USSR's borders.

Political leaders in the USSR from Lenin to Mikhail Gorbachev have articulated and tried to follow -- not always with complete success -- coordinated, coherent, long-range plans to advance Soviet national goals in the world arena. They have uniformly viewed international relations as a scene of irreconcilable zero-sum conflict between their totally government controlled socio-economic system and the pluralist states with economies based on private capitalist enterprise. They explicitly say they seek to expand Soviet influence until such time as all nations are Soviet-style socialist states governed under the principles of Leninist doctrine or at least weak client states dominated by the military and economic power of the Soviet Union.

At levels below total military warfare, the conflict with capitalist states goes on inexorably, in the Soviet view. This state of short-of-war geopolitical struggle is traditionally referred to by Soviet ideologues as "peaceful coexistence," a concept devised by Lenin and Stalin. This concept offers "peace" instead of "war" to non-communist nations until the final collision between communist and pluralist societies becomes inevitable or until capitalism fades away in economic decay, political revolution, or geopolitical surrender.

Soviet authoritative statements for the past seven decades have carefully restricted the meaning of peaceful coexistence to fit this classical Marxist-Leninist theory of social conflict. Lenin stated in 1919 the world view of the generation of Bolshevik rulers who had seized power in 1917:

> We are living not merely in a state, but in a system of states and the existence of the Soviet Republic side by side with imperialist states for a long time is unthinkable. One or the other must triumph in the end. And before that end supervenes, a series of frightful collisions between the Soviet Union and the bourgeois states will be inevitable.[1]

The clearest theoretical pronouncement of the Soviet world view came from Stalin, on the eve of the 19th Congress of the CPSU, shortly before his death in March 1953:

> The disintegration of a single universal world market must be considered the most important economic consequence of the Second World War . . . .
>
> This circumstance determined the further aggravation of the general crisis in the world capitalist system . . . . It follows . . . that the sphere of exploitation of world resources by the major capitalist countries (USA, Britain, France) will not expand but contract, that the world market conditions will deteriorate for these countries and that the number of enterprises operating at less than capacity will multiply in these countries. It is this essentially which constitutes the aggravation of the general crisis in the world capitalist system due to disintegration of the world market . . . .[2]

Brezhnev reaffirmed the Soviet adherence to Lenin's conception of the inevitability of the clash between capitalism and communism in his report to the 24th Congress of the CPSU, March 30, 1971:

> In recognition of its international duty, the CPSU will continue to pursue a line in international affairs which promotes the further activation of the world anti-imperialist struggle and strengthens the combat unity of all its participants. The total triumph of Socialism the world over is inevitable. And for this triumph, for the happiness of the working people, we will fight, unsparing of our strength.[3]

There are many statements by Soviet officials on this central idea. A particularly direct formulation was made December 21, 1972, when Brezhnev explained:

The CPSU always held and still holds that the class struggle between the two systems -- the capitalist and the socialist -- in the economic, political and also, of course, in the ideological spheres will continue. It cannot be otherwise, because the world outlook and class aims of socialism and capitalism are opposed and irreconcilable. But we will strive to shift this historically inevitable struggle onto a path which will not threaten wars, dangerous conflicts, an unrestricted arms race.[4]

Since the mid-1950s, under Khrushchev's leadership, military assistance and economic aid on a massive scale to countries which the USSR hoped could be won away from economic and political relations with the United States or West European "capitalist" powers have poured out in a mighty flood. While not so generous or ebullient as Khrushchev, Brezhnev continued to use arms and money to gain influence over peripheral areas and deny them to the West. Particularly in the Mideast, Soviet policy has brought a major change in the patterns of stability in this region and jeopardized the access of the United States, West Europe, and Japan to the oil which is vital to their industries.

Since Brezhnev's time, Soviet leaders have moved beyond the "peaceful coexistence" terminology and explained over and over that they are following a policy of "detente," a term that literally means, in French, a stopping or release of tension. Employed in 1971 and 1972, detente -- in the language of U.S.-USSR diplomatic relations -- originally meant a relaxation of tension which would permit Moscow and Washington to enter into a dialogue or a negotiating process that might reduce confrontations and dangers of war.

As time went on, the Nixon administration claimed such enormous benefits from personal diplomacy in Moscow and Peking that the term came to carry with it a connotation of peace and international harmony favorable to U.S. security. By 1975, many people in the United States had come to think that detente meant:

o a guarantee of peace, in the sense of avoidance of all kinds of war;

o stability in the international relations of governments and in social order;

o coordination and friendly cooperation between great powers, including the United States and the USSR; and o   tolerance of differing social systems, even as different as those in the United States and the USSR.

Unfortunately, this widespread U.S. understanding of detente conflicts with the USSR's basic interpretation. From the very beginning, Soviet doctrinal literature, in explaining to the cadres and officialdom as well as to the people of the Soviet Union what peaceful coexistence meant, took a quite different line.

As perceived in Moscow, it was a device to undermine the resolution of pluralist societies to pay the price of deterrence and containment for their own security. In effect, Brezhnev's detente was essentially the Leninist-Stalinist "peaceful coexistence."

The USSR puts a heavy emphasis on "peace" -- even as the United States does -- but Soviet leaders obviously mean by it only the avoidance of total nuclear war between the United States and the Soviet Union. This meaning was especially clear during the many years of U.S. weapons superiority. Soviet leaders did not want international issues settled in a contest in which the USSR was the weaker nation.

Soviet leaders have consistently espoused the right to fight a "just war" of "national liberation," that is, to assist a country to shake off external domination, as they would say they were doing in Vietnam. Beyond that, they have made painfully clear, especially for the benefit of their own citizenry, that peaceful coexistence, in addition to avoiding total war, means:

o   unrelenting class struggle;

o   worldwide support of the forces of revolution by the ballot if possible and by violence if necessary;

o   diplomatic moves to bring about political realignments in non-communist areas so as to restrict the parts of the world open to U.S. influence, trade, investment, and procurement of economic raw materials; and

o   permanent antipathy between the communist and capitalist social systems, the latter of which, according to Soviet doctrine, is still supposed to perish in the ultimate and long-heralded "world crisis of capitalism."

The heady impression Moscow gained from watching the removal of a U.S. president and the diffusion of leadership in the United States provided the strategic underpinning of the entire peaceful coexistence or detente policy of the 1970s.

In August 1973, after the touted summits held in Moscow and Washington, Moscow's official newspaper, _Pravda,_ unequivocally stated that the worldwide struggle between communism and capitalism would continue:

> Peaceful coexistence does not mean the end of the struggle of the two-world social system. The struggle between the proletariat and the bourgeoisie, between world socialism and imperialism, will be waged right up to the complete and final victory of communism on a world scale.[5]

This extraordinary frankness on the part of Soviet leaders seems somehow to have escaped most U.S. observers, who would like to think that peaceful coexistence is the same as their concept of detente and will certainly lead to "a generation of peace," as President Nixon promised.

On April 18, 1975, an authoritative *Pravda* editorial and a parallel *Izvestia* statement of the same day hailed detente as having brought about a "significant breakthrough" in "relations between the USSR and the U.S." Even the pre-eminent old Bolshevik theoretician, Mikhail Suslov, who gave the Lenin anniversary address at the CPSU's April 16 Plenum, suggested that capitalism was actually weakening.

The following year, at the 25th Communist Party Congress on February 24, Brezhnev, in high spirits about Soviet success in Angola and Vietnam, called capitalism "a society without a future" while stressing "mankind's progress" in socialism. He said:

> We make no secret of the fact that we see detente as the way to create more favorable conditions for peaceful socialist and Communist construction . . . . the international situation of the Soviet Union has never been more solid. We have entered the fourth decade of peace. Socialism's positions have grown stronger. Detente has become the leading trend.[6]

Soviet strategy has paid off very well in Asia. Five Asian states -- Mongolia, North Korea, Vietnam, Laos, and Kampuchea (Cambodia) -- are controlled by communist regimes strongly influenced by their Soviet supporters. Most importantly of all, the China mainland fell into communist hands in 1949.

On January 6, 1961, when Khrushchev reported on the findings of 81 Marxist-Leninist parties at a conference held in Moscow two months earlier, he praised their success.

> Almost 1.5 billion people have wrenched themselves out of colonial slavery . . . . New remarkable pages are opening in the history of mankind . . . Asia, this ancient cradle of civilization is one of the most important centers of revolutionary struggle against imperialism.[7]

This meeting was the high point of Marxist-Leninist international cooperation, occurring before the definitive Sino-Soviet split. In the Asia-Pacific region, a very loose grouping of diverse peoples, seldom thought of as a strategic unit, still remain free of Soviet domination. They are Japan, South Korea, China/Taiwan, the Philippines, Indonesia, Singapore, Malaysia, Thailand, Australia, and New Zealand. These ten nations constitute a significant body of international power associated with the United States rather than the Soviet Union.

Fortunately for the United States and non-communist states in Asia there is a deep fracture line between the very similar Russian and Chinese models of communist dictatorship. This fracture is not necessarily permanent, and a substantial reconciliation between Moscow and Peking appears to be taking place. Great-power rivalry has driven the two largest totalitarian states wide apart, only to veer back toward cooperation in the past two or three years.

It remains to be seen to what extent the bitterness between Stalin and Mao and their immediate successors can be overcome by common interests in the future, as it was overcome during the Korean and Vietnam wars.

China, the "Middle Kingdom" that shares its borders with eleven nations on the Eurasian continent, is unique among large states today, an enigmatic mix of Soviet-style ideology and political structure combined with many of the characteristics of a classical Chinese military dictatorship.

o   The People's Republic of China (PRC) is the largest of all nations in population, more than one billion people strong, and the third largest in territory.

o   China is especially baffling because it is not really yet a nation in the European sense but more an ancient culture based on a common written language giving a sense of identity to a numerous people.

o   While the literate 25 percent of the country read and write the same calligraphic language, dozens of mutually unintelligible spoken dialects separate regions and even local communities.

o   Religions are diverse and eclectic, with all of them treated somewhat negatively and usually with hostility by the Marxist-Leninist-Maoist oriented bureaucracy. Whether such a unique state, the largest in population ever to exist in the world, can hold together under any form of rule is a question only history will decide.

o   As long as the government in Peking remains a Soviet-style one-party dictatorship, however, it will be an adversary of the United States, potentially a hostile modern totalitarian nation completely controlling one quarter of the people in the world.

o   If it becomes strong enough to bargain effectively with Moscow, as it is beginning to do, Peking will try to strike a deal that leaves it the overlord of East Asia and an equal or superior rival of communist states everywhere.

o   Even now the PRC appears to be harking back to the foreign policy of Chou En-lai, which was based on building influence in the so-called Third World, mostly south of the Equator, to mobilize resistance to both Soviet and American programs there.

o   The PRC for the immediate future will be basically an adversary of both superpowers though at times possibly cooperative with one or the other for a limited purpose.

o   This ambivalent status must be faced by American and allied planners realistically, not over-simplified and not wished away by sentimental hopes for a friendly China on the mainland, a strategic ally, which the Peking regime adamantly denies it ever could be.

In theory, it was the Soviet view that peaceful coexistence did not apply to relations between communist countries. After the long estrangement with the People's Republic of China (PRC), however, Chinese officials suggested that relations between the PRC and the USSR should be an exception. Brezhnev's response was an acceptance. As recorded in Pravda on March 21, 1972, he said:

> I can tell you, comrades, that we not only proclaim our readiness, but translate it into the language of specific and constructive proposals on nonaggression, in the settlement of border issues and on improving relations on a mutually advantageous basis.

This exchange was at a time when the PRC had already decided to stand between the two superpowers, playing them off against each other while trying to solve its own difficult problems of economic growth and of orderly political succession to the elderly, failing Mao Zedong. Because this temporizing phase fitted in with the Nixon detente period of U.S. foreign policy, things have until now gone smoothly for Peking-Washington relations.

The Sino-Soviet rift, visible to all since 1960, is based on cultural antagonisms and historic border conflicts. At a crucial point in Sino-Soviet relations, the Soviet Communist Party expressed deep annoyance with the conciliatory approach the Chinese had been using in describing socialist and bourgeois ideologies. In a letter to <u>Pravda</u> on July 14, 1963, the Soviet Communist Party fumed, "It is permissible to ask the Chinese comrades: what means do they propose for the destruction of imperialism?" They have reduced "peaceful coexistence to an empty phrase" and ignored "the need for a resolute struggle . . . to the benefit of the imperialists."

Since then, the Soviet Union has concentrated on a strategy to surround the PRC mainland by dominating North Korea and Vietnam, both now Soviet proxy states. Mongolia is virtually Soviet territory. Laos and Cambodia are Vietnamese pawns dependent on Hanoi and Moscow for survival. The huge buildup of Soviet naval and air power worldwide cements these relations, while the PRC, at the present time, remains too weak to strike back or significantly alter the power balance.

There is a mountain of accumulated controversy to be climbed before Sino-Soviet relations can be fully harmonized. How the PRC will fare in the rest of the century is problematic, even under the leadership of Deng Xiaoping, whose "four modernizations" program has eased some of the economic problems in the countryside but has added complications to life in the cities. As long as the Soviet Union remains superior to the PRC in military strength, it will undoubtedly continue to hold the PRC hostage to its strategic goals.

On March 11, 1985, Gorbachev, in his first speech to the Communist Party after becoming General Secretary, appeared to be softening the Soviet view toward China. In terms of his desire to enhance the influence of socialism in world affairs, he said, "We would like to make a cardinal improvement of relations with the People's Republic of China, and believe that, given reciprocity, this is quite feasible."[8]

In planning for strategic operations should there be a shift in the correlation of forces, however, China is a prospective target. It is the center of the Soviet Union's Far Eastern Theater, one of the ten geographical theaters of the world designated for planned military operations. The nations surrounding the mainland also targeted in this theater are South Korea, Japan, the Philippines, Mongolia, Burma, Indochina, (excluding Indonesia), northern and central Siberia, as well as Alaska.

Moscow is continuing to build up military power in the Pacific and East Asia and counts on its massive strength, operating from bases in the Sea of Japan and the Sea of Okhotsk -- in its own territorial waters -- and from Cam Ranh Bay in Vietnam, to attract non-communist East Asian states to the Soviet flag.

The objective in tipping the "correlation of forces" in this region in this direction is to drive a wedge between the United States and its East Asian friends, making them doubt the reliability of American security guarantees, and gradually drawing Japan, the PRC, and the rest into more cooperative relations with the USSR. If this geopolitical maneuver is successful, the worldwide "correlation of forces" will undoubtedly shift against the United States and toward the Soviet Union.

NOTES

1. Lenin, V.I., <u>Selected Works</u> (New York: International Publishers, 1943), Vol. VIII, p. 282.

2. Kohler, Foy D., Mose L. Harvey, <u>et. al.</u> <u>Soviet Strategy for the Seventies: From the Cold War to Peaceful Coexistence</u> (Coral Gables, Florida: Center for Advanced International Studies, 1973), p. 28.

3. Kohler, Foy D., <u>Soviet "Peaceful Coexistence" is Not Western Detente</u>, Hearings of the Subcommittee for Europe, House Committee on Foreign Affairs, May 15, 1974, p. 24.

4. <u>Pravda</u>, December 22, 1972.

5. <u>Ibid.</u>, August 22, 1973.

6. <u>TASS</u>, February 24, 1976; excerpts of speech in <u>New York Times</u>, February 25, 1976, p. 14.

7. "Khrushchev Report on Moscow Conference," Moscow, <u>Soviet Home Service</u>, January 19, 1961, as published in <u>Kommunist</u>, No. 1, January 1961.

8. <u>TASS</u>, March 11, 1985; excerpts of speech in <u>Washington Post</u>, March 12, 1985.

Chapter 2

NATURE OF SOVIET GLOBAL STRATEGY

William Schneider, Jr.

Soviet strategy is driven not only by its Marxist-Leninist dogma which is at the core of the strategy, but also as much by the attitudes of some of the nineteenth century geopoliticians such as Mackinder, Mahan, and others. These factors combine to produce what has been a particularly belligerent and remarkably consistent global strategy over the past several decades. Soviet strategy in Asia also should not be considered in isolation from Soviet worldwide strategy. It is very much a piece of Soviet global strategy.

First, it seems fair to describe Soviet strategy as rather consistent worldwide. This strategy appears to be somewhat of an amalgam of the old Bolshevik notion of securing socialism in one country with some of the nineteenth century Russian notions of secure borders, warm water ports, and other matters of that kind.

The second dimension is the primacy of military power in support of Soviet global strategy. This can be measured in a number of ways that are quite obvious, such as the gross investment by the Soviet leaders in the military establishment, the dominant role of the Soviet military in the decision-making process, and even the domination of the Soviet state by what one can call the military culture which tends to reinforce the primacy of military power in Soviet strategy.

The third dimension which stands in fairly sharp contrast to the practice of free nations is the emphasis on autarky or virtual complete independence from dependence upon allies. This is not to say that the Soviet Union does not have states with which it works, but the relationship is not between free allies in a voluntary association for common ends. It is, rather, an association between a subject state and a master state where the association is neither voluntary nor in the mutual interest of all parties. Under Soviet strategy, Soviet alliances, so-called, serve only the interests of the Soviet Union.

The fourth dimension of Soviet strategy tends to be the opportunistic character of its operations. Despite the fact that Soviet global strategy has a strong element of consistency, the manner in which the Soviet leaders attempt to implement this strategy tends to be based not on some mechanistic or clockwork basis but rather on an opportunistic basis. When opportunities arise that facilitate or contribute to the achievement of the USSR's ends, Soviet leaders seek to exploit them.

It must be noted that over the last three or four years the Soviet Union has suffered very substantial reversals in carrying out its strategic policies. In some ways, this is a dangerous series of reversals because these failures have come at the time of the zenith of Soviet military power.

The most conspicuous failure is the failure of the Soviet policy of detente. The failure is especially spectacular because it is virtually complete, in the sense that there is no important area of the world where detente is an operating and influential policy. No doubt this is true because detente is now essentially viewed by Western democracies as a manipulative diplomatic scheme to conceal Soviet ambitions to establish the USSR as a preeminent military power, i.e., to undermine the ability of the Western powers to resist Soviet initiatives in the Third World.

Detente, on the other hand, was highly valued by the Soviet Union in the 1970s because it became the most effective means for Moscow to obtain Western military technology while at the same time discouraging allied defense revitalization. Fortunately in some sense for the Free World, the internal contradictions in Soviet foreign policy -- i.e., its opportunistic tendencies to try to seek worldwide advantage -- did not jibe with Western perceptions of how the Soviet Union should behave under a policy of detente. This ultimately resulted in the rejection of detente as a basis for doing business with the Soviet Union.

Looking at Soviet global strategy on a regional basis, a number of characteristics are worth noting. The region which has received the most attention in the past thirty-five or so years has been West Europe. There is no doubt that in the postwar period Soviet strategy could be described properly as Eurocentric. In part this is because this area is where the Soviet military deployments remained after World War II, and because Moscow was preoccupied with seeking compliant regimes in Europe upon the close of that war. The policy initiatives that the Soviet Union made in the late-1940s and even in the early 1950s to try to extend the dominion that it enjoyed after World War II were frustrated by the U.S. policy of containment which essentially denied Moscow easy opportunity to capitalize on Soviet military power in East Europe between 1950 and the present.

Nevertheless, the concern about Europe was very prominent in Soviet strategy. Since the objectives of Soviet strategy toward

West Europe have been largely frustrated, Moscow has focused on preventing the North Atlantic Treaty Organization (NATO) from taking concerted action, and it has tried to block any NATO efforts that might interfere with Soviet aims outside of West Europe. In general, the Soviet Union has been able to dissuade by a variety of means the West European allies from taking any active role in influencing events outside of the NATO area or the area of West Europe. But even here Moscow's strategy has not been completely successful because the French and British governments have retained their historic interests in various regions of the world and at times have seen fit to deploy forces to support those interests.

The Soviet leaders have failed manifestly in suppressing the ability of the European allies to act in a concerted manner. One needs only to look at the scale of effort that the Soviet Union made to suppress the Intermediate-Range Nuclear Force (INF) deployment in West Europe to appreciate how abjectly it failed in West Europe.

This is not to say, however, that the USSR does not have resources and that it has not gained something out of its efforts in West Europe. But despite a maximum Soviet propaganda effort, and maximum effort to influence not only the public policy choices of various West European governments but also the very composition of those governments, as with regard to the recent West German election, the Soviet leaders have failed dramatically in West Europe to implement some of their most cherished goals. These frustrated goals are directly related to the failure of their detente policy.

A second area of the world which certainly has been a recent preoccupation of the Soviet Union has been the United States itself. The Soviet leaders continue to view the United States as the principal enemy, both in ideological and military terms. The United States is feared as a military power, and as a global adversary, because it alone has the military power to frustrate Soviet ambitions in areas that are now of interest to the Soviet Union, particularly in the Third World.

During the detente period in the 1970s, the core of American-Soviet relations was in the field of arms control. One can characterize Soviet objectives in the arms control area, especially looking retrospectively, in terms of the Soviet attempt to deny the United States the ability to use its military power for diplomatic advantage. Specifically, the arms control agreements to which the Soviet leaders were willing to agree would have the effect of codifying Soviet military advantage.

The failure of the Soviet Union to agree to a SALT II arms control agreement that could win the support of the U.S. public and the Congress, and the persisting pattern of Soviet non-compliance with existing arms control agreements, have basically removed arms control from the center of the U.S.-Soviet relationship. In fact, with the removal of arms control from the center of this relationship, it has become apparent just how dependent U.S.-Soviet relations were on arms control.

In the Caribbean and Central America, Soviet objectives recently also have been at risk. The willingness of the United States to use its military power in the region to prevent the advancement of Soviet interests, as was displayed in Grenada, and which subsequently has been underscored by the very considerable effort that is now being made in Central America, particularly in El Salvador, where the fruits of this U.S. investment are beginning to be displayed with the rudimentary introduction of democracy, suggests that Soviet expectations in the area are likely to be diminished. It is not to say that the Soviet leaders will not continue to try. In fact, the use of the Soviet base in Nicaragua becomes more important than ever before.

Turning to East Asia, there are a number of reasons why the Soviet Union has had substantial trouble in increasing its influence. The first, and most important, dimension is the sheer economic dynamism of the East Asian region. The region's ready assimilation of advanced technology -- not only as an engine of economic well-being for its citizens but also as an economic model for developing countries -- demonstrates that the region has become an unalloyed success. This economic dynamism has no doubt contributed more directly than any other single factor to the inability of the Soviet Union to make much headway in this part of the world.

A second dimension concerning Soviet strategy toward East Asia is the anti-communist attitudes of both the general population and the elites in the non-communist societies. It has become quite apparent that communist ideology has had relatively little attraction in this area, and when the general anti-communist feeling is combined with the economic dynamism of the area, the result is certainly a very difficult environment for the Soviet Union.

A third dimension of the Asian situation is the good relations that the nations there have enjoyed with the United States, especially in the context of the security role that the United States has long played in the region. This has contributed to cooperative, and in many cases, alliance relationships with the countries in the region which have further complicated the task facing Soviet policymakers.

Finally, there is one fact of geography that is important but which is sometimes easily overlooked, especially when one is comparing with the European case. This is simply the lack of good overland invasion routes from the Soviet Union to the principal nations of the East Asian region. In fact, most of the nations of this region are accessible only by air or sea. This dimension tends to underscore the political significance of seeking to strengthen abilities to protect the air and sea lines of communication between the East Asian nations and their trading partners in the West.

As a consequence of these attributes of the new environment that the Soviets are finding in East Asia, the Soviets are turning to a policy of intimidation, as much out of frustration as calculation. A few points will underscore this. First, the Soviet Pacific Fleet is the USSR's largest. This is a considerable change from the earlier circumstance where the Northern Fleet, which is primarily Europe and Atlantic-oriented, was the largest. Second is the recent development of the Soviet air and naval facility at Cam Rahn Bay in Vietnam. It is now the Soviet Union's largest overseas air and naval facility and poses a direct threat to the southern approaches to the periphery of the Western Pacific. Third, there is the Soviet buildup of long-range nuclear striking power in the Far East, e.g., the deployment of SS-20 intermediate-range missiles and of intermediate- to long-range BACKFIRE bombers. These are among the many recent changes that tend to strengthen the perception of an overwhelming nuclear threat to the essentially unarmed nations of East Asia.

And in the case of Japan, the deployment of tactical air power and of a motorized rifle division in the southern Kurile Islands has once again underscored the reticence that we have found elsewhere in the world on the part of the Soviet Union to negotiate outstanding disputes. Instead, the Soviet Union seeks to settle disputes through acquiescence won through intimidation.

Finally, Moscow's efforts to increase its military strength in East Asia have been accompanied by a steady barrage of belligerent and blackmail-oriented rhetoric, warning especially of dire consequences if the East Asians support U.S. "imperialism." It is difficult to understand how the Soviet leaders are likely to gain from this rhetoric, but it does underscore the frustration that they are feeling because of the failure of their strategy in this region.

In the Third World, the picture is not dramatically better for the Soviet leaders, although this area is the primary focus of their diplomatic energy today. Their drive in Southern Africa has continued unabated but has been met with some substantial obstacles. The apparent recent withdrawal of Mozambique from active subversion in the region has been an important blow to Soviet aspirations in Southern Africa. The Soviet Union is currently bogged down in Afghanistan. Despite the massive investment of resources, the large-scale bombing of civilian targets by BADGER bombers based on Soviet territory, the indiscriminate use of fuel-air explosives against civilians, the use of chemical agents, and the deployment of well over 100,000 troops, Soviet policy in Afghanistan is not succeeding but is failing.

In short, it appears that the picture facing the Soviet leadership is considerably more gloomy than would have been expected by Soviet President Brezhnev when he made a speech in the early 1970s to a collection of East European communist officials,

16

stating that he expected that by 1985 the effects of the Soviet policy of detente would result in the substantial satisfaction of Soviet objectives. It is fair to say that Soviet objectives are now unlikely to be realized any time soon and that Soviet global strategy could be described fairly as being in disarray.

The best course for the Free World to adopt in the interim is to seek to deny the Soviet leaders easy opportunity to weaken its alliances and instead to adopt policies that force them to look inward, hopefully toward the end of more peaceful development. In short, the United States should seek to reduce not only U.S. military vulnerability through the effort which is currently underway, but also the vulnerability of U.S. allies.

The United States is hopeful that its allies in the East Asian region will, at least, attend to the minimum objectives of protecting the air and sea lines of communication, and of protecting land masses against air attack. Also necessary is increased political-military cooperation. Substantial movement in this regard can already be observed in Southeast Asia, with the increasing willingness of the countries of the Association of South East Asian Nations (ASEAN) to assume a quasi-political-military alliance.

Finally, referring to another dimension that deserves more attention in the Free World, is the need to develop an information policy which will transmit information to the Soviet Union which will tend to encourage forces inside to adopt policies that are essentially inward looking. It is to be hoped that the Soviet leadership is increasingly faced with other choices than merely attempting to sustain the status quo. One of the levers that the Free World has but that is insufficiently used is the power of ideas. I hope we in Free World nations can generate cooperation to use this power more effectively in the future.

Chapter 3

AWAKENING OF SOVIET INTEREST IN ASIA

James R. Blaker

Based on a review of Soviet actions with regard to Asia, one can present four hypotheses about how Asia fits into the Soviet world view and into the USSR's global strategy. These hypotheses are speculative and are designed to stimulate more detailed and systematic thinking. The hypotheses are: (1) Soviet interest in and concern with Asia is rising faster than Soviet interest in any other part of the world; (2) the goals that the USSR seeks in Asia are becoming increasingly complex; (3) the instruments by which the USSR seeks to secure its goals in Asia are expanding and becoming more diverse; but, (4) the base of Soviet influence and strategy in Asia will remain its military power. If these hypotheses are correct, they say something about the future.

Soviet international perspectives and strategy have traditionally been oriented to the West. Demographically, politically, and philosophically the Soviet Union has faced toward and been primarily concerned with Europe, and while the Soviet Union shares its longest borders with Asian nations, virtually all the measures scholars use to describe the international and military orientation of states point to the persistence of the priority of the Soviet western orientation. This year, about 60 percent of Soviet foreign trade will occur with Europe, and about two-thirds of the military manpower the USSR has deployed outside its borders will be in Europe.

But if one looks at the dynamic side of these measures, the picture is quite different. Demographically, it is the Asian populations in the Soviet Union which are growing the most rapidly. Where in the Soviet Union will one find the most rapid industrial expansion -- however limited? Where are most of the new roads and railroads being built? Where are the Soviet planners investing the most in agriculture, industry, social, and economic infrastructures? The answer is in the Soviet regions to the east of the Urals, that geographic backbone which divides European from

Asian USSR. And in terms of foreign trade, it is Soviet dealings with Asian nations which, over the last decade, have expanded at the fastest rate. Since 1977, Soviet exports to and imports from Asia have grown about 65 percent and 66 percent, respectively. In terms of military capabilities, the greatest rates of improvement are to be found in the Soviet Far Eastern military districts and the Soviet Pacific Fleet.

One can, of course, point out that rates of change depend on what is measured, over what period, and that in many of these measures, the reason Soviet activity in Asia seems to be increasing so much is that it started from such a low base twenty years ago. But the changes and increases and the rate of these increases were brought about in most cases by conscious decisions. Military forces do not automatically increase. Roads and airfields and barracks do not build themselves, and Soviet trade -- an integral part of the Soviet five-year plan -- expands in some regions of the world faster than in others because of conscious decisions. Changes in presence, activity, and resource commitments reflect human choices, and when changes are rapid in a given area of the world this is, it seems apparent, a strong indicator that interests on the part of decision-makers toward that region are increasing.

If it is true that the growth in Soviet presence and activity in Asia reflects a growing interest in or concern with this region of the world, what drives this increased interest? Part of the answer seems clear. The Soviet ground force capabilities exceed what would be needed simply to defend Soviet territory against Chinese attack. Indeed, the new intermediate-range SS-20 missiles, along with the longer-range intercontinental ballistic missiles (ICBMs), are theoretically far more than enough to deter Chinese nuclear attacks against the Soviet Union and exceed the force necessary if Moscow wishes to destroy all Chinese military and industrial capacity.

But, at least for now, Moscow has not deployed the air and sea transports which would allow the USSR's forces successfully to invade Japan or other Asian nations which do not share a common land border with the Soviet Union. China, then, is at the root of much of the Soviet concern which has led to the USSR's military buildup in Asia, but there are also broader purposes.

It is sometimes easy to overlook the intensity of this concern, despite the fact that it shows up in such strange places as some of the poetry of Yevtushenko and other Russian writers. It is quite strong. This analyst remembers the reaction of the Soviet negotiators with whom he dealt during the Mutual and Balanced Force Reductions (MBFR) negotiations in Vienna. There are few discussions that would seem to be less related to the state of Sino-Soviet relations. Yet, even there, the Soviet negotiators spoke of the threat to the USSR posed by China. And they did so with an intensity and vocabulary which was -- to put it mildly -- less than diplomatic. Presidents Ford and Carter relate similar experiences during their discussions with Brezhnev at summit meetings on strategic nuclear weapons at Vladivostock and Vienna, respectively. In short, the Soviet view of China seems almost more visceral and emotive than calculating or rational. Against such a background, what Moscow has done with regard to increasing its ground forces along the Sino-Soviet border is not particularly surprising.

But other aspects of the military changes are more ambiguous. It is difficult, for example, to account for the rate and extent of the Soviet naval and air force deployments in Asia solely in terms of the USSR's military concern with China. Nor can one argue convincingly that the deployment of Soviet air and naval forces to Cam Ranh Bay in Vietnam is due entirely to the Soviet view of China. We may never fully know why the USSR has taken these steps. But, whatever the reasons, doing so has given Moscow capabilities it lacked in the past. Twenty years ago, the USSR lacked the capacity to threaten the sea lines of communication through Southeast Asia. Now, the Soviet base at Cam Ranh Bay provides this capability. Ten years ago, the USSR lacked the capacity to project significant naval forces much beyond the immediate sea environs of Vladivostock. Now, the expansion and modernization of the Pacific Fleet make this possible. Five years ago, the USSR had only a limited air superiority or air attack range from the Japanese Northern Territories. Now, the improvements to and deployments of modern aircraft at its air base there give Soviet forces much greater range and potential effectiveness. The implication is direct. Soviet military increases and improvements in Asia are consciously designed by the Soviet leadership to give the Soviet Union the military capacity to promote Soviet interests that go far beyond the USSR's concern with China.

But what accounts for Soviet economic and diplomatic interests and increased activity? It seems that at least one factor is involved here. It has to do with the Soviet leaders' view of their position in the world. It is a view which emphasizes competition. To be sure, they see the United States as their rival and competitor. But their concept of competiton goes beyond a superpower framework. They see as rivals virtually all nations which differ from the Soviet Union in terms of political structures and, in particular, those nations which have been successful politically and economically.

We recall that the Soviet leaders discuss this competition in terms of the "correlation of forces" -- an argument which says it is not just the military balance which determines the relationship between states, but the economic, political, and psychological balances as well, and that in competitive situations, trade, economic ties, diplomatic initiatives, skill, and propaganda have important effects on the correlation of forces. Thus, to the extent that the

Soviet leaders see Asian nations as competitors, we can expect them to deal with Asia in their competitive terms. That is, they will seek to change the correlation of forces to their advantage by using the full range of economic, diplomatic, and political instruments available to them. The expansion of and increase in Soviet non-military activities in and directed toward Asia are because they see themselves in competition with many Asian nations -- in particular, Japan -- and believe they are slipping behind in this competition.

But here is the fundamental paradox faced by the Soviet Union. While the Soviet leaders may see this competition in broad, multidimensional terms, they compete badly in the non-military dimensions. Remember, for example, the visions proclaimed by the Soviets in the 1960s -- and then sometimes grudgingly accepted by the rest of the world. We sometimes forget -- and Pravda certainly no longer publicizes -- the statements made by Khrushchev in the early 1960s, that, by 1970 the Soviet Union and its East European communist neighbors would surpass the West and Japan in gross economic output, and, by 1980 would surpass the West and Japan in per capita output.

The fact of the matter is, of course, that this boast -- and it may have been a boast that the Soviets themselves believed -- was never attained. It is increasingly clear, even from the statistics the Soviets themselves publish, that this was a hollow forecast. The gross national product (GNP) has grown at about 3 percent over the last decade, and the annual rate of growth has declined, not risen. Forecasts made in the mid-1960s -- by both Soviet economists and non-Soviet observers -- were much higher, sometimes on the order of twice as great. Despite some industrial and agricultural investment -- much of which was directed toward Soviet Asia -- the Soviet industrial and agricultural sectors have failed to meet the goals of the last three Soviet five-year plans.

What about the vision of a revolutionary model? Twenty years ago, the Soviet Union was held up, by a number of revolutionary movements throughout the world, as the model for what they described as the post-revolutionary society. Today there is no revolutionary movement -- anywhere -- which proposes the Soviet Union as its post-revolutionary model.

And the vision of a better life? The Soviet government cannot claim to either its own population or to the world that the quality of life in the Soviet Union has improved over the last decade -- certainly not to the extent that was forecast in statistics they themselves have published: the average longevity of males in the Soviet Union has declined over the last twenty years. In 1964 the average life span of men in the Soviet Union was 66 years. In 1984 it was 61 years. The USSR shares this devastating but telling trend about quality of life with only one other nation in the world. It has the dubious distinction of being one of the two nations in which the expected life span of the population is declining. And it is not because people in the Soviet Union are having more fun. Alcoholism is one of the main causes reflecting a search for relief from drabness and tedium. So, despite the desires and hopes of the Soviet leaders in the 1960s and 1970s, the real leverage they have in economic, political, and social terms has remained limited and, relative to what is occurring in much of Asia, is declining.

This may point to another reason why Moscow has sought to expand its economic activity into Asia. The expansion may in part reflect a desire to provide quick fixes to an economic system in decline. Given the economic and technical dynamism of Asia, it is understandable why Soviet interest would turn there. But as the Soviet economy slips behind, both the USSR's competitiveness and its desire for economic and technical infusion increase. There are two basic paths by which those pressures can be released: internal reform or major infusions of assistance from outside.

Internal reform is difficult but not impossible. There is no lack of latent creativity within the Soviet population, and the population in general is not demoralized. The internal attention paid to Andropov's criticism of industrial problems and absenteeism was high, not out of fear but because of a general sense inside the Soviet Union that the economic system is not working. There was a deep resonance to the implication of Andropov's criticism -- namely, a sense that Soviet workers and farmers should be paid by their output, not according to the time they spend on the job.

Indeed, the ingenuity of the population to create and use the so-called second economy or black market within the Soviet Union attests as much to a willingness to innovate as it does to the shortcomings of the Soviet economic system. In short, the kind of economic reform which would stop the long-term decline of the Soviet economy is not out of the question. But if internal reform is possible it is by no means assured. Economic reform carries with it seeds of political reform and probably is possible only with political change. But the Soviet leadership is extremely conservative. It is an aging elite whose members have gotten to their positions by avoiding change and innovation. So the prospects for major and lasting internal reform are not high.

That leaves the Kremlin's need for technology and capital from abroad. But how is the Soviet Union to obtain such necessities? Perhaps -- and this is where the most serious problems may lie -- by depending increasingly upon the instrument of influence they have been most successful in developing over the last twenty years: military force; if not its direct use, then increasingly by the threat of its use.

That is why many observers -- including this analyst -- believe that the most salient development over the next half decade will be a continuing trend toward Soviet military modernization in

22

Asia. The perception of change and increased capability is not lost upon the Soviet leaders. To us, their rate of military improvement in the Far East is of concern. Their rate of improvement may be cause for some optimism in what must be, to them, an otherwise rather dreary assessment of military trends elsewhere in the world.

The danger is therefore two-fold: first, that the Soviet planners may opt to use the threat of military force to achieve the economic and technical inputs they hope will reinvigorate a declining economic system. And, second, that drawn by the momentum of their military improvements in Asia, they will turn increasingly to this region as the focus of such coercive threats. Japan, of course, with its high technology achievements, is a natural target for Soviet efforts to pressure nations to support their economic development of Siberian resources, and to otherwise assist the Soviet economy.

In sum, we can postulate in general terms about the character of the Soviet threat in Asia. It will remain multidimensional, and Moscow will continue to try to use a range of economic and psychological instruments to influence what it believes to be the correlation of forces in the region. But these are weak levers and have little prospect of becoming stronger in the next several years. The thing to watch is the extent to which Moscow increases its reliance on the one potentially strong lever of influence it has: its military power.

Chapter 4

SOVIET COLLECTIVE SECURITY PACTS

Osamu Miyoshi

Soviet strategy toward Asia should only be viewed in the context of Soviet strategy for all of Eurasia. The following discussion provides introductory comments on how all areas of Eurasia are interrelated in terms of Soviet strategy. It will be demonstrated that at the heart of Moscow's Eurasian strategy are collective security pacts incorporating similar Soviet methods and techniques for dealing with the Far East, South Asia, Southwest Asia, as well as Africa, and East Europe.

The Soviet Union's strategy in Asia is a part of its overall Eurasian strategy. On the one hand, it is clearly related to Soviet strategy toward Europe. On the other hand, it has been following its own process of development based on the geopolitical conditions of Asia. After World War II, the Soviet Union claimed itself to be an "Asian nation." The claim was officially made at the time when the Asia-African Conference was to be held in Algeria in 1964. However, that never took place because of a coup d'etat in Algeria. Recently, the Soviet Union has started claiming its voice as a Pacific nation.[1]

We cannot say that there is no legitimacy in the Soviet claim to be an Asian power. Seventy-five percent of its 1,376 million square kilometers of territory is in Asia. About one-fifth of its 267 million population is Asiatic, and this Asian population is growing much more rapidly than its Slavonic and Baltic peoples. If the Soviet claim of being an Asian power has provoked suspicion and resistance among Asian countries, it is because Moscow is forcing these countries to accept its claims mainly through political pressure based on its growing military power in the region. As an economic and political model, the Soviet Union is neither inspiring nor relevant to the development of the countries in the region.

Only the Soviet Union's overwhelming military power has commanded respect from these countries and has had some political effect. The Soviet Asian strategy was developed through the 1970s and took the form of the "Asian Collective Security System." The idea was publicly proposed at the World Conference of Communist Parties held in June 1969 in Moscow, with the participation of seventy-five communist parties. Leonid Brezhnev, in his speech at the conference on June 7, proposed the creation of "the Asian Collective Security System," while accusing "Mao's Group" of preparing for conventional and nuclear war against the Soviet Union. Moscow Radio reported on August 18 that India, Pakistan, and Afghanistan were expected to be the core of the security system which would eventually incorporate all of the countries from the Middle East to Japan, thus indicating Moscow's far-reaching strategic ambitions.

This Soviet proposal, however, has not been accepted enthusiastically by Asian countries. First, the proposal was presented in an ambiguous form which provoked deep suspicion among the Asian countries. Second, Moscow changed its tactics and adopted the policy of concluding similar bilateral treaties with friendly Asian countries and thus created a de facto collective security system by connecting these treaties to each other. In this way, Moscow concluded in 1971 both the Soviet-Egypt Treaty of Friendship and Cooperation and the Soviet-India Peace, Friendship, and Cooperation Treaty, and then entered into a series of similar treaties with Iraq (1972), Somalia (1974), Angola (1976), Mozambique (1977), Vietnam (1978), Afghanistan (1978), Ethiopia (1978), South Yemen (1979), Syria (1981), and North Yemen (1984). The expansion of these treaties into Asia and "Black Africa" (Angola and Mozambique) gave Soviet strategy its "Eurasian-African" character. Of these treaties, Egypt and Somalia abrogated the treaties one-sidedly in 1976 and 1977, respectively. In addition to the above-mentioned treaties, the India-Bangladesh Treaty of Friendship and Cooperation (1974), and the Vietnam-Cambodia Treaty of Peace, Friendship, and Cooperation, stimulated the role of India and Vietnam as protectors of their small neighbors forming the substructure of a collective security system of the Soviet Union. The countries of the Warsaw Pact and those of the socialist community, e.g., Mongolia and Cuba, are the core of the friendship-treaties-based global network of the Soviet Union.

Confronted with the intensification of conflict with China in the 1960s, the Soviet Union had strong motives to station Warsaw Pact troops along the Sino-Soviet border.[2] This intention, however, was crippled because Rumania strongly opposed such deployment on the grounds that the application of the Warsaw Pact was limited to the European front.[3] At that point, the USSR began to revise its mutual friendship treaties with all of the East European countries. The distinctive feature of the revised treaties was that the application area was not limited to Europe. The obligation of mutual support among member countries was, in addition, extended outside Europe.

By obviating the geographic restrictions inherent in the Warsaw Pact, the Soviet Union gained a legal basis on which to mobilize the troops of the Warsaw Pact (excluding Rumania) in any region outside Europe, including the Far East and Africa.[4] The Soviet Union provided the model of the Soviet-Mongolian Mutual Assistance Treaty which included an agreement of military assistance and pressured the other East European countries to follow suit, concluding similar treaties. In this way, the Soviet Union intends to create a legal basis upon which to expand the activity of the Warsaw Pact into the Far East.

Cuba, another active member of the socialist community, joined the Communist Council for Mutual Economic Assistance (COMECON) in 1972 and concluded the Mutual Cooperation Treaty with the Soviet Union in December of the same year. Since then, Cuba has played the key role of "proxy" in the process of expanding Soviet influence in Angola, Ethiopia, and South Yemen. Throughout the 1970s and 1980s Moscow has used this method for gradually expanding its collective security system, with the Warsaw Pact as its core.

Containment of China and Counterbalancing the U.S. Military Presence

What is the strategic objective of the Soviet collective security system, and how is it structured?

Soviet friendship and cooperation treaties resemble security treaties, in substance. For example, Article 4 of the Soviet-Afghan Treaty of Friendship, Good-Neighborliness, and Cooperation (1978) provides, "for the purpose of ensuring safety, independence and integrity of both states, both parties consult and take appropriate measures by mutual agreement." Moscow claims that the introduction of the Soviet forces into Afghanistan was based upon this clause.[5] Ironically, however, President Amin who should have called for "the Soviet military assistance" was slaughtered by the Soviet troops. This incident suggests that the Soviet Union has a unilateral right to interpret "the consultation clause."

Since 1975 the Soviet Union has repeatedly proposed the conclusion of a "Soviet-Japan Treaty of Good-Neighborliness and Cooperation," the title of which is similar to that of the Soviet-Afghan Treaty. Article 5 of the Soviet draft stipulates that in time of emergency both contracting parties contact each other.[6] In this case, "consultation" or "contact" are thought to have essentially the same meaning. All other friendship and cooperation treaties include either "consultation" or "contact" clauses. Furthermore, Article 9 of the Soviet-Afghan Treaty states that (the treaty) "establishes an effective security system .in Asia." These provisions are obviously

26

giving the Soviet Union friendship treaties the nature of collective security pacts.

Avigdor Hasselkorn, in his extensive research on the evolution of Soviet security strategy during 1965 - 1975, estimated that it was following the first experimental detonation of Chinese nuclear weapons (October 1964) that the Politburo in Moscow began to develop seriously a collective security strategy.[7] The emergence of a nuclear-armed, antagonistic power with a colossal population to the east of Soviet territory suddenly made its strategic environment more complicated than when the Soviet Union enjoyed the monolithic solidarity with China during the 1950s. From that time on, the Soviet Union had to prepare for the two-front enemies, the NATO states in West Europe and China in the Far East. The situation became more complicated when the United States began deploying POLARIS SSBNs (nuclear powered, ballistic missile submarines) in the Indian Ocean, raising strategic threats to Soviet security from the southern flank of its territory.

The border conflicts along the Ussuri River in March 1969 further aggravated Sino-Soviet relations. The Soviet Union markedly increased deployment of ground forces along the Chinese border. The troop strength, augmented from 15 divisions in 1964 to 27 divisions in 1969 (two stationed in Mongolia), went to 41 divisions in 1971, and 44 divisions in 1979. In 1983, the Soviet force size in Asia reached 53 divisions with 450,000 to 500,000 troops. Of these, some forty divisions with 370,000 troops are deployed east of Lake Baikal. In addition to this buildup of ground forces since the mid-1960s, all aspects of the Soviet military forces in the area were strengthened and modernized. One-fourth of the Soviet air and naval forces and one-third of the intermediate-range nuclear forces (SS-20s) are deployed in the Far East.

The development of the Soviet doctrine of collective security in Asia paralleled the Soviet military buildup in the Far East. It is obvious that a main objective of the USSR is the containment of China. Another equally important objective is to counterbalance the nuclear and conventional forces of the United States in the West Pacific and the Indian Ocean. Richard B. Foster, Director of the Strategic Studies Center, Stanford Research International, has noted that the Soviet objective in time of peace and war is to convert the international political, economic, and social systems into the socialist world order, with the USSR as its model. He further points out that, in order to fulfill these political objectives, Soviet global strategy tries to acquire a first strike capability against America with strategic nuclear forces to deny the U.S. access to the Eurasian continent and drive the United States into isolation.[8] This is how the Soviet global strategy is constituted: a quest for nuclear superiority over the United States and the implementation of their "collective security" arrangements in both near and remote regions.

Three Sub-Systems and Their Political Objectives

Soviet Military Power, published by the U.S. Department of Defense (1984), describes how the Soviet Union views the Eurasian landmass in terms of three main theaters: Western (Europe), Southern (Southwestern Asia) and Far Eastern, each with a set of political objectives affecting military operations within the theaters.[9] On the other hand, Hasselkorn, in his report, divides the Soviet collective security system in the Eurasian Continent into three sub-systems: the Warsaw Pact, the Middle East, and India and the Far East.[10] Hasselkorn's divisions approximately correspond to that of Soviet Military Power. Under Hasselkorn's formula, the political objectives of each sub-system are as follows:

1. **The Warsaw Pact**
    Standing face to face with the NATO powers on the European front, these countries, through the lessening of geographical constraints, serve as mobile task forces for the development of Soviet collective security strategy.

2. **The Middle East**
    The objectives of the Middle East sub-system are to assist Soviet activities in the oilfield areas of the Indian Ocean and the Persian Gulf, to deter nuclear strikes against Soviet territory by putting pressure on both the U.S. Sixth Fleet in the Mediterranean Sea and the U.S. SSBNs in the Indian Ocean, and to bring the oil fields in the Persian Gulf under control of the USSR. This sub-system includes seven states which are parties to security treaties with the USSR: India, Afghanistan, Iraq, Syria, South Yemen, Ethiopia, and North Yemen.

3. **India and the Far East**
    The major role of this sub-system is the containment of China. Another mission is to counter the American military presence (the Seventh Fleet, etc.). Concerning the Indian Ocean, the function of this sub-system coincides with that of the Middle East. This sub-system includes three states tied to the Soviet Union through security treaties: Vietnam, India, and Afghanistan.

Moreover, we might want to add the Black African sub-system to those listed above. The objectives of the Black African sub-system are to obtain political leverage against the industrialized

Western countries by the acquisition of control over mineral resources in Southern Africa.

The four sub-systems are commanded, controlled, and operated by the Communist Party and the military in Moscow. The objectives of the Soviet collective security strategy are:

o   to obtain, through its network of allies, strategic assets in Eurasia and Africa, which are necessary to realize the Soviet Union's ultimate political goals, and,

o   to control the strategic activities of the United States, its allies, and China, as well as to eliminate the strategic assets that they already have in the area.

The states which are parties to friendship and cooperation treaties with the USSR are asked to grant, in return for Soviet military assistance, the right to use and construct military bases, access to air and seaports, and transit rights through overland routes. One example is Soviet access to Danang and Cam Ranh Bay in Vietnam. These military arrangements are assumed to be provided for in the secret protocols attached to the friendship and cooperation treaties. In inverse proportion to this Soviet expansion, the retrenchment of a U.S. presence and restraint on U.S. activities have unavoidably taken place in the peripheral regions of the Eurasian continent. For example, the conclusion of the treaty between Vietnam and the Soviet Union signified the denial of America's access to Indochina and the development of the southern front as a means to encircle China. In this sense, the Soviet Union's gains led to constraints on the United States and China.

The Soviet Union also organizes mutual assistance programs with the states which are parties to the collective security treaties or among those sub-systems. In military terms, this objective is realized in the form of mutual logistical and defense arrangements such as military advisers, military equipment, and the right to use military bases. Mutual support is organized in the political sphere as well. During the time of the Vietnamese invasion of Cambodia, other friendship and cooperation treaty members were pressured to give diplomatic recognition to the puppet government which was established by Vietnam in Phnom Penh.

A strengthened Soviet naval force and large air transport forces are the main arteries which utilize the network of friendship treaties scattered over the Eurasian-African landmass. In order to counter the American SSBN forces (part of the triad of the U.S. nuclear strike forces against the USSR), the Soviet Union has developed "the Blue Belt of Defense" strategy since 1968. It has provided strategic bases for the enormous expansion of the Soviet naval forces, which are today composed of nuclear submarines, anti-submarine surface ships, naval aircraft forces, missile cruisers, missile destroyers, helicopter carriers, and the KIEV-class carriers which have recently come into service. The collective security system provides forward bases for the development of "the Blue Belt of Defense" strategy, and it also provides the "joints" which connect Soviet military assistance to its allies and mutual cooperation among the sub-systems.

Similarly, the airborne forces have the function of strengthening and unifying mutual assistance among the sub-systems of the Soviet collective security system which spreads over the Eurasian and African continents. According to <u>Soviet Military Power</u> (1984), the Soviet military air transport force, known as VTA, with about 600 aircraft at present, consists of more than 300 four engine propeller-driven An-12 CUB (range/maximum payload 1,400 kilometers), more than 200 long-range jet transport aircraft Il-76 CANDID (4,200 kilometers) and 55 heavy-lift An-22 COCK (4,200 kilometers). The VTA has been continuously improved in range, speed, and cargo capacity. A new heavy-lift CONDOR transport, comparable to the U.S. C-5A GALAXY and scheduled for deployment in 1987-88, will expand Soviet heavy-lift capability.

When Vietnam invaded Cambodia in November 1978, which was followed by the outbreak of the Sino-Vietnam War in February 1979, Soviet Tu-95 BEAR long-range reconnaissance aircraft, and new, powerful surface combat vessels (cruisers and destroyers) hurried one after another from the Maritime Province through the Tsushima Strait to Indochina and the South China Sea in order to carry out reconnaissance missions, demonstrate willpower, and deter Chinese responses. During this period, Soviet transport aircraft airlifted a large quantity of weapons and military materiel to Vietnam through staging bases in Iraq and India, both Soviet treaty countries, and through the territorial air space of Thailand.

Collective security strategy is an indirect strategy in which the Soviet policy objectives are usually carried out by backing friendship and cooperation treaty countries or by mobilizing Soviet proxies. Indirect strategy has an advantage in that the Soviet Union can achieve its political objectives relatively safely without provoking U.S. actions. If the U.S. response is judged to be passive, however, and if the Soviet Union is convinced that the opportunity has come, the Soviet Union would not hesitate to engage in direct military intervention. This prospect was endorsed by the Soviet invasion in Afghanistan, which can be considered as the leading example of direct intervention by the Soviet Union in an area outside of East Europe.

If we follow the Soviet collective security strategy -- its development and courses of action -- it reminds us of Mackinder's geopolitical theory that, "The power in the heartland of Eurasia advances to the crescent shaped rimland of the continent and expands," and further, "Who controls the rimland rules Eurasia, and who rules Eurasia controls the destinies of the world." Spheres of strategic operations of Russia, the heartland state, have now been expanding from the Eurasian continent to the African continent.

In the 1970s, the Soviet strategy of collective security resulted in at least four impressive achievements in and around Asia. First, there was the victory of India in its war with Pakistan in December 1971. This war erupted after the conclusion of the Soviet-Indian Treaty of July 1971, and led to separation and independence of Bangladesh from Pakistan. Second, with the threat of direct military intervention, the Soviet Union in effect saved one of Egypt's armies that had been surrounded and besieged by Israeli forces in the Middle Eastern War of 1973. The Soviet action was in implementation of the Soviet-Egypt Treaty of 1971. Third, Vietnam, with strong Soviet support, invaded Cambodia in November 1978, just after the signing of the Soviet-Vietnamese Treaty. Fourth, Soviet forces invaded Afghanistan in December 1979.

More globally, one can add the victory in the 1975 Angolan civil war of the Popular Movement for the Liberation of Angola (MPLA), with the crucial support by Cuban forces and Soviet military advisers. This operation made possible the 1977 victory by the Ethiopian government against Somali forces in the Ogaden. In all of these cases, Soviet military assistance extended through the medium of friendship and cooperation treaties, or direct intervention in the case of Afghanistan, played decisive roles.

The Soviet-supported Vietnamese aggression in Cambodia and the Soviet invasion of Afghanistan have had serious international repercussions in Asia and the world in general in the 1980s. Both these incidents presented new opportunities and problems to the Soviet Union as an Asian power.

NOTES

1. Statement of the late Dr. N. Inozemtsev, President of IMEMO (The Institute for the Study of World Economy and International Relations), at the third conference of the Japan-Soviet Symposium on "Peace in Asia," held in Kyoto, Japan, April 1976.

2. For example, Marshall Yakobovsky, Commander of the Warsaw Pact forces, insisted, in an article of _Journal of War History_, May 1970, that "the integrated forces of the Warsaw Pact share a common problem of the inviolability of the national border of each contracting member country. This obligation is not limited to Europe. As an inevitable corollary, we have to say that the integrated forces of the Warsaw Pact are obligated not only to defend the Soviet-Chinese border, but to defend North Vietnam."

3. The fourth article of the Warsaw Treaty defines that if one or more than one contracting party is attacked by the armed forces of any state or any group of states, every contracting party is obligated to provide immediate assistance by any means which it considers to be necessary, including employment of armed forces. The preamble of the same treaty also defines clearly that the objective of the treaty is to lead to the dissolution of the North Atlantic Treaty and to insure that the area of its application is limited to the European front.

4. The tenth article of the Treaty of Friendship, Cooperation, and Mutual Assistance between the USSR and Czechoslovakia states that if any of the contracting parties is attacked by any state or group of states, the other parties are obligated to provide immediately all necessary assistance including use of armed forces. Here the geographical limitation concerning the area of treaty application has disappeared. Concerning the Warsaw Pact, see Richard Szawlowski, _The System of International Organization of the Communist Countries_, Leyden, 1976.

5. The late President Brezhnev made the following remarks in an interview with _Pravda_ dated January 12, 1980: "Intrigues of a reactionary foreign government threatened the independence of Afghanistan. There was a danger that it might build an imperialist outpost near the southern border of our country .... The Government of Afghanistan requested our assistance on the basis of the Afghan-Soviet Treaty of Friendship, Good-Neighborliness, and Cooperation of 1978."

6. The Soviet draft text of the Good-Neighborliness and Cooperation Treaty between the USSR and Japan was first published by _Izvestia_, dated 23 March 1978. The term "Good Neighbor" is applied to neighboring countries of the Soviet Union including Afghanistan and Japan.

7. Hasselkorn, Avigdor, _The Evolution of Soviet Security Strategy, 1965-1975_, New York: Crane Russak, (1978), p. 5.

32

8. Foster, Richard B., *The Soviet Concept of National Entity Survival*, Washington, D.C.: SRI International, 1978, p. 5.

9. U.S. Department of Defense, *Soviet Military Power 1984*, G.P.O., Washington, D.C., 1984.

10. Hasselkorn, *Op. cit.*, pp. 67-90.

Chapter 5

GROWTH OF SOVIET MILITARY POWER IN ASIA

John T. Berbrich

It is a challenging task to summarize the large-scale Soviet military buildup in Asia, extending from the Eastern USSR and the Pacific to the Indian Ocean and the Persian Gulf region. The growth of the USSR's military power in Asia has been dramatic, especially when viewed in the context of Soviet posture from the mid-1960s.

Strategic Missiles

Traditionally, land-based missiles have the key responsibilities of fulfilling Soviet war-fighting objectives, and Soviet leaders have been consistently increasing missile capabilities and flexibility for employment under various wartime situations. The USSR has some 1,400 intercontinental ballistic missile (ICBM) launchers. The USSR has been embarked on a major expansion and improvement of its strategic forces since the 1960s, and it currently has eight ICBM variants available. For some of these forces, the USSR has stocked extra missiles, propellants, and warheads. Some ICBM silo launchers could be reloaded for additional missile firings. Especially significant are two missiles, the SS-X-24 and the SS-X-25. These missiles have been under development for many years, and they are currently being flight tested. The available evidence suggests both of these missiles can be deployed in mobile as well as silo modes. The current Soviet ICBM force has about 6,200 warheads, most of which have targets in the United States. A limited number of the ICBMs are probably aimed at Asian targets. Of course, these modern Soviet ICBMs can be re-targeted with considerable speed, giving the USSR flexibility in its strategic force posture.

The Soviet Union is also developing five new long-range cruise missiles that will have both strategic and tactical missions and applications, such as a submarine-launched variant. All five of these are now in their test programs, and initial deployments of some of these are likely in the next year or so. The deployment is expected to be throughout the Soviet Union, including Soviet Asia. Three of these cruise missiles are subsonic, similar in size to the U.S. TOMAHAWK, and they have a range of 3,000 kilometers. The other two are variants of a larger system, probably designed for long-range operations. This system has no U.S. counterpart.

The main missile threat to Asia over the next few years will remain the SS-20 intermediate-range missile, which has considerable improvements over the older SS-4 and SS-5 missiles that have been, or are being, retired. There are now 378 SS-20 missile launchers in the Soviet force, with some 135 (35 percent) capable of covering targets in Asia. Each SS-20 has three independently targetable re-entry vehicles, resulting in a total of over 400 warheads in Asia alone. Furthermore, this mobile, highly accurate system can be reloaded and refired with additional missiles. The SS-20 force continues to expand, and the number of deployed SS-20 launchers could increase by at least 50 percent by the late-1980s.

Ground Forces

Roughly 25 percent of the Soviet Union's motorized rifle and tank divisions are deployed in Asia, most of which are located along the border with China or in Mongolia. Since the mid-1960s the USSR has increased its ground force divisions from 20 to the current force of 53. In the Far East Military District opposite Japan, the number of divisions not only has doubled, but the personnel strength has increased some 150 percent. The ground forces are undergoing force-wide improvements. For example, Soviet forces in Asia have some 15,000 tanks -- or about 30 percent of the overall Soviet total. The tank units in Asia are currently being modernized with the T-72.

The Soviet Union is undoubtedly reviewing some of the lessons it is learning in Afghanistan and incorporating them into its forces. For example, the FROGFOOT ground-attack aircraft which supports ground forces was tested in Afghanistan.

In the future, there will probably be a slight expansion of the number of Soviet active divisions, presently about 194, and some of these will be in Asia. However, most of the improvements in Soviet ground forces will be qualitative. Further, about 25 percent of the total Soviet helicopter force is in Soviet Asia. It includes about 300 HIND helicopters for direct support to the ground forces.

Air Forces

The Soviet Union has about 2,100 strategic, tactical, and support aircraft in Asia, and this does not include aircraft assigned to the Soviet Navy. The Soviet Air Force recently completed a reorganization that combined the air defense fighters with the strategic and tactical air assets in most land border areas. This included air units in the Far East District opposite Japan. The old national air defense units became part of a new structure that not only improves defensive capabilities, but allows the Soviet generals to conduct massed offensive air operations more effectively.

The Soviet tactical aircraft inventory in Asia consists of some 1,800 fighters, ground attack and specialized aircraft. The USSR is replacing its older fighters with advanced models. For example in 1983, in the Soviet-occupied Northern Territories, the USSR introduced modern FLOGGERs to replace the older FISHBEDs. In addition to improving its basic aircraft, the USSR is increasing its emphasis on new missions, such as fighter escort and support of the ground forces. Soviet modern tactical aircraft, such as the FENCER which is deployed in Asia, carry greater payloads to much greater ranges than the older fighters. In the FENCER's case, it is able to carry over 5,000 pounds of bombs or missiles some 1,800 kilometers on return missions, which places Korea and Japan well within its range. About one-half of the some 200 FENCERs in Asia are assigned to the Far East Military District. The Soviet Union is currently testing at least two new aircraft, the FULCRUM and FLANKER. These are supersonic, all-weather fighters with a look-down/shoot-down system that has advanced air-to-air missiles, which will be the trend of the future. These will comprise the fourth generation of new fighters. Significantly, of the 1,800 Soviet tactical aircraft in Asia, about 90 percent of them are of the modern third generation models.

Additionally, there are over 250 long- and medium-range bombers and specialized variants in Soviet Asia. The Soviet forces are deploying a new version of their long-range BEAR bomber to carry more modern missiles. They are also currently flight-testing their latest bomber, the BLACKJACK, which could become operational in the next few years. It will be able to carry cruise missiles, bombs, or a combination of both.

The BACKFIRE is the USSR's most modern operational bomber, and some 40 are deployed with the Soviet Air Force in Asia. The BACKFIRE is capable of using nuclear or conventional bombs or missiles and has missions of both land attack and anti-ship operations. Its low-level penetration capabilities and its supersonic speeds make it a much more formidable weapons system than the BADGER, of which there are over 125 in Soviet Asia. Both the BACKFIRE and BLACKJACK have impressive combat ranges.

The USSR is also developing a new aerial-refueling tanker based on the CANDID jet transport design, which should be operational in the near future. When deployed, it will support both strategic and tactical aircraft. This will be a very significant development. The new CANDID tanker will greatly enhance the USSR's ability to conduct longer-range air operations.

Naval Forces

The Pacific Fleet, the largest of the four Soviet fleets, has grown steadily since the mid-1960s, increasing by some 30 percent to its current total of over 800 ships and submarines. In the strategic area, the Pacific Fleet has about 35 percent of the Soviet sea-based ballistic missiles on DELTA and YANKEE submarines. The latest Soviet SSBN -- the TYPHOON, the world's largest -- carries the SS-N-20 missile which has six to nine warheads that can reach Asian targets from the western Arctic area. The USSR is also flight-testing an even newer missile, the SS-NX-23, which is more accurate and eventually will replace the SS-N-18, currently carried on the most modern DELTA submarines.

The mid-1960s were watershed years for the Soviet Navy. It introduced its second generation missile-equipped submarines and surface ships, such as the KYNDA-class cruiser, and it began in earnest to deploy combat forces away from home waters. Since then, the Soviet Navy has developed into a globally deployed force composed of an impressive array of ships, submarines, and aircraft, including the nuclear-powered guided missile cruiser Kirov, which will probably be introduced into the Pacific Fleet in the 1980s.

The Minsk aircraft carrier, the second of the KIEV class, represented a visual sign of the Pacific Fleet expansion. The Minsk was delivered to the Pacific Fleet in 1983, further illustrating the emphasis the USSR places on this fleet. The future, however, lies in a port city in the Black Sea where the USSR is building a much larger aircraft carrier that will probably be nuclear-powered. This new carrier -- which probably will not be operational until the late 1980s -- will significantly improve Soviet fleet air defenses and enhance their power projection capabilities. The existing vertical take-off FORGERs on the KIEV-class carriers will be replaced. The new carrier will probably have a full-length flight deck for conventional take-off and landing fighters.

The Soviet Pacific Fleet's principal surface combatants represent about 30 percent of the total Soviet Navy's inventory. They have increased from 50 units in the mid-1960s to the current total of 90. Although the Pacific Fleet has two KIEV-class carriers, it has not yet received any of the other most modern types of ships.

Some of these newer major combatants, such as the SOVREMENNYY destroyer with its battery of eight supersonic anti-ship missiles will probably be deployed in significant numbers and will greatly enhance the anti-surface warfare capabilities of the Pacific Fleet. A gradual modernization program is also likely over the coming years in other naval warfare areas, such as anti-submarine warfare (ASW), as the Soviet Navy introduces other newer ships to supplement its current ASW combatants, like the KARA-class cruiser. Though somewhat smaller than the KARA, the new UDALOY destroyer is optimized for anti-submarine operations, having the most advanced ASW detection equipment, helicopters, and weapons as well as an integral air defense capability.

In addition, the Soviet Pacific fleet has hundreds of minor combatants, such as the NANUCHKA guided missile patrol craft designed for anti-ship operations. There are also 235 auxilliary ships in the Pacific Fleet. This fleet also has about 90 attack submarines, in addition to the ballistic missile submarines. Several new classes of nuclear-powered attack submarines will be introduced into the Pacific Fleet.

Just in the past year, two new nuclear attack submarine classes -- the MIKE and the SIERRA -- were launched in the Western USSR and are likely to be assigned to the Pacific Fleet in the next few years. The new submarines, such as the VICTOR III currently assigned to the Pacific, have improved technologies and capabilities, and are generally larger with greater weapons capacity. The Soviet Navy will also improve its diesel attack submarine force in Asia. New submarines, such as the KILO-class -- which is produced in the Far East -- will replace older diesel-powered units.

The Pacific Fleet has about 8,000 naval infantry, more than in any of the other three Soviet fleets. These forces are located at the main naval base at Vladivostok and are supported by a variety of amphibious ships, including the ROGOV-class. The only two ROGOV ships built thus far have been assigned to the Pacific Fleet. Additionally, there are numerous merchant ships in the Pacific area that can provide additional military sealift capability.

Soviet naval aviation in the Pacific has increased by 50 percent since the mid-1960s and currently consists of some 440 aircraft. Pacific naval aviation includes some 100 bombers, about 60 percent of which are missile-equipped BADGERs. Also in this force are about 40 naval BACKFIREs, in addition to those assigned to the Soviet Air Forces. Among the some 50 naval fighters are FITTER-Cs, which were introduced into the Pacific for the first time in 1983.

The Pacific naval air forces also include some 145 support and utility aircraft, like the BEAR-D reconnaissance variant which appears frequently over the Sea of Japan and has deployed to operate from Cam Ranh Bay in Vietnam. There are some 145 ASW aircraft including the modern BEAR-F and sea-based helicopters like the HORMONE. The HORMONE is already being replaced in the Pacific by the larger and more capable HELIX, which is expected to be deployed in both ASW and utility variants.

38

Power Projection Throughout Asia

Just a few years ago, the Soviet Navy had limited operations in Asia. Now the Soviet Navy is a visual sign of Moscow's global expansion. The expansion of Soviet facilities in Asia is most evident in Vietnam. Moscow subsequently gained access to Vietnamese military facilities. This was particularly significant at Cam Ranh, where the Soviet Navy is developing a full-fledged support structure for maintaining surface ships, submarines, BADGER bomber aircraft, and long-range BEAR reconnaissance and ASW aircraft.

Soviet forces periodically train with the Vietnamese, and in early 1984 Soviet units conducted an amphibious landing exercise on Vietnam's coast. The Soviet Union has provided more than $4.8 billion in military assistance to Vietnam during the past five years.

In South and Southwest Asia, the Soviet invasion of Afghanistan changed the geopolitical environment in that region. The USSR has over 105,000 personnel in Afghanistan supporting the war, plus many more inside the USSR. The USSR recently deployed a number of BADGER bombers to support its early 1984 campaign attempting to clear out the Panjsher Valley northeast of Kabul. This 1984 operation, like six prior Soviet and Afghan Army operations, failed to neutralize the resistance forces in the Panjsher. It appears the Soviet Union is facing the prospect of a very long occupation of Afghanistan -- with all the military and political implications that entails.

Growing Western interests and dependence on Persian Gulf oil have further increased the importance of Southwest Asia to the USSR. Iraq is a long-time recipient of Soviet military assistance, stemming back to the late-1950s. Baghdad ranks third on Moscow's all-time list of clients. Prior to Iran's crackdown on the Tudeh Communist party in early 1983 and the expulsion of 18 Soviet diplomats from Teheran, Moscow had provided some arms assistance -- under $2 billion -- to that country. Moscow's Warsaw Pact allies are also still providing some limited military assistance to Iran. Nevertheless, Iraq has received six times the amount of military aid provided to Iran. Syria has received more arms assistance from Moscow than any other country. Damascus has been allocated nearly $14 billion worth since the mid-1950s. Since the Lebanon crisis of 1982, Moscow has replaced Syrian losses suffered at the hands of Israel and has substantially upgraded many of Syria's weapon systems. This effort has included the enhanced SA-5 surface-to-air missiles and the SS-21 tactical surface-to-surface missiles, the only such deployments outside the Warsaw Pact.

On the Arabian Peninsula, Moscow and the East Europeans have been South Yemen's only arms suppliers for the past five years. Since the Moscow-Aden arms relationship began in the mid-1960s, Moscow has provided $2.2 billion worth of military equipment. The

Soviet Navy has access to South Yemen's ports and routinely has naval aircraft stationed in the country.

The USSR also maintains a constant military presence in the Horn of Africa where it has significant naval and naval air facilities in Ethiopia. This nation alone has received over 50 pecent of all Soviet military sales to Sub-Saharan Africa during the past six years. During the past three years, Moscow has provided about $1 billion worth of military support to Ethiopia.

Soviet military assistance relationships with countries, such as those in South and Southwest Asia, frequently develop to the stage where the Soviet Union receives military overflight privileges, obtains servicing agreements for ships and aircraft, and acquires direct access to military facilities. Such access enhances the USSR's abilities to conduct prolonged operations in distant areas and reduces the Soviet need for a larger number of ships in transit to maintain a naval presence.

Exclusive access to the naval facilities at Cam Ranh Bay in Vietnam permits the Soviet Navy to operate in Southeast Asia on a continuing basis. This facility provides major support to some 30 ships on an average in the South China Sea, which -- together with the aircraft access -- facilitates intelligence collection and ASW missions against U.S. and other naval units in the area, to include activities near the U.S. naval base at Subic Bay in the Philippines.

A similar situation exists in the Indian Ocean, where the Soviet facilities in Yemen and Ethiopia support an average of some 25 ships. The Soviet Navy is currently extending the runway at the airport at Aden, which could support larger aircraft, such as long-range BEARs. Soviet ship visits to Dahlak in Ethiopia have averaged about seventy per year for the past five years. Most of this activity has been for ships deployed in the area from the main Pacific Fleet. The Soviet Navy has an 8,500 ton floating dry-dock at Dahlak that services both Soviet and Ethiopian ships.

Arms Control

The USSR's efforts to increase its global reach include activities in the field of arms control negotiations. Moscow well understands that arms control agreements contribute to shaping the balance of military forces worldwide and provide an international forum for the USSR to use to its advantage. While some arms control agreements, such as the 1968 Nuclear Non-Proliferation Treaty, have made important contributions to global security, others have made contributions that are less clear.

The SALT process provides an example. On the one hand, in accordance with the SALT I interim agreement of 1972, the USSR has removed ten YANKEE-1s from service as ballistic missile carriers as newer submarines were produced to keep their overall SSBN force within the SALT I limits (62 modern SSBN/950 SLBM). These YANKEEs, however, have not been scrapped, and some may be returned to service as attack or cruise missile submarines.

The USSR has clearly violated the SALT II limits on encryption of missile test telemetry. The new SS-X-25 missile, which was mentioned earlier, is probably a second new ICBM type, prohibited by the SALT II agreement. A new large phased-array radar that the USSR is now building in the central USSR is almost certainly in violation of the 1972 Anti-Ballistic Missile (ABM) Treaty. In addition, the Soviet Union has on occasion refused to accept effective verification procedures in some arms control agreements. It has worked, for example, to impede international investigation of Soviet use of chemical and toxin weapons in Afghanistan, Cambodia (Kampuchea), and Laos.

The Soviet Union has violated arms control agreements when it thought it would be in its interest. It has used, or supported the use of, chemical agents and toxin weapons in Afghanistan and Southeast Asia. It is likely also, for example, that the USSR has violated the Threshold Test Ban Treaty limits on the size of underground nuclear tests. The Soviet record underscores the necessity of precise drafting and effective verification provisions in all future arms control accords. Furthermore, the Soviet Union will not have any incentive to accept such accords and reductions unless it is convinced that the West will not allow it to achieve unilateral advantage within or outside any arms control framework.

Conclusion

In summing up this discussion of Soviet military trends in Asia, three points should be kept in mind. First, the USSR's military buildup and modernization programs are impressive, and they cut across all Soviet forces. These programs are in consonance with basic Soviet doctrine and strategy, which call for superior forces to fight a war successfully at any conflict level. The basic modernization trend apparent in the overall forces is reflected in the military programs in Asia. Second, Moscow understands very well the military and political utility of its forces in Asia. Soviet forces are positioning themselves to challenge the West and promote their interests through a variety of means in the global arena. In the case of the Soviet military posture, this covers the spectrum of potential conflicts, including the capability to fight two major wars simultaneously. Third, and finally, the new programs and force modernization initiatives already apparent will further change the character of the Soviet military posture in Asia in the years ahead.

Chapter 6

BUILDUP OF SOVIET NAVAL POWER IN ASIA

S.R. Foley, Jr.

Programs which study the various aspects of Soviet global strategy are very useful to both Japan and to the United States. And in Asia, careful examinations of the USSR's intentions and capabilities are critically important to all nations concerned about the future. The threat from the Soviet Union becomes more serious every year. As free citizens of the world, it is our responsibility to recognize this very real threat and then ensure that proper defensive responses are taken.

The Soviet commitment of resources to military research and development is enormous and is helped considerably by acquisition of Western technology. It has narrowed the U.S. lead in nearly every key area of technology. With regard to the Soviet Navy, perhaps the most significant development in the past few years is its building of a large aircraft carrier. Speculation is that it will be nuclear-powered and displace approximately 65,000 tons -- about the size of our MIDWAY-class carriers -- and will have the capacity to carry approximately sixty aircraft. Initial sea trials could begin as early as 1988.

The Soviet submarine program provides daily evidence of an important role in Soviet naval strategy. The USSR is focusing on new and different undersea warships: TYPHOONs, OSCARs, DELTAs, ALFAs, VICTORs, and others. In the decade from 1972 to 1982, the Soviet Union built 50 nuclear attack submarines. The Soviet Navy of the 1990s will continue to possess the world's largest submarine fleet, one which is already highly capable and improving at a rapid pace. Soviet major surface ship programs reflect an increasing emphasis on size and complexity. They are becoming much more effective. In addition, Soviet naval aviation further modernized its long-range, anti-ship strike capability in 1983 with continued acquisition of BACKFIRE bombers. It must be stressed that BACKFIREs, of which there are now at least 80 in Asia, are used by naval aviation as well as the long-range strategic air force.

For more than ten years, Soviet military power has been expanded -- and employed either directly or indirectly through use of proxies -- out of all proportion to legitimate defense requirements. There is no way to rationalize the USSR's actions by the traditional claim of insecurity. What we are witnessing is historical Russian imperialism. Soviet strategy has come to involve wide-ranging overseas power projection including forward deployments by a technologically modern navy capable of sustaining operations thousands of miles from Soviet ports. With this growing Soviet Pacific Fleet, the United States must concede to the USSR a great improvement in its ability to project power in Asia. The Soviet Union can now project its forces into Third World activities or conflicts, as well as threaten the most vital sea lines of communication throughout the Persian Gulf, the Indian Ocean, and the Pacific region.

The common denominator for the nations of this Pacific area is that they are linked by water. No matter how diverse their cultures, nor how divergent their politics, all are dependent on the sea, and thus have a shared interest in how that sea is used and how it is protected. The threat resulting from the Soviet military buildup and Soviet expansionism should be of direct and urgent concern to the Japanese people. Like the United States, Japan is a maritime nation. Moreover, Japan is an island nation. Its survival as a free, democratic, and industrial nation depends upon its ability to keep the sea lines of communication open. Failing this, Japan will dry up and die like a cherry tree without water, factories will grind to a halt, lights will go out. Life as we know it will no longer be possible. The Soviet Union can control the destiny of the Japanese people by controlling the seas.

This fact is not lost to Soviet strategists. Soviet naval units are operating in virtually every part of the Asian region, and they are presenting challenges to security of the Free-World. This was not the case before the Soviet navy developed a "blue water" or open ocean, global capability. As vast as the ocean is, however, the landmasses that appear so fragile on a map exercise a great deal of influence on the ocean and its possible uses. That enormous expanse of water sometimes narrows down to a single strait or passageway, so that in strategic and tactical terms -- or simply in terms of moving from one part of the ocean to another -- a mere twenty miles of water between two points of land may be more important than thousands of miles of open sea.

The Soviet Union is taking increased advantage of this geopolitical reality. For example, Vietnam, South Yemen, and Ethiopia all support an expanded naval presence in the Asia-Pacific theater which positions Soviet power near such strategically vital places as the Red Sea, the Persian Gulf, and the Strait of Malacca, not to mention Japan's northern island of Hokkaido. Considering these developments together with the Soviet direct and proxy activities, the Soviet Union appears to be adopting a "choke point" strategy similar to that of the British in the nineteenth century. Just as the British ultimately established the capability to control world trade from Singapore, Gibraltar, South Africa, Suez, and Hong Kong, the USSR has created nodes of regional political and military influence which makes it potentially capable of power projection and the disruption of sea routes.

One such node is the establishment of a base at Cam Ranh Bay in Vietnam for Soviet power in Southeast Asia, representing a major change in the political and military structure in this part of the world. Cam Ranh Bay now provides support for some 30 Soviet ships usually operating at any one time in the South China Sea. In 1983 the USSR deployed BADGER aircraft to Cam Ranh Bay, signifying the first Soviet deployment of strike aircraft outside the Warsaw Pact since 1972. It should be emphasized that these are strike aircraft, not reconnaissance aircraft. Currently there are more than a dozen Soviet navy aircraft of all types, including strike and reconnaissance, operating out of the air facility at Cam Ranh Bay.

In April 1984, a Soviet naval task group in Vietnam conducted an amphibious exercise in the Gulf of Tonkin. This was another first. The eight-ship Soviet task group involved in this exercise included the aircraft carrier <u>Minsk</u> and an IVAN ROGOV-class amphibious assault ship.

What does all this say about the future? How will Moscow use its forces to exert influence? And finally, what should we do about it? Certainly Moscow will be searching for vulnerabilities in the non-communist world along with ways to employ its own strength. It will encourage and attempt to exploit instability, dissidence, turbulence, and ongoing conflict between nations. Similarly, if the Kremlin attained unquestioned military preeminence it would be in a position to intimidate, threaten, or divide anyone who opposed it. This is a negative but standard Soviet approach to foreign relations. Let there be no mistake, the Soviet Union will not hesitate to use its power brutally and directly, as it did in Afghanistan. And once Soviet forces come in, they do not leave.

Conversely, it is in our interest to foster stability, encourage a healthy economic environment, and support strong independent friends and allies. This is easy to say, but requires a wise mix of diplomacy, sound trade practices, and cooperative policies tailored to Asian sensitivities.

Japan cannot alone cope with the Soviet threat, nor can the United States alone. We share common interests, and our bilateral defense relationship must remain strong. Our mutual security treaty is stronger today than ever before. Japan remains in the shade of the strategic umbrella provided by America. The Japanese Maritime Self-Defense Force (MSDF) and U.S. Navy ships continue to train very closely together. Each year, officers and men of the MSDF become more proficient seamen. This U.S. naval officer, serving as the U.S. Pacific Fleet Commander, feels confident that the MSDF would fully serve Japanese defensive interest if called upon. It is most important that Japan and the United States continue to maintain very close ties and continue mutual defense cooperation for the security of the two nations as well as for international security.

To conclude, let us ponder a quote from a Japanese naval hero. It is as meaningful as when first spoken by Admiral Togo. A few short months after his one-sided defeat of the Russian fleet in 1905, the Japanese combined fleet was in Tokyo Bay for a victory celebration and dispersal. It was during this celebration that Admiral Togo warned of the often short-lived nature of victory. He said, "If we slack our fighting spirit because we are in peacetime, our armaments would be as easy to collapse as a castle built on sand, even though they may look strong and powerful. Heaven gives the crown of victory only to those who by habitual preparation win without fighting, and at the same time deprives that crown to those, who -- content with one success -- give themselves up to the cause of peace."

There is a saying in the U.S. Navy that wars are won in peacetime. It can be hoped that Japan and the United States will work closely together now to preserve peace in the future.

Chapter 7

INCREASE OF SOVIET ECONOMIC RELATIONS IN ASIA

Takehiro Togo

As is the case in other parts of the world, the USSR's presence in Asia is marked by its military strength. The stepping up of its power in naval and air forces, the ever-increasing numbers of SS-20 missiles deployed in the Far East, and the enhanced use of air and naval facilities in Vietnam add up to the fact that the Soviet war-fighting capabilities in Asia have been strengthened dramatically.

Politically in Asia, however, the Soviet Union seems to be on the defensive. The rupture of relations with China is only slowly being patched up. Moscow's efforts at fortifying Vietnam as a bridgehead in Asia have been met with hostility in China and neighboring countries, including in ASEAN (the Association of South East Asian Nations, which consists of Brunei, Indonesia, Malaysia, the Philippines, Singapore, and Thailand), especially after the Vietnamese invasion of Cambodia. Over the long run, the reliability of Vietnam may not be totally secure for the Soviet Union, taking into account the strong nationalism of the Vietnamese. The Soviet Union also supports North Korea, another isolated socialist country in Asia, but in this case friendship is shared with the Chinese in almost equal measure.

India is trying to remedy its image of too much dependence on the Soviet Union. Japanese-Soviet relations have gone through a deep chill, as the foreign ministers of the two countries admitted when they met in February 1984 during the funeral of the late Secretary General Yuri Andropov. In spite of the fact that the Soviet Union is a part of Asia and that a substantial and growing percentage of its population is Asian, it has a very uneasy political presence in Asia. This situation may be reflected in Moscow's frantic efforts at strengthening its military presence in this part of the world.

Also, this uneasy USSR political presence characterizes its economic relations with Asian countries. In some cases in the region, strong political ties are backed up by close economic

46

relations, and in others, economic interests are used to further political objectives. The overall economic presence of the Soviet Union in Asia is, however, small and in many cases negligible. It is important in Vietnam and in India for different reasons, and certain trends in ASEAN countries need closer attention in the future.

It was only in 1966 at the 23d Party Congress of the Communist Party of the Soviet Union (CPSU) that foreign trade was given a legitimate place as an important part of the national economy. At the 24th Party Congress in 1971, a further economic strategy was adopted vis-a-vis developing countries, and it was finalized by the Plenum of the Central Committee of the CPSU in April 1973. Soviet foreign trade then showed a sharp upturn.

In this general upsurge of Soviet foreign trade from 1974 to 1983,[1] the main part was occupied by the increase of imports from the advanced capitalist countries. This trade was directed to increase the efficiency of Soviet industrial production through import of advanced technologies and facilities, as well as to fill in the deficiencies in agricultural production through import of grain and meat from the United States and other countries.

Trade with developing countries and socialist countries declined in relative importance during this period. Trade with socialist countries occupied about 65 percent prior to this period, but in 1981 the share dropped to 53 percent.

In sharp contrast, trade with advanced capitalist countries increased from around 20 percent prior to this period to 34 percent in 1980.

Reflecting a setback in detente since 1980, trade with socialist countries increased up to 56 percent in 1983, while trade with advanced capitalist countries dropped to 30 percent in the same year.

The share of trade with developing countries stayed around 11 to 15 percent throughout this period.

Soviet trade with Asia expanded in line with the general trend of Soviet foreign trade since 1974, and its share from 1974 to 1983 stayed somewhere around 8 to 10 percent.

In Asia, there are three categories of countries: socialist countries (Vietnam, Mongolia, China, North Korea, and others, of which trade with Vietnam and Mongolia had the major share); developing countries (India, ASEAN countries, etc., of which trade with India had the major share); and, one advanced capitalist country (Japan).

With regard to the socialist group of countries, the share of USSR exports to these countries in its total exports to Asia has been increasing, from 36 percent in 1974 to 46 percent in 1983. The share of Soviet imports from this group of countries in total imports from Asia stayed around 22 percent, with a slight drop in 1981. The share of two-way trade with this group showed an upward trend from 29 percent in 1974 to 34 percent in 1983.

Mongolia had the largest share with Vietnam coming close to second. These two countries absorbed about 70 percent of the share of Soviet trade with the four socialist countries, and in each case the balance of trade was heavily in favor of these countries. This shows the great degree of dependence by Mongolia and Vietnam on the Soviet Union.

Especially in the case of Vietnam, trade with the Soviet Union increased almost five times from 1974 to 1983 (from 236 million rubles in 1974 to 1,139 million rubles in 1983), and the balance in 1983 was four-to-one in Vietnam's favor.

Since 1978, Soviet economic aid to Vietnam has been estimated at $1 billion a year, and Soviet arms deliveries since early 1979 have an estimated value of $2.5 billion.[2] This is a clear case where the Soviet Union is using economic leverage in order to consolidate its invaluable political and military foothold in Southeast Asia.

In contrast, Soviet trade with China and Korea is modest and has stayed fairly balanced showing only a slow growth. Even so, in the case of China, the trend reflects the delicate fluctuation of temperature in bilateral relations. The figure was lowest in 1981, at 177 million rubles, and the figure in 1983 doubled over that of 1982 (from 223 million rubles in 1982 to 488 million rubles in 1983). This is the result of the effort on both sides to normalize the relationship. This trend is continuing.

The economic role of the Soviet Union in China will continue to be secondary. It is to Japan and other advanced capitalist countries that China is turning for help and cooperation in order to attain its goal in the four modernizations program (which concentrates on agriculture, industry, science and technology, and defense). China's aim is to quadruple its national income by the end of the century.

Among the developing countries in Asia, India far surpasses other countries in trade with the Soviet Union. This does not include economic and military assistance that the Soviet Union gives to India. Because of India's geographical proximity to Soviet Central Asia, and because of its role as one of the leaders of the non-aligned countries, the Soviet Union wants to keep India as a trusted friend in the region. Although the Soviet Union is an important trading partner of India, there seems to be a diminishing market for Soviet economic assistance, because India is looking for the kind of technology that only the West can offer and for more capital which is in short supply in the Soviet Union. India is also trying to remedy its image of one-sided dependence on the Soviet Union with a tilt toward the United States.

In 1967, when ASEAN was established, the Soviet economic presence in the these countries was relatively insignificant.

48

Traditionally, these countries tried to keep the Soviet presence as small as possible,[3] since their relationship with the Soviet Union was an uneasy one.

Moscow tended to look upon this regional grouping with distrust until the mid-1970s, when it moved away from its denunciation of ASEAN as a group and began to promote closer bilateral ties with each member, using trade and economic cooperation as levers. Previously, the USSR had a trade relationship only with Malaysia, mainly purchasing Malaysian rubber.[4]

In more recent years, however, there have been some notable increases in ASEAN-USSR trade. The most important features of this trade are the already sizable value of ASEAN exports to the USSR, and especially the recent sharp growth in those exports.

The exports to the Soviet Union by the Philippines rose from $10 million in 1975 to $190 million in 1980, for a five-year increase of 360 percent. Exports from the Philippines to the USSR in the mid-1970s were only a few million dollars but rose to $123 million in 1980, for a five-year rise of 226 percent. Even Malaysia saw its exports to the USSR rise by 36 percent over a five-year period.

During this period, Soviet imports from all developing countries (excluding members of the Organization of Petroleum Exporting Countries) increased by around 18 percent.

Thus the USSR has become an important trading partner for ASEAN countries, especially for their exports. The USSR has filled in the gap of a falling export market for ASEAN at a time when ASEAN nations were encountering increasing difficulties in market access in Europe, Japan, and the United States.

The Philippines established full diplomatic relations with the USSR in 1976. Since then, the relationship has blossomed rapidly. A turnkey project of a Soviet-financed, quarter-billion-dollar cement plant in the Philippines with an annual production capacity of one million metric tons has been announced. It appears that the Soviet Union has gained a meaningful investment foothold in this country.

In its trade with ASEAN countries, the Soviet Union has not minded the heavy imbalance. The balance in 1983 for Singapore was three-to-one, for Malaysia twenty-to-one, for Thailand seven-to-one, and for the Philippines ten-to-one in their favor. Whether the Soviet Union will continue to bear the cost of such imbalance for the sake of compensating political gains remains to be seen. In any case, the long-term implications of such a trend in Soviet trade with the ASEAN countries merits closer attention.

Of all the Asian countries, Japan presents the greatest lure to the Soviet Union as an economic partner. As a highly industrialized and technically advanced country, Japan has a lot to offer in the way of high quality machine equipment, technology, and capital badly needed for the modernization of certain areas of Soviet industry. In return, Japan can provide an ever-increasing market for such items as the commodities of primary industry, lumber, coal, oil, non-ferrous metals, and cotton. There is a basic complementary element in USSR-Japan trade. Japan could be a very useful partner in economic development of Siberia, on which the Soviet Union will have to depend more and more as a source for natural resources such as oil, natural gas, and coal. At one time expectations were high. In 1973, then Secretary General Brezhnev spoke to then Prime Minister Tanaka in enthusiastic terms about the rosy prospect of cooperation in this field.

The volume of trade between Japan and the Soviet Union is the largest among the Asian countries. It almost doubled in the 1974 to 1983 period. Peaking in 1982 at 3,682 million rubles, it was almost four-to-one in Japan's favor. The Soviet Union did not seem to mind that.

Nevertheless, Moscow has a number of complaints about Soviet-Japanese trade. The bilateral relations have a generally cold atmosphere, stemming from overall strained East-West relations as well as from indigenous issues (such as the Northern Territories dispute), and Moscow complains that Japanese businessmen are not showing enough interest in the business opportunities in the Soviet Union. However, Japan will continue to be a desirable economic partner for the Soviet Union.

The BAM (Baikal-Amur Mainline) 2,000-mile railway project was begun in 1974 and will link Siberia's Lake Baikal with the Pacific Ocean. Completion of the line is expected to have not only significant economic consequences for the USSR -- especially because of the rich coal, copper, other mineral, and timber resources of the region -- but also strategic military implications in terms of Moscow's ability to deploy forces better in East Asia. Moscow hopes that commercial use of this second Siberian railway will make Japan more interested in developing the area.

It is in ASEAN, particularly in the Philippines, that we should follow Soviet activities with utmost attention. Never so blatantly has the Soviet Union exploited the economic opportunity to advance political objectives. In this strategically vital, yet politically vulnerable country, the Soviet Union may be waiting for a golden opportunity to increase its influence.

Generally, we in the advanced industrial countries should pay more attention to the economic needs of ASEAN and other Asian nations. Their prosperity under free enterprise is a very important factor in the political stability of Asia as a whole.

In any case, Western nations should continue to discuss and coordinate their positions concerning East-West economic relations. As clearly laid down in the declarations in the past three summit meetings among the leaders of the seven advanced industrialized nations, economic relations with the East should be compatible with the political and security interests of the West as a whole.

50

NOTES

1.   *Soviet Foreign Trade in 1982*, Ministry of Foreign Trade, Moscow, 1983. This document is the source of the statistical data years 1974 to 1983.

2.   Statement of Evelyn Colbert, before the Subcommittee on Asian and Pacific Affairs, Committee on Foreign Affairs, U.S. House of Representatives, July 26, 1983.

3.   Ibid. See also "New Kid on the Block: The Soviet Union in Southeast Asia," Testimony prepared by K. Gordon, Professor of Political Science, University of New Hampshire, for Hearings before the Subcommittee on Asian and Pacific Affairs, Committee on Foreign Affairs, U.S. House of Representatives, July 26, 1983.

4.   Gordon, Op. cit.

Chapter 8

SOVIET MILITARY STRATEGY IN EAST ASIA

Kenichi Kitamura

SunTzu, the famous Chinese strategist of more than 2,500 years ago, said that the best strategy is forcing an enemy to give in without actually waging a war.

It seems to be basic Soviet global policy to avoid a direct armed confrontation with the United States, to undermine the Western alliance, and to create a favorable strategic environment by reducing or eliminating the influence of the United States in strategically important areas of the world. In order to attain this purpose, the Soviet Union uses every available means, including political, economic, and ideological-psychological measures, armed intervention through proxy nations, and, only if the situation is propitious, Soviet armed forces.

Looking at what the USSR has achieved so far, Soviet leaders seem to have focused their attention on:

o   areas producing energy resources (especially oil) and essential non-fuel minerals (e.g., chromium, cobalt, and manganese); and

o   areas occupying strategic choke points crucial to control of the important sealanes of the world.

Considering future East Asian war scenarios, the present and future relations between the USSR and the People's Republic of China (PRC) should be taken into consideration. While the Soviet Union is now trying to restore its relations with the PRC, Moscow clearly has not given up its intention to envelop and contain the PRC. Thus Moscow continues to deploy some 43 divisions of ground troops along its border with the PRC[1] and is increasing its military presence in Vietnam.[2] Real Sino-Soviet reconciliation will not be realized so easily, because of history and deep cultural and political differences. Moreover, the USSR's dislike of the PRC's recent

52

advances toward Japan and the United States as well as armed conflicts between the PRC and Vietnam seem to make reconciliation even more difficult.

The Soviet Pacific Fleet has been remarkably strengthened in recent years, especially since 1978. It now has some 350 ships and 560 naval aircraft in this fleet.[3] Furthermore, as a result of a large-scale ship construction program now underway, several new types of powerful combatant ships will be completed in the near future. Some of these will be deployed to the Far East, and the Pacific Fleet will be strengthened all the more by the end of this decade. Most of the Pacific Fleet forces are stationed at Vladivostok and at other bases on the coast of the Sea of Japan, and powerful units (mostly submarines) are also stationed at Petropavlovsk on the Kamchatka peninsula. Units deployed in Vietnam have been increased since the end of 1982.

Strategy in Wartime

In pursuing its global strategy, the Soviet Union emphasizes military power as a political instrument.[4] It can be observed that the USSR's remarkable strengthening of its armed forces in recent years has been made on the basis of a long-term and comprehensive strategy which views naval power as an important instrument of Soviet foreign policy. A vital question in considering the future wartime behavior of the Soviet Navy is whether a large-scale U.S.-USSR war would terminate quickly. Some have said that the Soviet Union has a concept of a short-term war, even though it scarcely brings about a desirable effect to the winner. As SunTzu noted, "Rapidity even of some awkwardness is better and a long-term war, even if carried out skillfully, has scarcely won a success."

In relation to "the constant upgrading of readiness for immediate combat operations in the most complex situation," Admiral Gorshkov has stated "the old well-known formula is taking on a special meaning in naval battle under present-day conditions (conditions including the possible employment of combat means of colossal power)."[5] The armament of the Soviet major combatant ships suggests such an emphasis.

Consequently, capabilities for conducting a war effort over a long period of time are also important to the USSR and the United States, and to their allies. This is particularly the case with regard to naval capabilities. While it is necessary, needless to say, to stockpile oil, food, and important non-fuel minerals for emergency supply, each side should naturally be concerned about the sealanes needed to continue moving war materiel in a prolonged conflict. It is this analyst's viewpoint that the USSR has a strong interest in interdicting enemy sealanes in any conflict situation. Other analysts, however, insist that the Soviet Navy puts little emphasis on this.

In his The Sea Power of the State, Admiral Gorshkov noted that with the advent of nuclear weapons, the operations of the fleet against the land assumed a fundamentally new significance. He went so far as to say that fleet action against the enemy fleet becomes secondary to fleet operations against the shore.[6] He, of course, had in mind the important role of Soviet ballistic missile submarines which can rain destruction far and wide on the enemy. However, Gorshkov added that the fleet must still fulfill such traditional tasks as disruption of the sea lines of communications of the enemy and protection of one's own. The admiral also pointed out that operations to disrupt and cut off the sea shipments of the enemy now represent an essential way of waging war against the shore, i.e., through undermining the military-economic potential of the enemy.[7]

It may be true that the Soviet Navy has limited resources to interdict the Western sealanes during an early period of a war, because it will make a primary effort to destroy such powerful enemy combatant ships as nuclear powered, ballistic missile submarines (SSBNs) and aircraft carriers, along with important targets ashore.

However, when the Soviet planners judge that the war seems unlikely to terminate in the short term, they will surely begin to interdict enemy sealanes, striking at both shipping and supportive anti-submarine warfare (ASW) units. Sealane interdiction operations will include air and/or missile strikes on terminal harbors and ports, and mine-laying in harbors, ocean accesses, and coastal waters by aircraft or submarines.

In interdicting the sealanes, the USSR would attempt to undermine America's ties to its allies, since these ties are based heavily on the ability to keep open the sealanes. The sealanes are vital to the West. On the contrary, the sealanes are not necessarily essential for the USSR in time of war. The USSR could wreak much damage upon the West by denying or severely disrupting use of the seas.

Admiral Robert J. Hanks, USN (Ret.), has commented insightfully: "The theories of some notwithstanding, the Russians have not built almost 250 attack submarines solely to counter the U.S. sea-launched, ballistic missile threat to the Soviet homeland. Anyone who does not expect to find the bulk of those boats prowling the globe's oceans in a drive to sever the sea lines of communication connecting North America to Europe, as well as those sealanes over which critical raw materials flow to Europe and the United States, is suffering from a crippling delusion."[8]

54

Strategy in Peacetime

It should be noted that Admiral Gorshkov has pointed out the importance of naval power in peacetime:

Remaining a very effective and essential means of armed struggle, the navies are constantly used as an instrument of the policy of states in peacetime. The sea is no-man's-land and, therefore, the fleets do not encounter in their activity the many limitations which stand in the way of the use for political purposes of other branches of the armed forces in peacetime . . . . The mobility of the fleet and its flexibility where limited military conflicts come to a head enable it to exert an influence on coastal countries, employ and extend a military threat at any level, starting from a show of military force and ending with the mounting of landings.[9]

In general, the Soviet Union seems to apply the following peacetime strategy toward the East Asian countries:

o   Toward Japan, the USSR seeks to undermine Japan's cooperative relationship with the United States, to impede Japan's defense buildup, to interrupt the improvement of Japan's ties with the PRC, and to encourage Japan to move toward neutralism.

o   Toward the PRC, Moscow is trying to impede improvements in PRC-U.S. and PRC-Japan economic and military relations, to interrupt the PRC's modernization, to check PRC pressures on Vietnam, and to limit expansion of PRC influence on the countries of ASEAN.

o   Toward the Southeast Asian countries, the Soviet Union is trying to increase its own influence while limiting that of the PRC.

o   And the Soviet Union is building up its naval presence at its bases in Vietnam, taking advantage of Vietnam's economic and military dependence upon Moscow.

Large-Scale Conflicts

The USSR also has a strategy concerning East Asia which deals with contingencies for fighting a large-scale war as well as smaller conflicts. Under Soviet global strategy, the Soviet leaders do not make such a clear-cut distinction between peacetime and wartime as is usually made in the West. However, so far as the employment of military power is concerned, a clear-cut distinction is made between the case of a large-scale war involving a direct armed confrontation with the United States, and a local conflict (including a case in which either the United States or the USSR intervenes). A full-scale armed confrontation between the United States and the USSR seems unlikely to break out, because of the possibility of escalation to a mutual exchange of nuclear strikes. Consequently, the more likely armed confrontations involving the United States and the USSR will be of a more limited nature, perhaps involving, at least initially, only allies of Washington and Moscow, respectively.

One possible scenario may be a conflict in an oil-producing area in the Middle East. If a U.S.-USSR localized direct armed confrontation failed to be resolved quickly, the conflict might eventually escalate to a worldwide war, at least concerning naval and air operations. In such a case, East Asia would ultimately be involved, particularly involving Japan because of this nation's global trade, economic, and natural resources ties.

While many Soviet decision-makers would probably be reluctant to initiate any large-scale ground operations in East Asia until they knew what position the PRC was going to take, naval hostilities would seem more likely.

The threat from the seas to the Soviet homeland is greatest in the Far East. And a broad area for operations would be open to the Soviet Navy only if the Soviet Navy could deal a fatal blow to the U.S. carrier forces and/or could secure exits to the Pacific through the Soya Strait and passages in the Kurile Islands. Neither of these tasks would be easily accomplished.

Another important matter is the effect of geography on maritime operations in the East Asian region. Restrictive and unfavorable aspects of geographical conditions in Northeast Asia and the Western Pacific impede the advancement of Soviet vessels from bases on the coast of the Sea of Japan out into the Pacific. However, the geographical and meteorological conditions in this region make it easier for the Soviet forces to defend their Siberian territory.

Furthermore, if in a conflict the Soviet forces can secure local air supremacy and sea control over the areas around the various strategic straits, taking advantage of the defense deficiencies of their enemies, they could interdict the transit of enemy ships through the straits into the Sea of Japan and make it their own sanctuary.

The Soviet bases in Indochina also occupy such a favorable relative position as to be able to threaten the U.S. forces in the Philippines and the sealanes in the South China Sea. On the other hand, the Soviet bases in Indochina and their sea lines of communication through the Tsushima Strait will be vulnerable to interdiction by the West. During a war, Soviet maritime strategy in East Asia would probably have the following main objectives:

o   deployment of Soviet SSBNs in readiness and protection of them;

o   protection of Soviet territories against enemy strikes primarily from the seas;

o   neutralization of Japan and interdiction of sealanes; and,

o   offensive operations in accordance with circumstances.

Many Western analysts point out that the Soviet Union has built up ASW forces in order to better protect its own SSBNs. However, as long as the United States deploys powerful aircraft carrier groups in the Western Pacific, the Soviet ASW forces seem unlikely to be able to conduct safe and effective ASW operations in the open ocean beyond the coverage of landbased fighter aircraft. Consequently, the Soviet planners will probably make their own SSBNs operate alone or deploy them in safer coastal waters such as the Sea of Okhotsk or the Sea of Japan from which missiles can be launched against targets in the United States.

In a war, the Soviet Union will also attempt to secure air supremacy and sea control over the Sea of Japan and the Sea of Okhotsk and to deny access to Western ships in order to protect Soviet SSBNs, Soviet territory, and sealanes for Soviet naval units. The USSR also will endeavor to control the Soya Strait. For this purpose it will try to neutralize Hokkaido by air and missile strikes, and might direct commando raids, amphibious assaults, and/or airborne assaults against northern Hokkaido.

To neutralize Japan militarily, the Soviet Union will endeavor to destroy Japanese air and naval bases as well as aircraft and ships located there at the beginning of a war. It may also employ propaganda, political maneuvering, and even nuclear bluff in order to make Japan break its alliance with the United States. It can be recalled that the Soviet Union made intimidating statements, suggesting a possible nuclear strike, in response to Prime Minister Nakasone's remarks on Japan being or becoming an "unsinkable aircraft carrier." In this connection, the Soviet intermediate-range SS-20 missiles do indeed pose a serious threat to Japan.

In addition to missions involving the deployment and protection of SSBNs, the protection of Soviet territories from enemy sea-based strikes, the neutralization of Japan, and sealanes interdiction, the Soviet Navy in East Asia could participate in a number of other missions. For example, Soviet attack submarines and land-based bombers might attack U.S. carrier groups and other main combatant groups operating in the Western Pacific. Or, air strikes might be directed at U.S. bases in the Philippines.

Another possibility for action by Soviet naval forces might involve the Korean peninsula. In a large-scale war in East Asia, it is possible that North Korea will undertake an invasion of South Korea, on its own or at Soviet direction. If this happens, the USSR may support ground operations on the Korean peninsula with aircraft and ships, and even attempt to control the Tsushima Strait. Should the Soviet forces succeed in such an attempt, South Korea would be isolated and the western part of Japan would be threatened. And the PRC would directly face the Soviet threat from the Yellow Sea and thus be forced to decide to stand on the U.S. or Soviet side, or to try to remain neutral.

It has been said that the USSR does not have major strategic concerns in Southeast Asia. It is true that in a large-scale war with the West, the USSR would find it difficult to conduct major offensive operations in this area. It might be impossible to achieve much more than limited interdiction of the West's sealanes with submarines. However, as long as Moscow's broad strategy aims at expanding Soviet influence in this area, and avoiding a direct armed confrontation with the United States, Southeast Asia is of increasing importance to Moscow. This is because the Soviet sealanes extending from the main bases in the Far East to the Middle East and Africa pass through this area. Thus Southeast Asia is well positioned for the establishment of Soviet naval and air bases.

The countering defense strategy in which Japan must play a major role will generally be carried out in the following ways:

(1)   destruction of enemy bases;

(2)   denial or interruption of enemy units passing through choke points, including the three main straits around Japan;

(3)   defense of important harbors and passages, and patrol and anti-submarine (ASW) operations in coastal waters;

(4)   area patrol and ASW operations in the oceanic areas; and

(5)   protection of shipping.

Of the above, Japan has to expect the U.S. forces to carry out task number (1). Japanese forces should assume a primary responsibility for tasks (2) and (3) and should be able to conduct tasks (4) and (5) in the so-called "area within 1,000 nautical miles of Japan" under overall sea control by the U.S. forces.

Clearly, the defense not only of Japan but also of the entire East Asia/Western Pacific area depends heavily on U.S. aircraft carriers. Thus, the Soviet planners are sure to put great emphasis on the destruction of these carriers. While at this time it may be doubtful whether the Soviet strike concepts and weapons systems will be able to overcome U.S. Navy carrier protection measures, Japan should recognize the great importance of these carriers. In view of the limited number of U.S. carriers, and their essential missions all over the globe, Japan should do all it can to contribute to ensuring the safety of the U.S. aircraft carriers.

In particular, Japan should focus special attention on increasing the air defense capabilities of the Air Self-Defense Force (ASDF), including the air defense system to be deployed in the future along the Ogasawara (Bonin) Islands as well as the capabilities of the Maritime Self-Defense Force (MSDF) for area patrol and ASW. Japan also should be prudent so as not to burden the U.S. carriers too heavily and not to disturb their freedom of action. In this regard, Japan should strengthen and improve its own naval forces so that they can perform regular defense tasks in cooperation with the U.S. units deployed permanently in Japan, doing whatever can be done without the presence of the U.S. aircraft carriers.

In this context, the MSDF's surface units taking part in sealane defense operations in the open ocean should have sufficient capabilities for self-air defense against missile strikes by BACKFIRE bombers as well as to conduct ASW operations. Some Japanese insist that in a wartime situation there will be no U.S. aircraft carrier in the vicinity of Japan.

While the defense of the sealanes in the East Asia/Western Pacific region will be carried out largely by the United States and Japan, cooperation with other Asian countries is, of course, also essential. The establishment in the area of a collective security system like the North Atlantic Treaty Organization (NATO) seems unlikely in the foreseeable future.

On the other hand, the United States has bilateral defense treaties with Japan, the Republic of Korea, the Philippines, and Thailand. There is the ANZUS treaty among Australia, New Zealand, and the United States, and a five-power agreement on the defense of Malaysia and Singapore among these two Asian countries and the United Kingdom, Australia, and New Zealand. All of these Asian countries can improve their local defense arrangements to a considerable extent using their respective frameworks. But the defense of all of the sealanes extending over the broad East Asian/Western Pacific area is certainly a great task which needs more cooperation.

Need for Security Cooperation

Consequently, it is proposed that these countries including the United States and Japan undertake a joint study about ways, however informal, to promote cooperation in education and training and to enhance the defense capabilities of the respective countries. This proposed study effort for new cooperation and coordination measures could be undertaken without concluding any new treaties or formal arrangements. The members of ASEAN are important to the West because of their locations, resources, and free enterprise orientations. They are also strongly oriented toward independence and neutrality. Thus Japan and the United States should respect the desire of each free nation in Asia for independence while assisting each nation to maintain political and social stability and to achieve economic development. Military stability and security throughout the East Asian/Western Pacific region are inseparably related to political and social stability, and to economic development. Thus, cooperation in all these areas is necessary.

The behavior of the Soviet Union, Vietnam, and the PRC casts dark shadows on the stability and security of the East Asia/Western Pacific Area. Thus, Japan and the United States should jointly prepare a coordinated and balanced security strategy in Asia which takes into account the strategy of not only the Soviet Union but also that of the PRC. But any such enhanced Japanese-American defense collaboration must be cognizant of, and respectful concerning, the sensitivities of all the free nations of the East Asian/Western Pacific Area.

NOTES

1. The Military Balance, 1985-1986 (London: The International Institute of Strategic Studies, 1985), p. 29. According to Collins, John M., U.S. Soviet Military Balance, Concepts and Capabilities, 1960-1980 (New York: McGraw-Hill Publications, 1980), p. 355, in 1978 there were 43 Soviet ground force divisions deployed along the Sino-Soviet frontier. Two more were on Sakhalin, and another on Kamchatka. These are supplemented by 75,000 KGB border guards.

2. About 7,000 Soviet forces are stationed in Vietnam (Military Balance, Op. cit., p. 30).

3. Toth, Robert C., "Soviet Naval Power Growing in Pacific," The Korea Herald, August 8, 1985; Soviet Military Power, 1987, p. 9.

4. Gorshkov, (Admiral) S.B., "Navies in War and in Peace," Proceedings of the U.S. Naval Institute, January 1974, p. 20.

5. Ibid., November 1974, p. 63.

6. In The Sea Power of the State (New York: Pergamon Press, 1977), p. 280, Admiral Gorshkov wrote: "The imperialists are turning the World Ocean into an extensive launching-pad, less dangerous in their view to their countries as compared with land, of ballistic missiles, of submarines and carrier aviation trained on the Soviet Union and the countries of the Socialist community. And our navy must be capable of standing up to this real threat."

7. Ibid., p. 221.

8. Hanks, (Admiral) Robert J., The Unnoticed Challenge: Soviet Maritime Strategy and the Global Choke Points (Cambridge, Massachusetts: Institute for Foreign Policy Analysis, 1980), p. 44.

9. U.S Naval Institute, July 1974, p. 60.

Chapter 9

POLITICAL ASPECT OF SOVIET STRATEGY IN EAST ASIA

Hayao Shimizu

The political dimensions of Soviet strategy include diplomatic activities, propaganda, and the use of or threat of the use of military power for psychological and political purposes.

An important example of the Europe-Asia connection in Soviet global strategy, and of the increasing tension in East-West relations, is the recent problem of the installment of SS-20 missiles in the Far East. This issue for Asia first came up as a peripheral problem caused during the process of the negotiations on intermediate-range nuclear forces (INF) in Europe. More specifically, Soviet leaders, in order to obtain the attention of the West, started claiming in the January 1983 negotiations that the USSR, if pressed for reductions, would be justified in moving some of the SS-20s installed facing Europe to the east side of the Ural mountains or to the Far East.[1] Later, General Secretary Andropov retracted the statement saying that any SS-20 cutbacks made in Europe should not be compensated for on Asian fronts but would be reduced totally if an agreement could be reached between the United States and USSR.[2] Nevertheless, despite Andropov's softening, the Soviet Union now has deployed about 200 SS-20s east of the Urals.[3]

It is clear that the USSR is paying primary attention to the European front in its strategy toward the West. Asia is an area of secondary concern to Russia. But this does not at all indicate that the Soviet Union takes Asia lightly, especially East Asia.

The Soviet interest in East Asia is even more strongly apparent when one considers the sudden increase of Soviet military involvement in the Far East. One comes to the conclusion that the installation of SS-20s in the Far East is not merely a secondary side-effect of the INF negotiation in Europe but is primarily an expression of the huge strategic interest the USSR has in Asia. Looking at it another way, Moscow amended its traditional policy, maintained since the days of Imperial Russia, from that of avoiding hostilities on both frontiers, East and West, to that of a posture

62

which makes it possible to fight or exert political pressure on both the east and west borders.

What, one may ask, is Moscow's real reason for deploying SS-20s in the Far East? In the first place, Moscow intends to achieve nuclear superiority over Washington in the East Asian area and in the Western Pacific Ocean. Second, given that advantage, the purpose is to threaten, both politically and psychologically, Japan and other East Asian countries. From this perspective, one can view the intention of Soviet leaders of accumulating SS-20s and building up their military forces in the Far East as going well beyond what would be strictly necessary to defend their own borders. No doubt some of the SS-20s could be targeted on U.S. bases in South Korea and the Philippines where indeed U.S. nuclear weapons may be located. But such targeting does not warrant Soviet intimidation of Japan. The primary aim is political.

Soviet Interests in East Asia

What kind of meaning does East Asia have for the USSR? The Soviet Union, needless to say, occupies a huge expanse of land, extending through most of the northern part of the Eurasian continent, and it often likes to call itself an Asian nation. But Moscow has undeniably been tending more to its relationship with Europe than with East Asia. This is only natural when one sees that the dominant Russian populace of the USSR comes from the European side and that the history of the nation in the past has been focused westward. And even now in modern times, Soviet national life still has its center west of the Ural mountains, a range which geographically divides the Soviet Union into a European part and an Asian part. Simply speaking, though the USSR is geographically between Europe and Asia, it has been thought of largely as a country facing Europe.

In fact Moscow's interest in and concern for security are indeed primarily directed toward the European front. This Russian and Soviet attitude is unchangeble and has been so ever since the fifteenth century when the Mongolian control from the East terminated both in name and practice. After that, or since the sixteenth century during the so called "chaotic era," Moscow has been threatened in succession from the West by Poland, by Napoleon of France, by Hitler of Germany, and now by the countries of the North Atlantic Treaty Organization (NATO). This is quite natural. Not only is the cultural and political center of the Soviet Union geographically close to Europe, but there exist no other countries, save for those in NATO, which have the power to threaten its center. This has been the case since the termination of Mongolian control, with but few exceptions. The exceptions were the Ottoman

Turkish Empire, which posed a threat to Russia from the southern side, and the Japanese Empire from the east, beginning in this century until World War II.

More recently, though, during the period of the Cold War after World War II, the U.S. military extended its presence in Asia, stretching from the Western Pacific Ocean to the South China Sea. And China began to be a source of fear for Moscow as differences between China and Russia became clear in 1960. Due to these factors, the Soviet Union found its security threatened on the East Asian front in addition to the European one. Despite this, however, there is no substantial deviation from Moscow's primary concern, which is the European front.

Of course the USSR is not looking at the countries bordering it only from the point of view of security. Obviously that is a major concern, but the Soviet leaders are more interested in a step beyond, i.e., using the neighboring countries as a means by which they can spread Soviet political influence. This influence-seeking is by no means limited to the countries which directly border the USSR. The USSR, which has grown to be a superpower, is trying to interfere in problems and affairs all over the globe in its competition with Washington. Its superpower character, along with the traditional Russian ideological character, is what has made the USSR an expansionistic country that attempts to expand influence in, and to invade, if given the opportunity, any area. Such behavior carries the Soviet Union well beyond the range of what would be called a merely defensive nation.

Despite the fact that East Asia will pose no threat to the USSR for some time, Moscow knows that in the foreseeable future this region's population, economic power, and military power will all grow. The nations which already have great influence and power in this region are Japan, China, and the United States.

Thus, in order for the USSR to expand its power in East Asia, it has to remove or sharply diminish the presently existing influence of Japan, China, and the United States in the area. While the USSR urges Japan to withdraw from the Japan-U.S. Security Treaty, at the same time it frequently makes propagandistic statements about the threat of "Japanese militarism." Similarly, Moscow makes propaganda concerning the American threat in Southeast Asia. And, while stirring Indochinese feelings against Chinese merchants living abroad, the USSR also supports the deportation of Chinese-Vietnamese from Vietnam.

In implementing its political strategy toward Asia, or to enlarge its sphere of influence, Moscow tries to avoid arousing hostility in any country which would have enough power to threaten the interests of the USSR in any way in the future. Moscow thus seeks to make the Asian countries that border it friendly ones, or, at the very least, militarily neutral, while preserving a neutral zone in the area. This is the traditional policy, which has been pursued by both the Russian Empire and the present USSR toward its western and southern neighbors.

Yet in East Asia there are no nations, with the exception of Mongolia, that could be considered part of a "buffer zone" in the same sense as are neutral countries like Finland, Sweden, and Austria in Europe, and countries to the USSR's south like Turkey, Iran, Afghanistan, and Pakistan. China is too large and still too hostile. As for Japan, there is not, so far, any possibility for it to become a pro-Soviet or neutral nation unless the political left takes power. Nonetheless, in view of their traditional policy orientations, the Soviet leaders believe that they cannot keep the wide eastern border safe without having China and Japan effectively under Soviet influence. Thus Moscow's special efforts to expand influence over China and Japan will persist, whatever the difficulties.

Soviet Political Strategy Toward China

Moscow's long-term political goal in the Far East is to "Russianize" China. But for now, Moscow insists on restoring friendly relations with China based on the "principle of peaceful coexistence," the fundamental rule which is the basis for all relations between the Soviet Union and the capitalistic countries. This means, Moscow views China in the same way it views other non-socialist countries. However, when then General Secretary Brezhnev appealed in Tashkent for the improvement of PRC-USSR relations, he acknowledged China as a socialist country by stating, "We haven't denied, and are not denying at present, the existence of the socialistic social structure in China."[4] Thus while Moscow recognizes there exists a socialist economic foundation in China, Moscow's relations with Peking must be based on pressures and maneuvering similar to that employed in dealing with other powers like the United States and Japan.

In order to realize its final goal, the Soviet Union has surrounded China as much as possible on all sides. The USSR has placed some 43 divisions on the Sino-Soviet border as well as 5 more in Mongolia, put pressure on the Chinese southern front by using the Vietnamese military, and deployed its Pacific Fleet along the Vladivostok-Cam Ranh Bay axis.

Moscow's efforts to encircle China militarily include the continuing maintenance of friendly relations with India. Furthermore, despite efforts by North Korea to move closer to Peking, it must be remembered that Moscow supports Pyongyang's armed forces, and Soviet warships and merchant ships use North Korea's port of Najin. In short, there is no question that Peking feels encircled by the Soviet Union.

It seems unlikely, however, that the Soviet Union's strategy aimed at the Russianization of China will succeed in the long run. Russianization would mean that China would not be allowed by Moscow to deviate from the Soviet model of socialism. In short, the persistent Soviet theme of the Russianization of China in and of itself puts a certain limit on the improvement of Sino-Soviet relations.[5]

Soviet Political Strategy Toward Japan

It goes without saying that Moscow's approach toward Japan differs from that toward China. Even if the Kremlin would like to achieve the Russianization of Japan, it knows that realization of such a goal is unlikely in the foreseeable future. At present, the Soviet Union makes a three-fold request of Japan:

o   that it become powerless militarily;

o   that it politically depend on the USSR, or at least maintain a neutral and not anti-Soviet stance; and,

o   that it economically aid the Soviet Union.[6]

The biggest obstacle on the road to fulfillment of these Soviet desires concerning Japan-USSR relations is the Japan-U.S. Security Treaty. Moscow tries to pressure Tokyo to abrogate the treaty. When the high-ranking Soviet official Georgii Arbatov declared that Soviet SS-20s were not pointing toward Japan, he made the additional stipulation that this would be true only so long as Japan did not permit other nations (i.e., the United States) to transport or deploy nuclear weapons in Japan.[7]

This means that Moscow has no compunction about using nuclear weapons like the SS-20 to threaten Japan and, eventually, to force Tokyo to renounce American influence. In short, Moscow has been stockpiling nuclear arms to an extent far beyond defensive requirements, and it is using its tremendous military strength in an effort to bring about the demilitarization of Japan both politically and psychologically. The USSR seeks to bring Japan to a feeling of powerlessness[8] and, in this political way, to eliminate American nuclear weapons and military influence in the Western Pacific and Far East.

The strategy of Soviet leaders toward Japan will be successful only when Japan, powerless militarily and therefore isolated politically, is obliged to pour the bulk of its economic and industrial power into the Soviet Union, particularly into the economic development of Siberia and the Far East. It would be foolish to think that Japan could retain independence of action in the economic sphere if it became powerless both militarily and politically, and it severed its ties with the United States.

But as is the case of China, Moscow's policies toward Japan are presently deadlocked, and they are likely to remain so for the foreseeable future. This is because Soviet policies toward Japan are riddled with mutually contradictory elements. More specifically, even if the Soviet Union were to succeed in estranging Japan and the United States, and if either country would scrap the Japan-U.S. Security Treaty, it would still be very difficult for the Soviet Union to prevent Japan from heavily rearming itself for self-defense. Also, Moscow's self-seeking request to draw on Japan's economic power is restricted by the political relations of the two countries, and especially by the fact that the USSR still occupies Japan's Northern Territories.

Soviet Political Strategy Toward the Koreas

The policy of the USSR toward the Korean peninsula -- which is divided into two opposing countries, South and North -- is not as clear as that toward China and Japan. The peninsula has a high strategic value for the Soviet Union. Since the period of the Russian Empire, Moscow has viewed the area extending from Old Manchuria to this peninsula as a route leading toward the Pacific Ocean. Furthermore, Moscow has seen the Korean peninsula as an entity separating China and Japan, and causing disagreements between them.

So far Moscow's success in the Korean peninsula has been limited. Needless to say, Soviet influence is limited to the northern half. That influence is held in check since North Korea physically lies between China and the Soviet Union and keeps an equal distance in diplomatic relations with both countries. If the Soviet Union tried significantly to improve relations with South Korea, it would run the risk of losing influence presently enjoyed in North Korea. All things considered, the USSR still has not been able to discover a workable approach toward the Korean peninsula.

Observing recent activities, Moscow seems likely to try to improve its relations with Pyongyang. It seems that the Soviet leaders are now ready to consent to the transfer of political power from President Kim Il-Sung to his son Secretary Kim Chong-il. Moscow in the past has been reluctant in this regard. In contrast, Soviet criticism toward South Korea has been stepped up, especially after the Soviet downing of the Korean Airlines Flight 007 in October 1983. Anyway, as far as the south-north problem in Korea is concerned, the USSR seems intent on sticking to its present posture of supporting North Korea.

Soviet Political Strategy Toward Southeast Asia

Another area in East Asia which Moscow regards as important is Southeast Asia. From the beginning, this area has not had close relations with either Russia or the Soviet Union. After World War II, when the colonial powers of England, France, Holland, and Japan departed from the area, the popular movements toward independence were often accompanied by an interest in communism. This development gave Moscow an opportunity to start spreading its power in the area.

Moscow's opportunity increased greatly in 1975 after the departure from Indochina of the United States, which had become the dominant Western power in the region. North Vietnam annexed South Vietnam, gained ascendancy over the Indochina peninsula, formed an alliance with the Soviet Union, joined the Council for Mutual Economic Assistance (CMEA), and became a member of the Moscow-led "socialist community." Thus, in a number of respects, Indochina became an indispensable geographic, political, and military focal point for the Soviet Union with regards to its Asian and global strategy.

First, the Soviet presence on the Indochina peninsula can be used to put pressure on China from the south. This presence greatly aids Moscow's increasing efforts to reduce China's influence in Southeast as well as South Asia.

Secondly, by expanding its military power in this area, Moscow is able to threaten marine transportation routes from Japan to Southeast Asia and all the way to the Middle East.

Thirdly, the enlargement of Soviet influence throughout the Indochinese peninsula forms a counterbalance to the U.S. defense line from Japan through Taiwan to the Philippines.

And finally, in a general sense, this area is at the confluence of sealanes which run through the Pacific Ocean, the South China Sea, the South Pacific, and the Indian Ocean.

The Soviet Union is hurrying to upgrade two Kampuchean (Cambodian) ports, Kompong Som and Ream, to augment the existing, superb Soviet bases at Cam Ranh and Danang in Vietnam. So far, though, Moscow has not been able to surpass the United States in exerting influence over the Indian Ocean region, but it certainly has the intention of expanding its own power in this area while diminishing and ultimately excluding U.S. power.

Southeast Asia not only includes the three communist countries of Vietnam, Laos, and Kampuchea, but also the non-communist countries of the Association of South East Asian Nations (ASEAN): Thailand, Malaysia, Singapore, Indonesia, the Philippines, and Brunei. The Soviet leaders intend to expand their influence in the Indochina peninsula, using Vietnam as a lever. For a time, the Soviet Union maintained a hard-line, hostile attitude against the

68

ASEAN countries, portraying them mainly as an American bulwark of anti-communism. But just before and following the "Russianization" of Vietnam, Moscow adopted a softer attitude in order to woo ASEAN countries from American influence. Moscow now apparently hopes to establish normal political and economic relations with all of these countries, supporting this overture by promoting dialogue and communication between pro-Soviet Indochinese countries and the U.S.-oriented countries of ASEAN. Compared to the past, relations with ASEAN countries have improved, for example, the development of trading links and the conclusion of technical cooperation agreements.

It should be noted that the relationship with Vietnam is not going forward as smoothly as Moscow expected. Naturally, the Soviet view of Vietnam in its overall global strategy is one of a general directing a soldier in the front line. Vietnam is valuable to Moscow strictly as a tool to further Soviet power expansion throughout Southeast Asia and beyond. However, Vietnam has its own interests, and these do not necessarily coincide with Soviet global strategy.

Vietnam apparently would like ultimately to annex Laos and Kampuchea to create a Hanoi-led confederation of all Indochina peoples. Moscow, however, seems opposed to this notion and at times operates contrary to Hanoi's desires. For example, the Soviet Union expressed its intention to give military and economic support to Laos and Kampuchea -- bypassing Vietnam.

On the other hand, the USSR is valuable to Vietnam in that the former can be used to divert China from threatening Vietnam militarily. Disturbing to Hanoi is any progress in improving Moscow-Peking relations. Such improvements in relations seem to Hanoi to arise out of a kind of superpower egoism which ignores the interests of small nations. When the USSR raises the price of oil or cuts back in economic support to Vietnam, relations between Moscow and Hanoi are hurt. The fact that the Vietnamese must send laborers to the Soviet Union in order to pay back their debt also humiliates them.

Moscow's influence over the ASEAN countries is limited. There exist hardly any common cultural elements between the Soviet Union and these countries. Moreover, ASEAN members traditionally have had closer ties to China, West Europe, Japan, and the United States. Not only is the Soviet Union a relative newcomer to Southeast Asia, but also technology and merchandise that it offers are inferior to what can be provided by other countries. Under these circumstances the main thing that Moscow can provide is military power including weapons. The ASEAN countries are especially reluctant to be militarily dependent on Moscow.[9]

Concluding Comments

The biggest concern which Moscow has in mind when it tries to deal with East Asia is basically the desire to enlarge its sphere of influence.

There are fundamental differences of culture and civilization which determine just how deep, how wide, or how long one powerful nation can affect another. If China has been positively affecting politics in neighboring countries for some time, it is because the light of the Chinese culture is strong enough to illuminate outlying areas. If West Europe once was able to dominate Asian countries, it is because Europeans at first overwhelmed this area culturally.

The principal element which is sorely lacking in Moscow's foreign activities is this power of cultural assimilation. Admittedly, if one takes into account a specific time period and a limited area, the Soviet leaders' Marxism-Leninism and the culture based on it might be said to have had some influence. But it has been verified already what sort of destiny they offer. Russian language cannot be used beyond the immediate borders of the Soviet Union. The great fountainhead of literature, which was a source of pride for Russia from the nineteenth to the early twentieth century, has, with a few exceptions, dried up. East Asia has many countries, some economically poor and most militarily weak, but culturally they are far from being underdeveloped countries, having cultural traditions far surpassing those of the Russians. For this reason, people in East Asia tend to be hostile to Russians.

All things considered, the only means by which Moscow can satisfy its desire for self-expansion in East Asia is through its military power. Enlarging the Soviet sphere of influence in East Asia essentially through military means will deny Moscow political agreement on the part of the peoples in the area and, in fact, will invite their antipathy instead. The only political hope of the Soviet Union is that it can break down the weakest links in the present chain of non-communist nations in East Asia by spreading a feeling of powerlessness among the people and undermining their will to resist Soviet military expansionism.

70

NOTES

1. Interview on January 17, 1983, with Soviet Foreign Minister, Der Spiegel, January 24, 1983. Furthermore, General Secretary Andropov commented concerning intermediate-range nuclear missiles based in Europe in Die Welt, January 17, 1983.
2. Pravda, August 27, 1983.
3. The Military Balance, 1985-1986 (London, England: The International Institute for Strategic Studies, 1985), p. 29; Weinrod, W. Bruce, ed., Arms Control Handbook, A Guide to the History, Arsenals and Issues of U.S. Soviet Negotiations (Washington, D.C.: The Heritage Foundation, 1987), p. 12.
4. APN Press News, March 26, 1982; for deployment of Soviet troops, see The Military Balance, 1985-1986, p. 29.
5. Soviet officials coming to Japan are eager to present the impression that the relationship between China and the Soviet Union has been improving rapidly, and there are some Japanese scholars who advocate the restoration of the Sino-Soviet union. There still is a big gap in these two countries' attitudes, however, and especially as regards the Kampuchean problem, differences are strong.
6. The rough draft of the Japan-Soviet Good-Neighborliness Cooperation Treaty, the terms of which the Soviet government disclosed in February 1978, indicate the basic attitude of Russian strategy toward Japan, i.e., Japan is to be put under the obligation that it refrain from letting other countries use its territory for the purpose of actions which "would bring damage to Soviet security." Furthermore, the Soviet Union proposed that, in the case of war, an urgent consultation between Japan and the USSR be held in advance. According to Article VII, it would be necessary after conclusion of the agreement to involve the government in matters of mutual economic cooperation, which had heretofore been taken care of by the initiative of private enterprises.
7. Asahi Newspaper, Tokyo, April 1983.
8. This Soviet policy has been more or less successful. For example, Japanese professor Dr. Morishima, at London University, has stated that the Japanese should capitulate to the Soviet Union if invaded and support the "non-armed neutral theory" -- the same policy as put forth by the Japanese Socialist Party Secretary General, Mr. Ishibashi.
9. When Soviet Deputy Minister Kapitsa visited Singapore in April 1983 he hinted that Soviet military support would be given to anti-government guerrillas in the ASEAN countries saying, "If ASEAN refuses to quit taking a stance in opposition to Laos and Kampuchea, which are countries allied with Vietnam, they (ASEAN) will get into trouble." In response to this statement, a large-scale anti-Soviet demonstration was staged in Malaysia and Kapitsa's warning ended up producing the opposite reaction to that intended.

Chapter 10

BASIC SOVIET STRATEGY TOWARD JAPAN

Osamu Miyoshi

An increasing concern for Soviet strategy in Asia is the emergence of Japan as a political power. Rajan Menon has analyzed Moscow's heightened uneasiness about Japan as follows:

If recent Soviet analyses of China are calmer, Soviet analyses of Japan display a new alarmism. As Marxists, the Soviet leaders respect Japan's economic attainments. They are also in awe of the military potential inherent in the advanced Japanese economy; this is probably increased by an awareness that, according to some calculations, Japan's industrial production has surpassed the Soviet Union's to become the second largest in the world. Unlike poor and technologically backward China, Japan has the prerequisites to emerge as a modern military power.[1]

Soviet concern about Japan has been strengthened since 1975 when the Sino-Japanese rapprochement came to the surface. A staff member of the International Department of the Central Committee of the Communist Party of the Soviet Union (CPSU) warned in a 1976 book on collective security in Asia that a U.S.-China-Japan "alliance" would unavoidably lead to instability and conflict. He cautioned particularly against "the dangerous effects of U.S. policies which allow Japan to seek to expand its military and political power in Asia, and Beijing to seek to involve Tokyo in its anti-Sovietism." From this point of view, he stressed the importance of the Soviet concept of collective security in which all Asian states must be involved.[2]

The basic purposes of Soviet strategy toward Japan were made clear by a set of Soviet postwar diplomatic documents. In a letter to President Harry Truman on August 16, 1945, the day after the war ended, Stalin demanded allied agreement to Soviet occupation of the northern half of Hokkaido, north of the line connecting Kushiro and

72

Rumoi, in addition to Soviet possession of the southern half of Sakhalin and the Kurile Islands, which the Allies had secretly agreed at the Yalta Conference to cede to the USSR after the war. Subsequently, in September 1951 at the signing in San Francisco of the Allied-Japan Peace Treaty, the Soviet delegation headed by Vice Foreign Minister Andrei Gromyko introduced an amendment to the original draft treaty presented by the United States and Great Britain. The amendment stipulated that Japan:

o   agree to full Soviet sovereignty over the southern part of Sakhalin Island and the Kurile Islands;

o   limit Japanese rearmament;

o   prohibit Japan from entering into any military alliances; and

o   agree to exclusive rights of free passage for Soviet warships through Japan's four strategic straits (Tsushima, Tsugaru, Soya, and Nemuro).

The Soviet strategic intentions with regard to Japan implicit in the draft amendment were described by the U.S. delegate, John Foster Dulles, and the Australian delegate, P.C. Spender, to be:

o   the encirclement of the Japanese archipelago by Soviet occupation of the northern territories and conquest of the Korean peninsula;

o   the separation of Hokkaido and Honshu (suggested by the Soviet demand to an exclusive right to patrol the Tsugaru Strait);

o   a weakening of Japan's defense capabilities;

o   the prevention of a U.S.-Japanese alliance;

o   the international isolation of Japan; and

o   control over Japanese industrial power.

Despite the fact that the Soviet Union failed to realize its strategic plans for Japan through diplomatic means at the San Francisco conference, Moscow has continued to strive for the same strategic objectives of encircling and controlling Japan by expanding Soviet military forces around the Japanese archipelago. To this end the Soviet Union has developed a system of military bases in the Far

East, linking the bases at Vladivostok, Sovetskaya Gavan (in the Khabarovsk region) and Petropavlovsk (on the Kamchatka peninsula). This complex of bases is said to be the USSR's second most powerful after that on the Kola peninsula in Europe.

The militarization of the Northern Territories (southern Kuriles), claimed by Japan but occupied by the USSR since World War II, can be clearly seen to be a part of this Soviet plan. Soviet forces on the islands have been rapidly expanded in recent years to division level (about 10,000 men) and their weapons and equipment have been modernized. In 1983, the USSR doubled the number of MiG-23 fighters stationed there to about 40, a development which might be intended as a means of countering the two squadrons of U.S. F-16 fighters deployed at Misawa in northern Honshu in 1985.

The Soviet militarization of the Northern Territories might have been undertaken with two objectives in mind:

o   to control the Pacific entrance to the Sea of Okhotsk; and

o   to indicate Soviet determination to maintain the status quo of illegal occupation of Japan's territories.

The Sea of Okhotsk, because of the recent deployment in the region of the newest DELTA-III class nuclear powered ballistic missile submarines (SSBNs), has clearly increased in importance as a strategic offensive base area from which missiles can be fired at the United States.

Parallel to the recent growth of Soviet military power in the Far East, the activities of Soviet naval vessels and aircraft around Japan have been increased as well as the frequency of incidents of military planes and vessels intruding into Japanese air and sea space. The Soviet fleet's deployment in the "Okean II" global exercises demonstrates that the wartime strategic objectives of the Soviet Pacific Fleet are:

o   to paralyze Japan's economy by disrupting its merchant shipping to and from Southeast Asia and beyond; and

o   to neutralize Japan by isolating it from U.S. military protection, as Soviet forces attack and destroy U.S. air and naval bases on the Japanese mainland, Okinawa, and the Philippines.[3]

With the expansion of Soviet military power in the Far East, the southern flank meant to encircle Japan has extended to Indochina primarily by the establishment of major bases at Danang and Cam Ranh Bay. The Soviet invasion of Afghanistan also has increased the threat to the Persian Gulf. In reality this means that the front line for the defense of Japan, which vitally depends on oil imported from the gulf, has been extended to that area. This, in turn, poses a grave and difficult challenge to Japan's original postwar concept of national security which has limited the geographic bounds of national defense strictly to Japanese territory.

The increased Soviet military power can also be utilized as an instrument of political pressure on Japan. Article III of the Soviet draft of its proposed "Good-Neighborliness and Cooperation Treaty" with Japan, for example, would obligate Japan to remove U.S. bases from its territory, suggesting that one of the basic purposes of Soviet policy toward Japan is to estrange Japan from the United States and nullify the U.S.-Japan Security Treaty.[4] This is but one of many examples where the USSR is attempting to carry out coercive diplomacy against Japan.

A TASS report dated January 19, 1983, commenting on Japanese Prime Minister Nakasone's remark about Japan being "an unsinkable aircraft carrier," warned that, "if Japan became an aircraft carrier equipped with an American nuclear arsenal, she might suffer a more serious disaster over the whole land than that which occurred 37 years ago." It is evident that this TASS warning was intended to threaten possible use against Japan of Soviet SS-20 missiles deployed in the Far East.

The greatest Soviet concern about Japan at present is to prevent Japan's enormous economic power -- roughly equivalent to that of the USSR but with Japanese technology more advanced in some areas -- from being used to enhance Japanese military capabilities. The principal cause for Soviet uneasiness is not Japan's present defense budget, which is less than 1 percent of GNP, but "the possibility that the Japanese public might come to support in majority a real and substantial increase of its defense capability, instigated by Mr. Nakasone's militaristic statements."[5] Similarly, Soviet concern today is not due alone to the modest growth of Japan's self-defense capabilities which are still very limited, but their importance in conjunction with U.S. power in the region, whereby "according to the extent that Japan increases its defense burden in the Northwestern Pacific, the U.S. forces in the area will have an increased ability to swing to the Indian Ocean and the Middle Eastern front and threaten the southern flank of the USSR."[6]

Japan's postwar pacifist attitude, as expressed in such popular concepts as "the Peace Constitution" and "the three non-nuclear principles," has been an important factor in restricting the growth of the Japanese defense capability. Taking note of this fact, the CPSU Central Committee sent letters in February 1983 to Japan's Democratic Socialist Party (DSP) and Japan Socialist Party (JSP) which supported Japanese political forces committed to maintaining this attitude.

75

The CPSU warned that three factors "implicitly endanger the present correlation of forces in the Far East." They are:

o   the U.S. decision to deploy F-16 fighters at Misawa in Japan;

o   the U.S. decision to provide U.S. Pacific Fleet ships with TOMAHAWK cruise missiles equipped with nuclear warheads; and

o   Japanese plans to blockade its international straits.

These Soviet letters promised the Japanese friends of "sure guarantees" if they "would continue to strictly observe the three non-nuclear principles in the future."[7] Clearly, the USSR considers it in accordance with Soviet national interests to help perpetuate Japanese postwar pacifism.

Soviet efforts to intervene in Japanese politics are sometimes very blunt. The Soviet Union, for example, has consistently pressured Japan to decrease the overall volume of its fishing catch in the northern Pacific through annual bilateral fishing negotiations. At the same time, however, it has tried persistently to entice individual Japanese fishermen in Hokkaido by offering them fishing privileges on the condition that they not support the national movement to return the Northern Territories to Japan. The Soviet Union has also tried to recruit Hokkaido fishermen to gather information for the USSR on Japanese forces in the area. By closing eyes to selected encroachments into Soviet-controlled fishing areas, the USSR has succeeded in converting many Japanese fishermen into a pro-Soviet political force.[8]

The Nakasone cabinet was, in 1985, pursuing a policy of relaxing tension with the USSR as one of its main diplomatic objectives. However, the Soviet reactions to the new Japanese approaches were proving to be inflexible. For example, Soviet Foreign Minister Gromyko, invited by Japanese Foreign Minister Abe to come to Tokyo to resume regular ministerial dialogues which had long been suspended, posed the unacceptable condition that Japan not include in the agenda the issue of the Northern Territories. Meanwhile, through the dispatch to Tokyo in October-November 1984 of a high-level delegation led by Politburo member D. Kunaev, Moscow showed revived interest in improving its relations with Japan in non-political, especially economic, fields. The Soviet visit indicated Soviet interest in promoting Japanese cooperation in the development of Siberian resources, with the recent opening of the BAM railway (Baikal-Amur Mainline) as a new impetus. It seems that Moscow's basic position is a " 'yes' to relaxation of tension, but with Soviet conditions."

76

NOTES

1. Menon, Rajan, "The Soviet Union in East Asia," Current History, 1983.

2. Kowalenko, I.I., Sovetskii soiuz v bor'be za mir i kollektivniu bezopasnost' v Azii," (The Soviet Union in the Struggle for Peace and Collective Security in Asia) ("Nauka," Moscow 1976). This quotation is derived from Lilita Dzirkals, "Soviet Perception of Security in East Asia, A Survey of Soviet Comment." Rand Corporation, P-6038, November 1977, pp. 5-10.

3. Spur, Russel, "Moscow: Drawing the Asian Battle lines," Far Eastern Economic Review, October 31, 1975.

4. The third article of the proposed Soviet Japanese Treaty Draft states that the contracting parties (U.S.S.R. and Japan) agree that any part of the territories of each contracting party shall not be used for any activity which may risk harm to the security of the other party.

5. Remark of G. Arbatov, Director of the Institute for U.S. and Canada (Moscow), in Tokyo, Fall 1982.

6. Remark of a Soviet representative at the 7th conference of the Japanese-Soviet Experts Symposium on "Peace in Asia," Tokyo, December 1983.

7. Asia Shimbun, February 3, 1983.

8. Miyoshi, Osamu, "The Global Strategy of Soviet Imperialism" (in Japanese), PHP Institute, Kyoto, 1980, pp. 291-299.

Chapter 11

JAPAN'S DEFENSE OF HOME ISLANDS AND WATERS

Ray S. Cline and James Arnold Miller

There is a very lively debate in Japan among scholars, government officials, and the general public on the Soviet threat toward Japan -- and on what Japan needs to do about the threat. One of the most critical elements in the discussions is the strength and capability of the Japanese Self-Defense Force (SDF).

There are numerous legal, historical, and societal factors in Japan that argue strongly against the buildup and the expenditure for the defense force. Much of the debate rages over the extent to which the National Defense Program Outline (NDPO), approved in 1976, should be expanded. The NDPO is the "standard defense force concept" which held that Japan should have a peacetime SDF of minimum size that is large enough to repel a "limited and small-scale aggression" and to prevent a fait accompli.[1]

The NDPO force structure essentially reflects the current levels of the SDF. In the Ground Self-Defense Force (GSDF) there are thirteen divisions, including an armored division on Hokkaido, two mixed brigades, eight anti-aircraft HAWK artillery groups, with a statutory strength of 180,000 men. The Maritime Self-Defense Force (MSDF) has 54 frigates and destroyers, 14 submarines, and 180 aircraft for tactical purposes. It has 41,819 men. The Air Self-Defense Force (ASDF) flies some 770 aircraft, of which 340 are designated as combat planes. For defense against high-flying aircraft, it has six groups with obsolescent NIKE-J missiles.[2]

While a capable force, the Japanese Self-Defense Force is sorely underequipped, with Japan's arsenal being considered obsolescent by U.S. and NATO standards. For example, the GSDF still in part has to rely on U.S surplus equipment, such as the World War II 75mm self-propelled anti-aircraft gun and the Korean War vintage N-42 tracked anti-aircraft rapid firing gun, for defense against low-flying aircraft.[3]

The Japan Defense Agency (JDA) in its Defense of Japan, 1982, expressed the view that "the Soviet Union shows no sign of easing its policies of building up large-scale military capabilities or . . . of expanding its influence by taking advantage of its military strength."[4]

Speaking in particular about the Far East, the document states, "Due partly to the 1969 border skirmishes with China and the 1972 Sino-American rapprochement, the Soviet Union has been making intense efforts to reinforce the military strengths in the Far East/Pacific Region."[5]

Hiroshi Kimura, a noted Japanese specialist on the Soviet Union and Professor of Political Science at the Slavic Research Center at Japan's Hokkaido University, commented in 1984 on what is perhaps the major aim of Soviet strategy toward Japan:

> It can be safely said that Moscow will continue to attempt to separate Toyko from Washington. To divide and conquer is one of the favorite tactics of the Kremlin. Besides this Bolshevik tradition, there is another, perhaps more important, reason why Soviet leaders, whoever they may be, will continue to apply this policy toward Japan. Soviet leaders do not perceive Japan to be, in itself, a significant power in military terms; however, when Japan commits its resources to the support of U.S. foreign policy, it becomes a formidable power in the Kremlin's eyes.
>
> Thus the Soviet Union will attempt to do its utmost in order to drive a wedge between Japan and the United States by resorting to persuasion, bluffs, encouragement, entreaties and all other means available to it. One kind of Soviet effort is persuasion. Moscow will try to explain to the Japanese what the new U.S. global strategy is and how dangerous is the role Japan is expected to play in that U.S. scheme.[6]

Numerous factors help explain the growing interest in Japan for increasing the capabilities and missions of the SDF. These factors include the Soviet invasion of Afghanistan in December 1979, the stationing of about two hundred intermediate-range SS-20 nuclear missiles in Asia, the continuous large-scale Soviet military and naval buildup in East Asia in general, and the Soviet buildup north of Japan in particular.

The Soviet military buildup in recent years has made the Northern Territories issue much less of a symbolic matter and increasingly a strategic question for Japan. The contested islands are part of the Kurile Islands chain that runs to the northeast from Hokkaido, the northernmost of the four main Japanese islands, to the USSR's Kamchatka peninsula. Japan's government seeks return of Habomai, Shikotan, Kunashir, and Etorofu islands. The whole chain extending up to Kamchatka was Japanese territory from 1905

79

to 1945, and Japanese claims on the southernmost four islands are based on nineteenth century treaties between Japan and the USSR. Of major concern to Japan is that some 10,000 Soviet troops and about 40 MiG-23 Soviet fighters are stationed on the four disputed islands, and the Soviet Navy is making use of a deep-water port at Etorofu Island.[7]

The Japanese are increasingly realizing that Japan's strategic location makes it of critical importance to the Soviet Union in the event of any East-West conflict. This recognition, plus the recognition that the United States alone will be hard pressed to meet all of its defense commitments, has heightened interest in ways to improve its own defense of the straits and sealanes around Japan, particularly the vulnerable northern island of Hokkaido.

Japan's defense involves the fact that, from the main Soviet naval base at Vladivostok, the Soviet Pacific Fleet has the choice of three routes to the open seas of the Pacific Ocean. Only if all of these routes are closed at choke points, where the straits narrow, can the fleet be locked in the Sea of Japan.

o   The Soya Strait between Hokkaido and the Soviet island of Sakhalin averages 175 Soviet passages per year. (It is approximately 45 miles wide.)

o   The Tsugaru Strait between Hokkaido and Honshu, narrower than the Soya Strait, averages some 60 passages a year. (It is approximately 15 miles wide at its entrance and exit.)

o   The Tsushima Strait between the southern tip of the Korean peninsula and Kyushu has averaged 170 passages a year over a five-year period. (This strait is about 135 miles wide at its broadest point.)

In time of conflict, free passage through the straits would allow Soviet forces to contest the use of the Pacific sealanes over which Japan's supplies travel from its trading partners. Any severing of these sealanes would mean the instant withering of Japanese strength and security. The protection against this eventuality is at present modest. The United States has a naval installation at Sasebo, flanked by a South Korean naval base at Chinhae, overlooking the Tsushima Strait. The U.S. First Marine Aircraft Wing at Iwakuni could play a major role in providing protection. On Honshu, near the Tsugaru Strait, the U.S. Air Force has stationed two squadrons (some fifty aircraft) of F-16s at the Misawa Air Base.[8]

During a visit to Washington in May 1981, Japanese Prime Minister Zenko Suzuki for the first time defined the relationship

80

between Japan and the United States as an "alliance" and announced Japan's intentions to assure the security of vital sealanes in the Pacific Ocean in a radius of 1,000 nautical miles, extending as far south as the Bashi Channel between Taiwan and the Philippines, and eastward to the vicinity of Guam.

Japan's commitments to share "the U.S. and Japanese roles for peace and security in the Far East" were reinforced during a visit to Washington by Prime Minister Yasuhiro Nakasone, who in December 1982 succeeded Mr. Suzuki. Nakasone announced his intention of turning Japan into an "unsinkable aircraft carrier," a statement to which Moscow's propagandists continually return, contending that it reveals Japan's "militaristic and revanchist designs."[9]

A major issue in Japan in recent years, and a significant bone of contention between Tokyo and Washington, has been the amounts devoted by Japan to defense spending. Japan's military spending has been held down to around 1 percent of the national GNP under a decision made by a cabinet headed by the dovish Takeo Miki in 1976. A Defense White Paper issued in late-September 1984 said this amount is much lower than that of European nations, when measured by the same yardstick.

Opponents of Japan's military buildup retort by pointing out that since Japan's GNP is 1.5 times that of West Germany, twice that of France, and 2.5 times greater than that of Great Britain, the amount in cash is actually larger in the case of Japan as compared to these ountries. Further, the critics contend, Japan's military outlays are increased 1.6 to 1.7 times when computed according to NATO standards. This is because, they point out, Japan's military budget does not include expenditures for pensions for former soldiers and allotments for their survivors, nor the amount spent to maintain the Maritime Safety Agency (coast guard).[10]

In 1985, the Japanese government was considering a $100 billion, five-year military spending plan that would expand sealane and air defense capabilities. The plan would continue Japan's gradual increases in military spending in recent years; however, it would not involve radical changes in the speed or in the direction of this spending.

The Japanese defense plan reportedly would increase the number of U.S.-designed P-3C ORION anti-submarine patrol planes from about 50 to 100; increase combat ships from 49 to 63; increase submarines by five to 15 or 16; increase F-15 fighter aircraft from 125 to 190; replace the old NIKE surface-to-air missiles with the new PATRIOT missile system; increase from 8 to 12 the number of Grumman E-2Cs, a small, propeller-driven radar reconnaissance plane; reorganize Ground Self-Defense Force divisions on Hokkaido; and, provide the GSDF with 40 new anti-tank helicopters.[11]

Admiral William J. Crowe, Jr., Chairman of the U.S. Joint Chiefs of Staff, commented in May 1985 while he was Commander-in-Chief, U.S. Pacific Command (CINCPAC), on what the Japanese need to do:

> We strongly believe that to achieve that 1,000-mile sealane capability they are going to have to spend more than they are now. For example, given their current resources, we estimate that they are probably a year behind in their mid-term defense program. They have even stretched some of those programs further and are working on a "longer-term" mid-term defense program, trying to adjust some of their goals to their assets . . . .

> I guess there are a couple of problems here: One is that those goals remain their goals, and number two, that they go ahead and meet their program, and we don't know whether they'll do that or not. If they do, it looks like it will be the early or mid-1990s before they have the kind of capability they are talking about.[12]

Admiral Crowe also commented on the need for the Japanese to place more emphasis on ground forces, especially with regard to the main northern island of Hokkaido which is so close to the Soviet-occupied islands, the Northern Territories:

> It's true that they have devoted the bulk of their appropriations to air defense and to naval matters. And this has naturally resulted in the neglect of their ground forces, in terms of equipment, sustainability, and modernization. I do believe strongly, and I've had some reinforcement from Japan itself, that those forces being dedicated to defending Hokkaido need to be modernized. They need to be more mechanized, and they need more firepower, and they should definitely have more sustainability.[13]

Besides the level of Japanese defense spending and the resulting capabilities and commitments of Japan's Self-Defense Force, another important defense issue involving Japan, the United States, and the Soviet Union is Japan's three non-nuclear principles: not to possess nuclear weapons, not to manufacture them, and not to allow their introduction onto Japanese soil.

The third principle conflicts with the U.S. guarantee of Japanese security. To implement the guarantee, U.S. ships and aircraft -- some of which are presumably armed with nuclear weapons at least some of the time -- must operate in Japanese waters and airspace. When they do, anti-nuclear Japanese have protested their presence on the grounds that they violate the prohibition of nuclear weapons in Japan.

82

But Tokyo does not require the United States to confirm that no nuclear weapons are present. In short, Tokyo's attitude is "what we don't know won't hurt us." For public consumption (its tatemae stance), Tokyo proclaims a strong anti-nuclear posture, while its more candid and pragmatic position (its honne stance) winks at and implicitly sanctions what is necessary for Japan's defense. Some observers fear that if New Zealand persists, and succeeds, vis-a-vis the United States on the nuclear weapons issue, then it will be very hard for the ruling party in Tokyo to deflect the strong anti-nuclear forces in Japan. In this view, it will be forced by circumstances and public opinion to press for convergence of Tokyo's tatemae and honne positions. American-Japanese relations, and ultimately the security of free Asia, might be severely harmed if Tokyo felt it necessary to follow New Zealand's example -- e.g., when New Zealand's Prime Minister David Lange rejected a requested visit by the U.S. destroyer Buchanan because Washington would not guarantee that the ship did not carry nuclear weapons.[14]

Over the years, Moscow has attempted to convince Tokyo to bar U.S. nuclear weapons from Japan. For example, in April 1983, Soviet Vice Foreign Minister Mikhail Kapitsa offered Japan a non-nuclear-strike pact in a meeting in Tokyo with senior Japanese officials. Japan's Foreign Ministry later told newsmen that Kapitsa denied his country has nuclear weapons aimed at Japan, and he said Moscow is ready to sign an agreement pledging not to use nuclear weapons against Japan. In return for Moscow's agreement, noted Kapitsa, Japan would have to assure Moscow that it would uphold its policy of not making, possessing, or bringing nuclear arms into Japan. In short, Moscow wanted Tokyo to adhere rigorously to the three non-nuclear principles.[15]

It should be emphasized in addition that Moscow's propaganda machine attempts to create among Japan's neighbors, especially in Southeast Asia, fears about a revival of a militarily powerful and militaristic Japan. For its part, the Japanese government has attempted assiduously to ameliorate such fears on the part of its Asian neighbors. In his first state visit to Southeast Asia in May 1983, Prime Minister Nakasone participated in delicate talks on defense, trade, and foreign policy. On the surface, the purpose of the visits to the five countries of the Association of South East Asian Nations (ASEAN) and oil-rich Brunei (which was to become an ASEAN member) was for Nakasone to lay out a variety of Japanese commitments aimed at increasing Japan's access to the resources and markets of the ASEAN states in exchange for technology transfer and economic aid. Underlying the meetings, though, was what observers point to as Nakasone's need to reassure ASEAN governments -- especially Indonesia and the Philippines -- that Japan has no intention of returning as a major military power in Southeast Asia. Nakasone reportedly tried to indicate to the

Southeast Asian leaders that Tokyo-Washington discussions about Japanese assistance in defending sealanes in the Western Pacifc would not infringe on the sovereignty and independence of ASEAN region nations. It should be recalled that Nakasone's visit to the area followed the 1982 controversy over revisions of Japanese textbook histories of World War II Japanese atrocities in occupied Asian countries.[16]

Despite an improved Japanese image in Southeast Asia in the last decade, observers point out that what has happened is that ASEAN feelings toward Japan have changed from negativism merely to a kind of ambivalence. ASEAN leaders reportedly indicate that they would tolerate Japanese rearmament only to the extent that it frees U.S. ships and planes to operate in greater strength in Southeast Asia. But ASEAN is deeply uncomfortable with any implication that America is asking Japan to take up part of its defense burden in East Asia as a whole, to include Southeast Asia, or to act as a surrogate for Washington in the Pacific area.[17]

It should be clear from this discussion that the extent to which Japan increases its military spending, and commensurately expands its forces and defense commitments, will be heavily influenced by Japanese official and public perceptions of the threat posed to Japan's home islands by Soviet global strategy. Of vital importance to U.S. policymakers, then, will be the extent to which they can convince Tokyo, in a way which is persuasive but not shrill or overly alarmist, that the Soviet threat is permanent, growing, and especially pernicious for Japan in its home islands because of the long-term, multidimensional, and global nature of the threat.

84

NOTES

1. Mochizuki, Mike M., "Japan's Search for Strategy," _International Security_, Vol. 8, no. 3, Winter 1983-1984, pp. 153, 175, 178-179.

2. Horiguchi, Robert V., "North-East Asia: Vigorous Soviet Buildup," _Pacific Defence Reporter_, Vol. 11, nos. 6/7, December 1984/January 1985.

3. _Ibid._

4. _Defense of Japan, 1982_, the White Paper published by the Defense Agency, Japan, p. 7.

5. _Ibid._, p. 30.

6. Kimura, Hiroshi, "Soviet Policy Toward Japan," _Washington Quarterly_, Vol. 7, no. 3, Summer 1984, p. 24.

7. Elder, Timothy, "Soviet Grip on Northern Islands, Creates Sore Point for Japanese," _Washington Times_, September 27, 1984, p. A-6; and, Burgess, John, "Island Dispute Impedes Japanese-Soviet Relations," _Washington Post_, November 15, 1984, p. A-23.

8. Linn, Tom, "On Soya Strait and Soviet Pacific Deployment," _Defense and Foreign Affairs_, December 1983, p. 9ff; the Nemuro Strait lies between Hokkaido and Kunashir, the southernmost of the Kurile chain. Two serviceable Soviet airstrips overlook the strait. See Collins, John M., _U.S. Military Balance, 1980-1985_ (Washington: Pergamon-Brassey's, 1985), p. 141.

9. Horiguchi, "North-East Asia: Vigorous Soviet Buildup," _Op. cit._; and Oberdorfer, Don, "U.S. Accuses Soviets of Trying to Intimidate Japan," _Washington Post_, January 21, 1983, p. A-1.

10. Horiguchi, "North-East Asia: Vigorous Soviet Buildup," _Op. cit._

11. Burgess, John, "Japan Plans New Outlays for Defense," _Washington Post_, April 29, 1985, p. A-13; and ---- "Japan Sets More Arms Spending: Nakasone Proposes Increase of 6.9 Percent," _Washington Post_, December 30, 1984, p. A-17.

12. Meyer, Deborah G., "Interview with Admiral William J. Crowe, Jr.," _Armed Forces Journal_, May 1985, pp. 106-108.

13. _Ibid._

14. Olsen, Edward A., "Antinuclear Posturing: New Zealand vs. Japan," _Christian Science Monitor_, March 19, 1985, p. 17; and, Krauss, Melvyn, "If the New Zealand Syndrome Spreads," _New York Times_, February 17, 1985, p. E-19.

15. "Soviet Official Offers Japan No-Nuke Pact," _Washington Times_, April 13, 1983, p. A-4.

16. Lee, Dinah, "Nakasone Broadens Japan's Influence in Visit to Southeast Asia," _Washington Post_, May 11, 1983, p. A-26.

17. Oka, Takashi, "Southeast Asia Wary of Changing Roles of Japan and U.S. in Pacific," _Christian Science Monitor_, July 10, 1984, p. 10.

Chapter 12

SOVIET STRATEGIC OBJECTIVES ON THE KOREAN PENINSULA

Kim Yu-Nam

Of great importance to the Soviet Union is securing the Korean peninsula from both the Soviet Union's and North Korea's common enemies: South Korea and the United States. Today, Moscow is treaty bound to defend the Pyongyang regime just as Washington is to defend South Korea. Moscow is burdened with an additional requirement of ensuring that Pyongyang does not move too far into Peking's orbit and attempt to improve its own control over the North Korean regime. It is fair to say, however, that Moscow is becoming increasingly aware of the fact that there exists a certain limit as to the control that it can exercise over Pyongyang under the current regime. As a result, Moscow has attempted to give North Korean issues a low priority in recent years and has apparently hoped that the People's Republic of China (PRC) would do the same. Over the last ten years Moscow has not dispatched any new major weapons systems or made substantial increases in its economic support to North Korea.[1] In effect, Moscow has "maintained" its relationship with Pyongyang but has shown no real interest in improving it.

In the meantime, Moscow has become increasingly concerned about a growing Seoul-Tokyo-Washington alliance. With the recent planned expansion of the Vladivostok-Vostochnyy-Nakhodka Soviet naval complex, the near completion of the BAM railway (Baikul-Amur Mainline), and the planned development of Siberia and the Far Eastern Maritime District, Moscow can no longer ignore its national interests in Northeast Asia nor the West's challenge to Moscow's self-image as the leader of the "socialist community"[2] in the region. The Soviet Union logically seeks a peaceful and stable environment in the Far East, particularly on the Korean peninsula which is adjacent to the Soviet Far East Maritime Territory. As will be shown below, Moscow has proposed confidence-building measures as an apparent means of accomplishing this national foreign policy or strategic goal.

86

Moscow-Pyongyang Relations

Relations between the Soviet Union and North Korea have never remained on an even keel for any extended period of time. Kim Il-sung's personality cult, dating back to his great-grandfather and extending now to his son Kim Chong-il, and the nationalistic "Juche" (self-reliant) ideology of North Korea do not seem to sit well in Moscow. North Korea consistently seeks to apply indigenous traditions and experiences to build its own socialist system. Leading Soviet apparatchiki, scholars, and intellectuals in their private conversations with Western counterparts have all been critical of the North Korean regime and especially so of Kim Il-sung. North Korea is significantly absent in Soviet foreign policy writings and official documents. Soviet foreign policy textbooks since 1975 offer only formal, rather than substantive, references in support of the socialistic system established by the Soviet "liberation of Korea" in 1945.[3] The official policy statements made by the Secretary General to the 25th Party Congress of the Communist Party of the Soviet Union (CPSU) in 1976 and to the 26th Party Congress in 1981 make no reference to North Korea, and the Soviet news media also appear to be extremely reluctant to give more than "lukewarm support to Kim Il-sung."[4]

Nonetheless, North Korea's geostrategic location has become increasingly important to Moscow in terms of Soviet national interests. Furthermore, during the last decade and a half of Sino-Soviet rivalry, the Soviet Union could ill afford North Korea being drawn too close into China's orbit. From Moscow's point of view, China has gone to considerable length to court North Korea. Since the death of Mao Zedong, top Chinese leaders such as Deng Xiaoping, Hu Yaobang, and Zhao Ziyang have all visited Pyongyang and have had extensive discussions with Kim Il-sung and other North Koreans. Additionally, in 1983 Kim Il-sung and his son were both warmly received in Peking in a gesture that appeared to indicate top Chinese acceptance of and a willingness to support Kim Chong-il's succession. This warming of relations between North Korea and China has forced Moscow to reconsider its interests in Northeast Asia and particularly in North Korea.

Not wanting to find itself isolated in Northeast Asia, Moscow extended an invitation to the North Korean leadership to visit the Soviet Union. On May 23, 1984, Kim Il-sung arrived in Moscow and spent five days. During the visit, Kim Il-sung and General Secretary Konstantin Chernenko reportedly had at least one private closed-door session and two other sessions with other members of both delegations. At a banquet that evening, Chernenko set the tone of the discussions by reading a statement expressing concern with

North Korea's intensely nationalistic brand of communism. Inherent in Chernenko's text were Moscow's expectations for closer Soviet and North Korean positions on international and foreign policy issues especially with regard to the PRC, South Korea, Japan, and the United States.

Moscow surely recognizes that Pyongyang is quickly approaching a change in leadership and has not ignored the fact that China has apparently already acceded to the selection of Kim Chong-il as his father's successor.[5] The close ties between North Korea and China, and North Korea's open criticism of the Soviet invasion of Afghanistan have been regarded with growing concern in Moscow. In addition, in the last two or three years Moscow has viciously accused the United States and Japan of forming a triple alliance with South Korea against the Soviet Union and other socialist states in the region.[6]

The Soviet Union already uses North Korea's warm water port facilities of Najin in accordance with a series of agreements aimed at promoting economic cooperation between North Korea and the Soviet Union. It is possible that Moscow is now beginning to think of increasing its military cooperation with North Korea and increasing its use of North Korean bases.

The Soviet Union has been cool toward Pyongyang's public proposal in January 1984 for tripartite talks among Pyongyang, Seoul, and Washington. It is apparent that the Soviet Union is not comfortable with the idea of having the United States as a major party to peace talks on the Korean question. It has been Moscow's firm position for years that the Soviet Union should be "one of the main participants in any peace negotiations which bear on the direct interest of the Soviet Union."[7] Moscow is also sensitive to the fact that the Soviet Union was excluded from the North Korean proposal concerning tripartite talks. Moscow prefers to apply its own suggested confidence-building measures to the Korean problem. In 1981, General Secretary Leonid Brezhnev had introduced these measures as a Soviet peace program for the Far East. In essence, they are a scheme for holding an Helsinki-type security conference in the Far East. Accordingly, the USSR would be a participant in any talks.

From the Soviet point of view, the USSR's ultimate trump card over North Korea is the succession issue. If North Korea is willing to improve its relations with the Soviet Union and become a much more respectful ally, Moscow will support Kim Chong-il's succession. If these conditions can be brought about, a new era of Soviet-North Korean relations could emerge.

North Korea's foreign policy toward the Soviet Union and China over the past 23 years has often been categorized as a "zero-sum game." What China won in terms of concessions, Moscow lost. North Korea has done little to attenuate this perspective and has

88

actively pursued its own national interests by courting both suitors. Kim Il-sung's historic visit to Moscow in late May 1984 is no exception in that it was preceded by a North Korean visit to Peking and by a two-week visit by the Chinese General Secretary Hu Yaobang to Pyongyang in early May.

Pyongyang-Moscow versus Pyongyang-Peking

North Korea's relations toward its communist allies can be viewed in terms of both long- and short-term foreign policy objectives or goals. Its long-term goal is to maintain close ties with both the Soviet Union and the People's Republic of China in order to ensure their continuing support for Pyongyang's reunification policies and struggle against South Korea. Although relations between Pyongyang and both Moscow and Peking have vacillated over the last two decades, China and the Soviet Union have been important sources of political, economic, military, and diplomatic support for North Korea.

In the short-term, while officially maintaining an equidistant policy towards both of these communist superpowers, North Korea continues to capitalize on the volatile relations between the two. In effect, North Korea has sought its own national interest by playing one superpower off against the other in this strange courtship.

A pertinent question to ask at this point is why have North Korea's relations with these two communist superpowers fluctuated so dramatically? The answer is relatively simple. North Korea is acting in terms of its own national self-interests, and as the relations between China and the Soviet Union have deteriorated, North Korea has taken advantage of the situation by courting one or the other for its own gains. When Soviet policy goals and support to North Korea become detrimental to Pyongyang's reunification policy, North Korea wastes no time in focusing its attention towards Peking. Such changes have been easily accomplished due to China's phobia over its Soviet neighbor since the armed clashes on the border in 1969.

From Pyongyang's point of view neither the Chinese nor the Soviet offers of friendship are without qualification. For example Peking's recent contacts with Seoul, such as the visit of Director Shen Tu of the Civil Aviation Administration of China (CAAC) in May of 1983, increasing levels of indirect trade through Hong Kong, and more frequent sports and cultural contacts between China and South Korea have left some doubt in North Korean minds as to China's true intentions.

North Korea's perceptions of the Soviet Union are just as suspicious, if not more so. Pyongyang knows that Moscow has on a few occasions sent its "feelers" to South Korea apparently in an expression of Moscow's displeasure over Kim Il-sung's June 1983 visit to Peking.[8]

Kim Il-sung's statement during his May 1984 visit to Moscow reminded the Soviet Union of the difficulties that North Korea faces in its economic development efforts, partly due to its almost exclusive dependence on the Soviet Union for economic assistance and partly due to its heavy defense expenditures. North Korea in recent years has spent almost 16 percent of its gross national product (GNP) on its defense efforts and another 25 percent of its GNP on defense-related industries.[9] Kim Il-sung highlighted the fact that part of North Korea's economic problems arise directly from its staunch support of Moscow and Peking, at the expense of possible economic relations with Western countries. Whether North Korea and the Soviet Union will move closer towards a concrete military alliance remains to be seen. Soviet national interests in Northeast Asia appear to be on the increase and a closer Moscow-Pyongyang axis is possible. The Soviet willingness to shoulder a heavy economic burden in Vietnam to counter the Chinese threat in Southeast Asia could be repeated with regard to North Korea.[10]

North Korea's Objectives

A review of the limited publications available both from Moscow and Pyongyang tends to indicate that North Korea has these objectives vis-a-vis the USSR:

o   obtain Soviet approval and support for the North Korean proposed tripartite talks which would allow North Korea to open its doors to the United States;

o   acquire a Soviet pledge to increase Moscow's economic assistance to North Korea and consolidate Pyongyang's socialistic economic ties with the Soviet Union. This would not prohibit Pyongyang from preparing for economic contacts with non-communist countries;

o   gain Soviet acceptance of the dynastic succession of Kim Chong-il as Kim Il-sung prepares to retire gradually;

o   increase Soviet transfer of modern weapons systems to North Korea in exchange for Pyongyang's global security cooperation with the Soviet Union. This objective would further allow the Soviet Union to obtain base rights at a number of additional North Korean bases and could allow for joint exercises between the Soviet Union and North Korea in the future.

90

Following Kim Il-sung's visit, the long-standing issue of increased Soviet economic assistance to North Korea remains just as cloudy. The Soviet Union, facing its own economic setbacks, is already heavily committed to North Korea, not to mention its commitments to Vietnam and Afghanistan. In 1981 Moscow promised Pyongyang its support on eight new projects under North Korea's second Seven-Year Development Plan (1978-1984). These new projects included the Kimchaek Steel Refinery Complex, the Chongjin Thermal Power Station, the Aoji Chemical Plant, and the Pyongyang Generator Plant.

These new commitments were in addition to some 51 existing projects under construction.[11] With North Korea's foreign debt currently standing at U.S. $3 billion, it is doubtful that the Soviet Union is in a position to significantly increase its economic assistance to North Korea without substantial concessions on the part of Pyongyang.

Soviet Interest in South Korea

The Soviet Union has taken several visible measures towards easing tensions on the Korean peninsula. Over the past two years and in response to South Korea's "nordpolitik," the Soviet Union has presented several amiable gestures to South Korea whenever the opportunity presented itself. Although unofficial trade and contacts between Seoul and Peking still dwarf those between Seoul and Moscow, the Soviet Union seems to be moving slowly toward a "two-Korea" policy.

Moscow is additionally interested in South Korea's fast-growing industrial potential, and Moscow will face the dilemma of the 1988 Seoul Olympic Games. Moscow will be hard put to boycott the games in 1988 because of its 1984 boycott of the Los Angeles games. The Soviet Union thus will probably like to participate in the 1988 Seoul Olympic games as "the eyes of the world will then increasingly shift to South Korea."[12]

In addition, the Soviet Union knows that it owes an apology to South Korea for shooting down a Korean Air Lines Flight 007, a Boeing 747 "jumbo jet," on the night of September 1, 1983.[13] It seems clear that the longer the Soviet Union waits to begin building stronger contacts with South Korea, the more difficult the process will become.

In terms of its relations with Seoul, the Soviet Union realizes that it stands in a position behind China. For example, the first sports exchange in forty years between South Korea and China occurred at the Davis Cup Eastern Zone elimination rounds held in China on March 2 to 4, 1984. At that event, China hoisted the South Korean national flag for the first time.[14]

The Soviet Union also realizes that the North Korean economy's disarray requires more access to Western goods, capital, and technology. Since South Korea's wage rates in certain sectors of its industry are no longer cost-competitive, South Korea could even assist the North. Moscow thus foresees that Kim Il-sung's foremost objectives in wooing the United States are, first, to get the American troops out of South Korea and, second, to weaken the South's military strongholds and allow for the introduction of more economic assistance.[15] In terms of its economic leverage, the Soviet Union's window of opportunity is closing as Pyongyang steadily, though slowly, increases its commercial links with the West and particularly with Japan. These economic motives are yet another important consideration in Pyongyang's growing interest in cultivating links with the United States through the tripartite talks.

The above scenario provides Kim Il-sung with a better opportunity for playing his "American card" than at any other time since the 1950s. Though the Soviet Union understands that Pyongyang would never wish to align itself totally with China, Kim Il-sung nevertheless retains the capacity to move somewhat closer to the Chinese and in doing so use its American card against the Soviet Union. The tripartite talks proposals could become an ideal medium through which this maneuver could take place. Moscow is already psychologically and diplomatically pressed by China to support the tripartite talks or else be left out in the cold. Conversely, if the tripartite talks do become a reality, the Soviet proposals for confidence-building measures would pass into obscurity, and China, the United States, and Japan would become the major superpower actors in the talks.

Soviet Global Objectives

In conclusion, for the Soviet Union, the Korean question has to be treated in terms of its global requisites while North Korea's peripheral vision is much narrower. Soviet interest in the Korean peninsula is no longer limited to the small nation north of the Demilitarized Zone (DMZ), and its strategy on the issue must also address all of Northeast and Southeast Asia and the Pacific as well.[16] Soviet long-term interests are much more focused on China, Japan, and the United States than they are on a nation of less than 20 million.[17] In this sense, for the Soviet Union the settlement of the Korean question is but a means of accomplishing its global objectives, not an objective itself.

Another conclusion concerns the relative number of options open to both the Soviet Union and North Korea. North Korea is in the advantageous position of being the holder of the key. It can open tripartite talks with the United States and South Korea, call for bilateral talks with South Korea alone, enlist China's support for any of these efforts, and then use these efforts or proposals to pressure Moscow. Although Moscow does provide substantial military and economic aid to North Korea, it is still North Korea's ball game. Moscow has but one option and that option is contingent upon North Korea's request for the USSR's participation in the talks. If Moscow does not accede to Pyongyang's positions, it will find itself left out of negotiations on an area that is vital to Soviet national interests.

This is a shortened and edited version of a paper entitled, "Changing Relations between Moscow and Pyongyang: 'The Odd Man Out,' " prepared for the Conference on North Korea in a Regional and Global Context, Cheju, Republic of Korea, August 20-23, 1984.

NOTES

1. For details, see Ha, Joseph M., "Soviet Perceptions of North Korea," Asian Perspective, Vol. 6, no. 2, Fall-Winter 1982, pp. 105-131.

2. Stephen, John J., "Asia in the Soviet Conception," in Soviet Policy in East Asia, edited by Donald S. Zagoria, (New Haven: Yale University Press, 1982), p. 37.

3. For books in English, see A Study of Soviet Foreign Policy (Moscow: Progress Publishers, 1975), pp. 68-69; Kovalenko, Ivan, ed., Soviet Policy For Asian Peace and Security (Moscow: Progress Publishers, 1979), pp. 72-78; and Kykov, O., V. Razmerov, and D. Tomashevsky, The Priorities of Soviet Foreign Policy Today (Moscow: Progress Publishers, 1981), pp. 166-176.

4. David, Steven R., "Third World Interventions," Problems of Communism, May-June 1984, p. 66.

5. For more on the growing ties between Peking and Pyongyang, see, among others, Pollack, Jonathan D., "Chinese Policy Toward Korea: A Continuing Dilemma?" Asia Pacific Defense Forum, Special Supplement, Summer 1983, pp. 13-17.

6. Petukhov, Valentin, "The U.S.-Japan-South Korea: NATO's Double in the Pacific?," Asia and Africa Today (Moscow), no. 2, March-April 1984, p. 11.

7. Ponova, E.I., Americanskiy Senat i Vneshnaya Politika (Moskva: Institut SShA i Kanady, 1978), p. 16.

8. See The Pyongyang Times, May 26, 1984, p. 2; and Pravda, May 24, 1984, p. 2.

9. Hoivik, Thomas, "Korea -- Is Peaceful Unification Still Possible?," Washington Quarterly, Vol. 7, no. 1, Winter 1984, p. 81.

10. For more on Moscow-Hanoi relations, see Shan, Tan, "Kremlin-Hanoi Pact: Sources of Southeast Asian Tension," Current World Leader, Vol. 27, no. 1-3, February 1984, pp. 100-102.

11. For more on the Soviet foreign policy cooperation, see The Priorities of Soviet Foreign Policy Today, Op. cit., p. 2.

12. Olsen, Edward A., "The Evolution of the ROK's Foreign Policy," Washington Quarterly, Vol. 7, no. 1, Winter 1984, p. 71.

13. In defense of its action, Moscow accused Washington of dispatching the passenger plane on a spying mission. At the same time, there were noticeable indications that Moscow tried hard not to offend the grieved South Koreans. See the content of the Soviet statement made at a news conference led by Marshal Nikolai V. Ogarkov, Chief of the Soviet General Staff, on September 10, 1983, in New York Times, September 10, 1983.

14. China sent its two basketball teams (boys and girls) to the 8th Asian Youth Basketball Championship Games which took place in Seoul on April 7 to 19, 1984. China also sent 20 athletes and nine officials to the 2d Asian Swimming Championship Games

94

which were held in Seoul, April 27 to May 3, 1984. Each time the Chinese five star flag was hoisted.

15. "Doves over Korea," The Economist, January 21, 1984, p. 13.

16. In a recent Soviet press report on South Korea, the Soviet Union recognized the strategic importance of South Korea to the interests of all major powers of the region. See Kapustin, Dmitriy, "Koreya: Reportazh c 38-y Paralleli," Literaturnaya Gazeta, May 24, 1984, p. 21.

17. For details, see Dmytryshyn, Basil, "Soviet Perceptions of North Korea," Asian Perspective, Vol. 6, no. 2, Fall-Winter 1982, pp. 105-131.

Chapter 13

DEVELOPMENT OF STRATEGY IN SINO-SOVIET RELATIONS

Shinkichi Eto

Historical Background: Slavs versus Chinese, CPSU versus CPC

Historically, the Chinese have feared the Slavs, essentially because of centuries of their eastward expansion. As early as the seventeenth century, they confronted Slavs along China's Amur River. Geographically speaking, the Slavs were centered around Moscow in the western part of the Eurasian landmass, east of the Ural Mountains. Unlike the steep Rocky Mountains in the United States, the Urals tend to be gently sloping, often with extensive rolling hills. Thus these mountains are relatively easy for people to pass over. History says that a Cossacks headman, Yermak, went over the Ural Mountains and conquered the State of Sibir Khan, which he offered to Ivan the Fourth, the sixteenth century Russian Czar. It is said that Sibir Kanh is the origin of the name Siberia.

When the Boxer Rebellion broke out in China in 1900 a series of incidents occurred in Manchuria in which Chinese people molested many Slavs. In retaliation, the Slavs removed some 5,000 Chinese from their homes in Blagoveshchensk, gathered them by the Amur, and killed them. It is also a fact that the Russians stationed a large number of troops in Manchuria. These forces suppressed the Boxers, and virtually put most of Manchuria under their control. These kinds of historical events have led to a basic Chinese dislike of the Russians. For example, when White Russians fled from the Bolshevik Revolution to Manchuria, they experienced a hard time living with Chinese people there.

Another example of bloody hostilities between Slavs and Chinese occurred when the Chinese Revolution erupted in 1911. Russia immediately put pressure on Outer Mongolia and made it a pro-Russian state. At the outbreak of the Russian Revolution -- the "October" Revolution -- in 1917, China dispatched troops and drove the Russian forces out of Outer Mongolia. When the Bolshevik Revolution spread to Siberia, Japan supported Gregori Mikhailovich

96

Semijonov, a Slav/Mongol mixed-blood of the White Army. Japan supplied him with many weapons and military advisers. Semijonov wielded power for some time with China as his base. He had a subordinate, Baron Ungern von Sternberg, who led troops into Mongolia and either drove away or killed a great many Chinese merchants and officials. Then the Red Army came on the scene, defeated Sternberg's troops, and put all of Outer Mongolia under its control. The Red Army installed a puppet party called the Mongolian People's Party, which turned Mongolia into Moscow's first satellite nation. Similar Russian-Chinese hostilities took place in Xinjiang (Sinkiang) Province in China.

Not surprisingly, Sino-Soviet relations since the Russian Revolution have been characterized by much distrust, bad feelings, and periods of outright hostility. An appreciation of the conflicts in this period is essential to understanding relations between the two communist states.

After the revolution, the Lenin-led Communist Party of the Soviet Union (CPSU) formed the Comintern, an international organization of communists, in Moscow, and revolutionaries from India, Holland, and other foreign countries joined. But very few persons from East Asia were among the initial members.

Eventually, the Comintern decided to recruit Chinese members. A large number of Chinese were invited to the "Workers University of the Far East," located in Moscow. Some of the recruits later became members of the Chinese Communist Party (CCP). One of these recruits was Chang Tai-lei, a young intellectual who graduated from the Peking National University. He was ordered by the Comintern to go to Japan to distribute travel money to Japanese socialists, which was used by a number of Japanese to smuggle themselves into the Soviet Union. After the Japanese socialists returned to Japan, they founded the Japanese Communist Party in 1922.

Through such actions, the Comintern exerted a significant influence on the foundation and development of many communist parties in East Asia. Lenin was the leader of both the Soviet Communist Party and Comintern, and Stalin succeeded Lenin in these capacities.

The Sino-Soviet Split

Following is a list of factors which contributed to the Sino-Soviet split in 1960, and have helped keep the two big communist states at odds since then:

o   Mao was a doctrinarian who literally interpreted the ideology of Marx and Lenin, whereas Khrushchev was somewhat flexible in his interpretations. Although not known in the West at the time, an intense Moscow-Peking ideological dispute erupted about 1957.

o A major manifestation of the ideological differences between Mao and Khrushchev was Mao's opposition to the "peaceful coexistence" policy adopted by Khrushchev with regard to relations with the United States. Khrushchev held that such an approach was necessary in view of U.S. predominance in nuclear weapons. In contrast, Mao advocated a more active or even aggressive approach to the West.

o Mao and his followers began in 1958 to take an approach, different from that of the USSR, to building socialism in China. Initiated were "the great leap forward," and "one-state socialism," which were supposed to increase industrial and agricultural production. The results of these efforts were generally poor. In 1958, Khrushchev made a highly negative remark about people's communes in China.

o In response to China's desire for nuclear weapons, in late 1958 Moscow signed an agreement with Peking to supply Soviet nuclear weapons technology to China. However, as the Sino-Soviet ideological dispute intensified, Moscow did not adhere to the agreement and unilaterally withdrew its engineers from China. Peking questioned Soviet reliability in technological cooperation.

o In 1961, 2,000 Soviet technical advisers who had been working in China returned to the Soviet Union.

o In 1963, Moscow and Peking differed sharply concerning the nuclear test ban treaty.

o Because of nomadic farmers, and shifting islets in rivers cultivated by farmers, border disputes between China and the USSR often erupt, usually during periods of general tension between the countries. For example, border disputes resulted in a military clash in Damanskii -- to give it the Russian name; in Chinese it would be Chenpao -- island on the Ussuri River, in March 1969, and at Yümen in Xinjiang in June 1969.

o Bilateral relations had deteriorated greatly by 1963 at which time Moscow stationed elite troops along the

98

border. Some observers believe the USSR was considering, or at least pretending to be considering, pre-emptive war against China. The Chinese certainly feared the Soviet military buildup on the border and began storing food, digging shelters for possible nuclear attacks, and training for guerrilla warfare against any Soviet occupying force.

o   Moscow and Peking collaborated somewhat in support of Hanoi during the Vietnam War. But differences with Moscow still led Peking to agree to improved relations with the United States, culminating in President Nixon's dramatic visit to China in February 1972.

o   In 1975, to get away from the Soviet model, the PRC enacted a new constitution which described China as a nation based on social capitalism.

Moves Toward Sino-Soviet Reconciliation

After Mao died in 1976, after the arrest of the "Gang of Four," and after the discrediting in China of the ideology that underpinned the Cultural Revolution, the climate changed to one in which Sino-Soviet relations could improve.

On March 24, 1982, Brezhnev gave a lecture at Tashkent in which he called for reconciliation between the Soviet Union and China. Rather than remain cool to such a proposal as on previous occasions, Peking responded to this call at once. The result was a meeting of deputy foreign ministers from the two nations. Similar periodic meetings have continued since then. At the 20th meeting of the Chinese Communist Party in September 1983, General Secretary Hu Yaobang noted the growing possibility that Sino-Soviet relations would be improved. However, Peking set three conditions for such an improvement:

o   reduction of Soviet troops on the Sino-Soviet border,

o   end to the Soviet invasion of Afghanistan, and

o   end to the Soviet-backed Vietnamese invasion of Kampuchea.

The Soviet troop presence along the Sino-Soviet border thus continues as an important Sino-Soviet issue. Since 1969, Chinese leaders, including Chou En-lai, have said that over a million Soviet troops are stationed along the border. Japanese Government sources, however, have put the number at 400,000 to 500,000. Peking has proposed for a long time that both nations withdraw their troops 100 kilometers behind their respective borders. This analyst believes, however, that at the present time China no longer sees any possibility of the Soviet troops invading its territory. And, conversely, the Soviet Union does not fear a Chinese attack.

Thus even though Peking is still holding to its three conditions for improved relations, there appear to be no longer any real causes for further conflicts between China and Soviet Union -- despite the long history of unhappy incidents in the past. Peking still publicly holds it will not reconcile with any nation which adheres to hegemony. Whatever the verbal posturing, though, it seems that both sides want improved relations. The USSR remains open to such improvement, a desire expressed consistently by the words and actions of Brezhnev, Andropov, Chernenko, and Gorbachev. General bilateral relations have indeed improved in recent years. Moscow and Peking have agreed each year to conclude agreements on the shifting river border. Cross-border trade was resumed in 1983 after a decade's suspension.

This observer believes that China and the Soviet Union will normalize their relations on the national level, and that there will be more trade and interchanges of people. This is because reconciliation to a certain degree will benefit both nations in their negotiations with the West.

It seems that China will improve its relations with the Soviet Union in order to maximize its diplomatic maneuverability against the United States. In the past, China considered the Soviet Union as an enemy. This deprived China of what may be called the "Soviet card" in negotiating with the United States. Even if Washington tried to be dominant over Peking, China would not be able to say, "If you behave like that, we will go with the Soviet Union." In the absence of normal relations with Moscow, China's diplomatic maneuverability vis-a-vis the United States is narrowed.

For several years, President Reagan acted in a way sometimes deemed unfriendly by China. For example, Washington delivered advanced weapons to Taiwan. Washington took a long time from, September 1982 to January 1983, to decide whether or not to grant political asylum to the tennis player Hu Na. The Reagan administration publicized the matter in the newspaper before deciding to grant asylum. This was like throwing mud at China's face. If Washington did intend to accept her, it could have done so without publicizing it so much. Another example is seen in the decision of the U.S. Congress to grant permission to Pan American World Airways to resume its flights to Taiwan.

Thus the United States has been taking actions which mean or portend loss of face for China. The Chinese leaders no doubt realize that if they have a confrontational relationship with Moscow, they cannot play the Soviet card against the United States. Improved relations with the Soviet Union, they believe, will strengthen their bargaining position with Washington. It seems that such reasoning is behind the prompt response on the part of China to the Soviet call for reconciliation in 1982. However, leaders of the Peking government deny this interpretation.

While Peking will no doubt seek to improve relations with Moscow so as to have increased bargaining leverage with the United States, a revived Sino-Soviet alliance does not seem likely. A major reason is the Chinese desire to achieve the four modernizations. Peking recognizes that the Soviet Union is not an adequate nor reliable source of the technology that China needs to modernize. For example, post-purchase spare parts and services are poor when China buys Soviet Ilyushin commercial jets. On the other hand, when British Trident or American Boeing 707s are purchased, quality parts and services are immediately supplied from depots in Shanghai. In addition, Chinese pilots say that Boeing 707s have better maneuverability than the strongly built but heavier Soviet planes. Likewise, Western nations provide far better automobiles, communications equipment, polymer chemistry products, and computers than the Soviet Union.

Chapter 14

SOVIET STRATEGIC CONCERNS IN SOUTHEAST ASIA

William R. Kintner

Southeast Asia has long been of interest to the USSR. Indonesia was one of the first Third World states and the first in Southeast Asia to receive Soviet attention and assistance. The initial Soviet overture to Indonesia took place in 1956 at a time when Sino-Soviet relations were still relatively cordial. Hence, Soviet aid took into account both the fact that the Indonesian archipelago was situated astride the sea routes connecting the Indian and Pacific oceans and that the country possessed great natural resources. In the three decades that followed, the Sino-Soviet split took place and widened, and the Soviet Union became firmly entrenched in Vietnam. Because of its massive military buildup in Southeast Asia and elsewhere in Asia, the USSR poses an increasing threat to the countries of the Association of South East Asian Nations (ASEAN), all of whom except the Philippines have flourishing economies.

PRC-USSR Relations

Soviet strategic concerns in East Asia are dominated by the present and potential capabilities of the People's Republic of China (PRC). Consequently, the USSR has attempted to encircle the PRC. While striving for a cordon sanitaire, however, fears of Chinese potential have led Moscow to periodic attempts to improve relations with Peking. The competition for leadership in the world communist movement creates some tension betweeen the two powers. Their rivalry is often a by-product of competition for Asian regional political influence. Peking perceives that Moscow's support of Vietnam against Pol Pot's regime in Kampuchea (Cambodia), its occupation of Laos, and invasion of Kampuchea represent Soviet attempts to increase pressure on Peking in a vise-like fashion.

PRC attempts to escape this encirclement have led it to abandon a highly ideological foreign policy stance and to cultivate

102

ties with non-communist or "reactionary" regimes in Southeast Asia. In February 1981, PRC Prime Minister Zhao Ziyang declared: "We will try to take further action to prevent our relations with the Communist parties of the ASEAN region from affecting friendly relations between China and the countries of ASEAN."[1]

Though the accession to power by Deng Xiaoping somewhat eased tensions between the PRC and ASEAN, the intentions of the Soviet Union in the region led ASEAN to hold a conference on June 26 and 27, 1983, at which time the ASEAN countries discussed the "Soviet threat in Asia."[2] However, although ASEAN attention has focused most heavily on Soviet expansion, Chinese refusal to abandon support of the guerrilla insurgencies in Malaysia and the Philippines is a source of considerable concern to the non-communist countries. Chinese efforts to cultivate ties with ASEAN have been matched by similar Soviet efforts. The methods employed by the USSR are the familiar combination of military presence, foreign assistance, and political manipulations.

Soviet Expansion of Influence

The massive Soviet military buildup in the Asian theater in the past decade and a half is the most significant change that has occurred in that vast region. It has been on land, in the seas, and in the air. Southeast Asia has played an important role in this buildup.

With the acquisition of naval and air bases in Vietnam, the USSR's ability to monitor and, if need be, interfere with sealanes of communication has been greatly enhanced. At Vietnam's Cam Ranh Bay, the USSR bases an average of 22 naval ships, half of which are combatants. At times, these have included up to four nuclear and conventional-powered submarines. In November 1983, nine 1,500-mile-radius Soviet Tu-16 BADGER medium bombers were deployed to the Cam Ranh airfield. In addition, nine more BADGERS were deployed in June 1984.[3]

In April 1984, a Soviet-Vietnamese joint amphibious naval landing exercise of unprecedented size was held south of Haiphong. Vietnamese landing ships and frigates were joined by a Soviet Naval Infantry battalion transported by the large amphibious assault ship Aleksandr Nikoleyev, which was escorted by the anti-submarine carrier Minsk and other Soviet combatants.[4]

Soviet access to Vietnamese bases gives Moscow the ability to threaten sealanes and U.S. naval forces in the South China Sea, to strike targets in southern China, and to monitor activity in the Indian Ocean. Moscow also has the capability to support Vietnamese moves in the Tonkin Gulf if it so desires.

Southeast Asia has become the most active arena of political, psychological, and subversive confrontation between the Soviet

Union and Communist China. Because of geographic proximity, Southeast Asia offers the best opportunity to China for expanding its influence. Recognizing this, the USSR has commented that "Southeast Asia has always had a special place in the policy of the Chinese leadership."[5]

Both the USSR and the PRC perceive Southeast Asia as intrinsically important because of the perceived intentions of the other power. Moscow is convinced that the Chinese will use their influence to contain Vietnam and to create an anti-Soviet, anti-Vietnam coalition with the ASEAN states. Peking fears that Moscow is using Vietnam to oppose Chinese influence in the region and is encouraging Vietnamese dependence on the USSR to insure an anti-Chinese foreign policy on the part of Hanoi.

Each ASEAN nation represents an obstacle as well as an opportunity for the Soviet Union. Thailand, in particular, is vulnerable to Soviet influence should Vietnam successfully consolidate control over Kampuchea. Facing mounting domestic pressures, Indonesia is also susceptible to Soviet penetration.

For many years, the PRC was the only communist power that supported Ho Chi Minh's struggle against the French and subsequently against the United States. It was Chinese artillery that led to the surrender of the French forces at the battle of Dien Bien Phu. The USSR began to supply military aid to Hanoi in the late 1960s, and by the time of the U.S. military withdrawal in 1973 the Soviet Union had become Hanoi's principal partner.

Competition from Chinese Forces

The ability of the PRC to compete with Moscow was severely constrained by the traditional ethnic enmity between China and Vietnam. Hanoi's perception of its regional role and the policies it initiated have brought it into conflict with Peking. This tension is complicated by Hanoi's ideological affinity with Soviet doctrine. Somewhat muted during the 1965-1975 Vietnam War, the Vietnam-related hostility between the two communist powers blossomed when Hanoi began to side openly with Moscow after 1975.

The PRC courted Vietnam with a $400 million economic assistance package and an interest-free loan awarded in 1976. Conscious of the Chinese competition, the Kremlin cancelled all Vietnamese repayments of previous loans and agreed to "coordinate" national economic development plans. The USSR then extended a $500 million assistance package to Vietnam for Hanoi's first five-year plan, 1976-1980.

The Chinese perceived that the Soviet Union had gained both from the American withdrawal and the emergence of Vietnam as the most powerful Indochinese nation. One year after the defeat of

104

South Vietnam, Pravda stated, "the victory of Vietnam has opened up new horizons for the whole of Southeast Asia."[6]

The Soviet-Vietnamese relationship became a concern of other regional states as the degree of Vietnamese control in Laos and Kampuchea grew. The Pathet Lao elimination of Lao nationalist leaders and their replacement by pro-Vietnamese members of the Indochinese Communist Party reflected continuing Vietnamese expansion of political influence in neighboring states. By 1976, Hanoi had stationed 40,000 to 60,000 troops in Laos.[7] The Lao People's Democratic Republic was established in September 1976. Since then Soviet activity in Laos has been intense. The degree of Soviet and Vietnamese influence in Laos has led Laos to support Soviet and Vietnamese policy at the expense of the PRC.

Marking the second anniversary of the communist victory in Vietnam, Premier Pham Van Dong visited the USSR in April 1977. Dong requested Vietnamese admission into the Soviet-led Council for Mutual Economic Assistance (CMEA). Vietnam's admission to this body was announced at the June 29, 1978, CMEA meeting of prime ministers in Bucharest and was quite unexpected by other CMEA members.[8]

Moscow and Hanoi entered into a Treaty of Friendship and Cooperation on November 3, 1978. A Soviet spokesman stated the treaty was motivated by "the political climate in Southeast Asia which is being poisoned by the Chinese leadership."[9] The USSR also intimated that the treaty would contribute to the policy of encircling China. Unlike mutual assistance treaties, which Moscow has with other countries, committing the USSR to provide "immediate aid," including "military aid in the case of attack on the other party," the Soviet-Vietnamese treaty calls on each party to begin "immediate mutual consultation" in the case of a threat or attack. Both sides pledged to take "appropriate effective measures for the preservation of peace and security . . . ."[10]

In December 1978, Hanoi launched a military offensive into Kampuchea with around 100,000 troops. Hanoi quickly announced the formation of the Kampuchean United Front for National Salvation, composed of dissident Cambodians loyal to Hanoi. The Vietnamese forces seized the Kampuchean capital of Phnom Penh on January 7, 1979. On February 18, Vietnam signed a Treaty of Peace, Friendship, and Cooperation with Kampuchea. After Vietnam, the Soviet Union was the first nation to recognize the new Hanoi-aligned government, headed by Heng Samrin, a former commander of the Khmer Rouge Communists. The new government replaced the brutal regime of Khmer Rouge leader Pol Pot, who ruled Kampuchea and murdered over one million Kampucheans between April 1975 and January 1979.[11]

Despite the apparent success of the invasion of Kampuchea, the Vietnamese discovered that Kampuchean nationalists had withdrawn to the high mountains of the Cardamon and Elephant ranges in southwestern Kampuchea. These forces began a full-scale resistance against the Vietnamese troops. As the fighting escalated, Hanoi was forced to deploy additional troops along the Vietnam-PRC border to counter Peking's massing of troops and aircraft. Despite the heavy deployment of troops opposite the PRC, Hanoi doubled the occupation forces in Kampuchea from 100,000 to 200,000 troops.

The global consensus opposing Vietnamese and Soviet policy toward Kampuchea was evident when the USSR was forced to veto a watered-down resolution of the United Nations Security Council calling for the withdrawal of all foreign troops from Kampuchea. Moscow and Hanoi had initially refused to admit that Vietnamese forces had taken part in precipitating the fall of Pol Pot's Khmer Rouge regime.

Clash in Vietnam

Meanwhile, the Chinese began to deliver supplies to the Khmer guerrillas. Initially using Thai ports,[12] the Chinese established a land-based supply link with the nationalists using the so-called "Deng Xiaoping Trail." The supply route enters northeast Thailand from China via Laos, winds through Thailand and ends at the northwestern Kampuchean frontier. In return for Thai acquiesence to this passage, the Chinese curtailed their support of the pro-Chinese Communist Party of Thailand.[13]

Peking also had a number of options for overt retaliation against Vietnam. The easiest would have been seizure of the Spratly Islands in the South China Sea. Statements from Peking in December 1978 laying claim to the islands coveted by both the PRC and Vietnam indicated that this was under consideration. The Chinese condemned "any foreign country's invasion or occupation of the Nansha (Spratly) Islands" as constituting "encroachments on China's territorial integrity and sovereignty."[14] The previous time that China had officially asserted its claim on Spratly Islands was in June 1976. A Chinese move against the islands could have taken advantage of easy logistics by utilizing Chinese naval capabilities. However, the questionable effect on Hanoi and the threat of Soviet naval intervention apparently argued against such a move.[15]

In the meantime, the Chinese massed over half a million men along the Vietnamese border. Another sign of Chinese seriousness was the assignment of Yang Tezhi, the general who fought the American-led United Nations forces in Korea, to command the Chinese forces along the border with Vietnam.[16]

The Chinese buildup was matched by a larger Soviet effort along the Sino-Soviet frontier. The size and speed of the buildup caused some anxiety in Washington as fears of escalation grew. After the beginning of the Vietnamese offensive into Kampuchea in December 1978, the Soviets deployed a small naval task force off the Vietnamese coast. These vessels were divided into two groups, one positioned between the Chinese island of Hainan and the Vietnamese coast and the other in the South China Sea. The first group was composed of intelligence-gathering vessels and a few gunboats. The mission was apparently to eavesdrop on Chinese communications to gather possible clues of intentions and timing. The second group had two heavy KRESTA II cruisers as well as several frigates. This mission was apparently a "trip wire" should the Chinese move to take the Spratly Islands and served to warn the Chinese that such a move would escalate into Soviet involvement.[17]

The Chinese invasion of Vietnam on February 17, 1979, was an effort both to demonstrate that Hanoi's relationship with Moscow would not checkmate the PRC in Southeast Asia and to "punish" Vietnam and the USSR. Meanwhile, Moscow airlifted supplies to Vietnam, though not on a large scale, indicating that Vietnam was not seriously short of supplies. The Soviet Union also deployed more ships to the South China Sea after the invasion, including the flagship of the Soviet Pacific Fleet which was capable of directing air and naval operations. These 1979 deployments marked the first Soviet show of force in the region.[18] As the Vietnamese military position along the PRC-Vietnam border gradually worsened, Moscow began to warn Peking in sharper language. There were reports that the Soviet military was calling for action against the Chinese. When the battle began for the Vietnam provincial capital of Lang Son in early March, the USSR for the first time warned that the war could spread and publicly underscored its obligations under the Soviet-Vietnamese Treaty of Friendship and Cooperation.

In any case, the Chinese forces withdrew from Vietnam in mid-March 1979. The Peking leadership could credibly argue that its "limited" objectives had been achieved by capturing Lang Son and diverting Vietnamese troops from Kampuchea, but most analysts agree that the poor showing of the People's Liberation Army and numerous casualties suffered made the PRC effort less than successful. The Chinese attack on Vietnam was clumsy and poorly executed. Ironically, though the purpose of the Chinese invasion was to teach "Vietnam a lesson," it was instead a significant factor in strengthening Soviet-Vietnamese ties.

Soviet Support for Southeast Asians

Moscow has gained more than political and psychological benefits from its ties with Hanoi. The collapse of Vietnam-PRC relations and the 1979 border war led Hanoi to allow Moscow use of the U.S.-built Cam Rahn Bay naval complex and other facilities. The Soviet facilities at Cam Ranh Bay and at Danang are reportedly strictly under Soviet administrative control and are entirely separate from the military command line of the Vietnamese forces.[19] The implications of the Soviet use of such facilities are vast. In addition to threatening vital Western sea lines of communications between the Indian and Pacific oceans, the bases provided facilities for Tu-95 BEAR aircraft to monitor U.S. vessels in the South China Sea and Indian Ocean. In addition, the bases enable the USSR to increase its presence on approaches to the Strait of Malacca and to outflank the PRC's naval forces in the South China Sea based in Whampoa, Zhanjiang, and Yulin. The effectiveness of America's Subic Bay naval base and Clark Air Base in the Philippines is threatened by the proximity of Soviet forces and nearby support.

In March 1979, Soviet ships were also reportedly using facilities in Danang and Ho Chi Minh City (formerly Saigon).[20] To impress both Hanoi and Peking, in early March 1979, the USSR dispatched a large tank-landing ship and a KRIVAK destroyer.[21] It is possible that this use of the facilities was grounded on Soviet arguments that the bases would be necessary to resupply Hanoi should the Chinese border war escalate. In any case, after the Chinese withdrew from Vietnam, the new V/STOL aircraft-carrier Minsk and a task force group were stationed in Vietnamese waters. This became the Soviet South Seas Eskadra (Squadron) in 1980 and greatly expanded the intervention/interdiction capabilities of the Soviet Union in the region. This South Seas Eskadra and the operational base facilities in Vietnam were quickly accorded the same organizational status as the principal base of the Pacific Fleet operating from Vladivostok.

The USSR also began to build naval facilities at Kompong Som in Kampuchea, less than 100 miles from the Thai border. When completed, this will provide the Soviet Navy with a deep bay submarine base as well as an excellent fleet anchorage.[22] Soviet use and development of bases in Indochina pose a challenge to America's naval position in the Western Pacific. The Soviet Union has already gained a tremendous advantage from its new position in Southeast Asia. It now has a southern base against China to match the Soviet forces deployed on the long Sino-Soviet frontier.

Another important long-term advantage conferred to the Soviets is the ability to exploit Vietnam as a surrogate. Thus Vietnam has provided assistance and training to Marxist movements in Africa, e.g., in Mozambique.[23] Vietnam worked closely with Cuba at the Columbo Conference of the non-aligned states to ideologically link the non-aligned movement to the Soviet Union.

The advantages the Soviet Union obtains from Vietnam are not without cost, since the Vietnamese economy requires substantial

108

assistance, apparently beyond what the Soviet-led Eastern bloc is willing or able to render. For example, it has been estimated that $9 billion in agricultural investment will be required to enable Vietnam to rebuild agricultural self-sufficiency.[24] Prior to the collapse of the regime in Saigon, South Vietnam had been a major rice exporter.

Senior PRC officials asserted to this writer in 1980 that the Soviet plan for dominating the "southern tier," or the area stretching from Southeast Asia to the Persian Gulf, involves a gigantic pincer movement. One pincer, following the Soviet conquest of Afghanistan, would be to establish a Soviet naval base in an independent Baluchistan, carved out of Pakistan, Afghanistan, and southeastern Iran. Simultaneously, with Kampuchea remaining firmly under Vietnam's control, Thailand would be destablilized and then subverted. The same process of destabilization and subversion would be repeated in Malaysia and, ultimately, in Singapore. The USSR would be able to "squeeze" the Strait of Malacca. In short, the Soviet Union in concert with Vietnam would pick up the dominoes in Southeast Asia and, by controlling the Japanese oil line, force Tokyo to accommodate with Moscow.

Besides the Soviet invasion of Afghanistan and the Vietnamese effort to subjugate Kampuchea, the Chinese pointed to other developments that should be a cause for concern: the Soviet bases in Vietnam that will strengthen the Soviet projection of power in the South Pacific, and the Soviet troop buildup in the occupied islands north of Hokkaido, Japan. And while it cannot be denied that at least one aim of Soviet policy in Asia is to intimidate China, noted the Chinese, the Soviet activities are not aimed exclusively at China. The Kremlin, they pointed out, is trying to "decouple" Asia from the United States, just as it is trying to "decouple" West Europe from the United States. In effect, Moscow is seeking to neutralize all of Asia and to wipe out all traces of U.S. influence.

In Southeast Asia, a "political solution" is simply not in sight. The Chinese do not believe that the Soviet-Vietnamese effort can be halted by negotiations; nor do they believe that the Vietnamese can be eased out of their association with the Soviet Union by economic aid. Neither the USSR nor Vietnam are led by "supermen" of course, yet it will take more than a little effort to stop them. One must consider Soviet difficulties, e.g., the burden of simultaneously supporting operations in distant places such as Afghanistan, Vietnam, Angola, Cuba, and South Yemen; the historical and geographical remoteness of the Soviet Union vis-a-vis Indochina; and, the Soviet Union's own economic problems. Furthermore, Vietnam has not succeeded (thus far!) in crushing the forces of the Kampuchean resistance movements.

Vietnamese Resistance

At present, there are 180,000 to 200,000 Soviet-supported Vietnamese troops in Kampuchea, in addition to another 80,000 in Laos. Employing repressive measures, chemical warfare, and annual military offensives, the Vietnamese have been increasingly successful in efforts to control the population and to defeat resistance forces. The Vietnamese and the Heng Samrin puppet regime are opposed by a comparatively weak, uneasy coalition that has been recognized by the United Nations. Its president is the former Cambodian monarch Norodom Sihanouk. The coalition consists of some 30,000 Khmer Rouge guerrillas under Pol Pot; the 15,000 fighters of the nationalist Khmer People's National Liberation Front (KPNLF), led by former Cambodian Prime Minister Son Sann; and, the 10,000 nationalist fighters of the Armee Nationale Sihanoukiste loyal to Sihanouk. Recent offensives by Vietnamese forces have forced most of the resistance fighters, and their families and followers, to operate out of camps across the border in Thailand.[25]

The length of the resistance struggle in Kampuchea will depend no doubt on the actions of the United States and the PRC. It should be recalled that the defense line of Thailand is in Cambodia, just as the defense line of Pakistan is in Afghanistan. The Thais must be vigorously supported, say the Chinese, who clearly appreciate U.S. support of Thailand. But it is wrong to draw the line in Thailand.

Vietnam has not relied on military force alone to achieve its objectives; diplomatic means are used as well. In July 1984, the Vietnamese held a meeting of the region's foreign ministers in Vientiane, Laos, where they sought to pressure Thailand into holding talks with Heng Samrin, Vietnam's puppet in Kampuchea. They also sought to establish a demilitarized zone between Thailand and Kampuchea in order to prevent support for resistance forces from reaching Kampuchea through Thailand. If Thailand is to avoid succumbing to such pressure, it needs strong U.S. backing.

PRC View of Soviet Strategy

What, then, is China's policy in Southeast Asia? First, it is holding down two-thirds of the Vietnamese forces on the Chinese-Vietnamese border. Second, it is providing material support directly to the resistance forces in Kampuchea. Third, it is trying to get the former Kampuchean leaders, such as Pol Pot, to back away from the brutal policies they pursued when in power. Fourth, it is trying to focus world attention on the Soviet-Vietnamese aggression in Kampuchea. Finally, the PRC is trying to convince the member countries of ASEAN that China has no aggressive designs on them. For in Peking's views, the ASEAN countries, Japan, West Europe, China, and the United States will all have to cooperate to reverse the perilous trends toward Soviet hegemony. Obviously, the Chinese conceive the Soviet threat as global. In this context the strategic importance of Southeast Asia ranks high on the global scale.

Soviet planners understood the strategic significance of the passages between the Indian and Pacific oceans long before their American counterparts. The initial Soviet move toward Indonesia in the early 1960s telegraphed their subsequent strategy: Soviet hopes to regain influence in Indonesia. The Soviet leaders are staking their claim for a dominant position in Southeast Asia. Now there is no easy way of getting them out.

NOTES

1. New York Times, February 2, 1981.
2. New York Tribune, June 14, 1983.
3. Jane's Defence Weekly, July 21, 1984, p. 55.
4. "The Russians Are Landing," The Economist, April 28, 1984, p. 47.
5. Pravda, March 1, 1974, p. 4. In this vein Chinese foreign policy has sought to ally Peking with a wide variety of anti-Soviet actors and movements regardless of their ideology.
6. Pravda, June 24, 1976, p. 4. Also see, Choudry, Goalm, "Changing Pattern in Asia," Problems of Communism (January 1979).
7. Horn, Robert C., "Moscow and Beijing in Post Indochina Southeast Asia," Asian Affairs, September 1976.
8. Christian Science Monitor, July 3, 1978, reported that even some East European governments appeared to be caught off guard by the Vietnamese admission.
9. New Times, November 1978, No. 46, p. 5.
10. The text of the Soviet-Vietnamese Friendship and Cooperation Treaty, New Times, November 1978, p. 6.
11. Notably they include only dyed-in-the-wool Soviet allies. In order of recognition they were after Vietnam: East Germany, Bulgaria, Laos, Hungary, Afghanistan, Czechoslovakia, Poland, Mongolia, Cuba, Angola, Ethiopia, and South Yemen.
12. New York Times, February 8, 1979.
13. Newsweek, March 12, 1979, p. 23.
14. Christian Science Monitor, January 2, 1979, p. 9.
15. As cited in Kulkarni, W.G., "Oil Islands Heat Up Vietnam-China Diplomatic Front," Christian Science Monitor, January 3, 1979, p. 3.
16. Burt, Richard, "Soviet Places Ships Off Vietnam Coast," New York Times, February 8, 1979, p. 13.
17. Ibid.
18. This conclusion is based on a review of the figures on the Soviet naval diplomacy in McConnel, James, and Bradford Dismukes, "Soviet Diplomacy of Force in Third World," Problems of Communism, January/February, 1979.
19. Moritz, Frederick, "Vietnam: No Sign of Backing Off," Christian Science Monitor, March 27, 1979.
20. New York Times, March 29, 1979.
21. New York Times, March 7, 1979. The 4,100 ton landing ship carries up to thirty tanks and 300 troops with combat gear.
22. Hahn, Bradley, Threat Perceptions in ASEAN, Japan and the PRC (Philadelphia: Foreign Policy Research Institute, 1980). See also Intelligence Digest Weekly Review (Cheltenham, England) September 17, 1980, pp. 3-4.

112

23. The Daily Telegraph, August 10, 1979, p. 4.
24. Pike, Douglas, "Vietnam's Foreign Relations: 1975-1976." Report prepared for the Subcommittee on Asian and Pacific Affairs, House Committee on Foreign Affairs, June 1979, p. 8.
25. See "Cambodia: Year Ten," Wall Street Journal, January 28, 1985, p. 16; Branigan, William, "Vietnamese Forces Attack Last Resistance Stronghold in Cambodia," Washington Post, March 6, 1985, p. A-22; Foffet, George D., III, "Cambodian Resistance Leaders Lobby in U.S.," Christian Science Monitor, April 15, 1985, p. 9; and, Oberdorfer, Don, "State Department Details Evidence of Chemical Warfare in Asia," Washington Post, September 15, 1981, p. A-1.

Chapter 15

ASSESSMENT OF SOVIET PRIORITIES
IN AUSTRALIA, NEW ZEALAND, AND OCEANIA

Paul Dibb

The Region in the USSR's Strategic Priorities

Viewed from the Kremlin, Australia, New Zealand, and Oceania are distant parts of the globe. New Zealand, for example, is as far away from Moscow as is the southern tip of Latin America. The USSR has no land access to the region and even the region's closest part, northern Australia, is over 3,300 nautical miles (more than 6,000 kilometers) by air or sea from the nearest Soviet base at Vladivostok in the Maritime Territory. This is similar to the gap across the Atlantic that separates the United States from West Europe or, to put it another way, it equals the air distance from Peking to Moscow. As we shall see later, these distances make the region a formidable invasion task of the USSR. The nearest regular Soviet military presence in the region is at Cam Ranh Bay in Vietnam, which is almost 2,000 nautical miles (3,700 kilometers) from northern Australia -- or similar to the distance from England to eastern Canada.

Nevertheless, it is important to establish a realistic assessment of the relative priority of this region in the USSR's global strategic priorities.[1] Although it possesses formidable military power and, increasingly, it is extending its global reach, it is clear that the Soviet Union cannot be equally powerful in every part of the world. Like any other nation state, it has finite resources -- including limited military assets -- and Moscow has to decide where its priorities lie. In this writer's judgment, the USSR's vital national security interests are elsewhere and are not directly engaged in this part of the world -- the Australia-New Zealand-Oceania region -- with the important exception of U.S. military and intelligence facilities in Australia.

Although Southeast Asia (that is Indochina and the nations of the Association of South East Asian Nations, or ASEAN) is of less direct strategic interest to the USSR than the other parts of Asia that are closer to Soviet territory, the region also probably ranks higher in the Soviet Union's priorities than Australia, New Zealand, and Oceania. This is because Southeast Asia stands astride narrow straits and confined waterways that are an important strategic route between the Pacific and Indian oceans for Western powers (Japan, America, Australia, New Zealand, South Korea, and Taiwan) that are hostile to the USSR. Southeast Asian waters are also of strategic value for the Soviet Union. Ships of the Soviet Navy need to pass through the area on their way from Pacific Fleet headquarters at Vladivostok to patrol areas in the Indian Ocean. And, in the event of war in East Asia, when the Trans-Siberian railway would be interdicted, this sea route may assume a higher priority for Soviet defense planners.[2]

Soviet forces based in Vietnam have the range to deploy in the vicinity of Australia and New Zealand. But the USSR has no regular military presence in the Australia, New Zealand, and Oceania region, and no Soviet military aircraft or surface ships have been detected operating this far south. According to the Australian Minister for Foreign Affairs, the Soviet military presence in Vietnam does "not yet pose a major military threat to the region."[3] Even so, the Soviet military lodgement in Vietnam is of direct strategic concern to Australia because this is the first time that Soviet conventional military forces have gained access to a base in the region from which they could conceivably threaten Australia.

Soviet Wartime Strategy Towards the Region

The most dangerous threat to the national security of Australia, New Zealand, and Oceania would arise from nuclear war between the Soviet Union and the United States. Soviet nuclear strikes would be concentrated in the northern hemisphere because that is where enemy nuclear forces (U.S., British, French, and Chinese) are located that are capable of destroying the USSR as a modern functioning society.

According to Desmond Ball, the Very Low Frequency (VLF) facility at North West Cape in Western Australia is the largest and most powerful of the two principal VLF stations in the U.S. world-wide submarine communication system, the other one being at Cutler, Maine, in the northeast of the United States.[4] The primary mission of North West Cape is to maintain reliable communications with submarines of the U.S. fleet, particularly fleet ballistic missile submarines, that operate in the Pacific and Indian Oceans. With the withdrawal of U.S. POSEIDON submarines from their patrol areas in the western Pacific and their replacement with longer range TRIDENT boats, the United States may possibly come to rely more on the VLF station at Jim Creek in the state of Washington, especially when the 11,000-kilometer-range TRIDENT D-5 system is deployed late in the 1980s. The Soviet Union, however, would have to assume that North West Cape would transmit firing orders in the event that VLF facilities in the United States were destroyed or if the patrol areas of TRIDENT submarines remained in the western Pacific in order to be able to hit targets deeper in European Russia.

Ball describes Pine Gap and Nurrungar, in Central Australia, as ground stations for U.S. satellite surveillance systems, the first being concerned with gathering intelligence by the interception of a wide range of electronic signals, including missile telemetry, radar emissions, and communications; and the second being involved with the detection of Soviet missile launches and the provision of early-warning to the U.S. National Command Authorities (NCA).[5] He observes that some of these operations are extremely critical and could not be done anywhere else because of technical and geographic reasons, which include the fact that the middle of the Australian continent is electronically a very quiet location.[6] Ball believes that this applies most specifically to Pine Gap and that, in the case of infrared intelligence, Australia is only one of two places where this intelligence is passed down to the ground, the other one being in the United States.[7]

As a result of the crucial role that these U.S. facilities in Australia play with regard to early warning, accurate targeting (and therefore retargeting during a nuclear war), and relaying commands for nuclear strikes on the USSR by American submarines, it would be prudent to assume that they are on the Soviet targeting list. North West Cape, Pine Gap, and Nurrungar could be destroyed by a variety of Soviet nuclear forces, including SS-11 and SS-18 intercontinental ballistic missiles (ICBMs) located in Siberia or submarine-launched ballistic missiles (SLBMs) from DELTA-class submarines of the Soviet Pacific Fleet. Even if these three sites were destroyed by nuclear weapons the consequences for Australia would not be very great because they are located well away from major concentrations of population. In the worst-case situation, in which the nearby towns of Exmouth, Alice Springs, and Woomera, as well as the cities of Whyalla, Port Augusta, and Port Pirie (south of Nurrungar) were affected, total casualties would probably be less than 30,000 people.

The consequences of a Soviet nuclear attack would be much greater if the military bases at Darwin (which is presently used by American B-52 bombers staging through to the Indian Ocean) and at Cockburn Sound near Perth (which is regularly used by U.S. warships, including nuclear hunter-killer submarines and sometimes aircraft carrier battle groups) were attacked. In the case of a one-megaton weapon detonated on the ground near these two bases, fatalities could exceed 150,000 people. It is not highly likely, however, that U.S. naval and air forces would be using Darwin and

116

Perth during a nuclear war because Australia is remote from key targets that the United States needs to destroy in the USSR. New Zealand is of even less military utility to the United States in wartime because of its remote location.

What about Soviet strategy towards Australia, New Zealand, and Oceania in a conventional phase of war? The first point to make is that these countries would not be easy invasion targets. Even for a country with the USSR's clearly impressive military forces, mounting an invasion over such great distances from Soviet territory in the Far East would be hazardous. Not only would the Soviet Union have much more important priorities in the northern hemisphere, but an invasion force would have to transit areas in the northern and central Pacific controlled by the United States and its allies. The transportation of a force sufficient to invade Australia (at least nine divisions) would require a large concentration of troop transport vessels -- an inviting target for maritime strike forces -- requiring a large escorting force of warships and aircraft.[8] The USSR would have to be capable of obtaining and then securing against attack port and airfield facilities, probably in the Indonesian-Melanesian island chain to the north of Australia. It would also need to be capable of commanding the maritime and air approaches to Australia, which would require a large naval force, including a maritime air power component, and large air forces based in the adjacent islands. These same maritime bases would have to continue to secure the lines of supply of the invading force for the duration of the hostilities.[9]

A Soviet invasion of Australia itself, even if it used Cam Ranh Bay and an intermediate staging base to provide the attacking force with effective air cover and to keep its shipping operational, would involve a very difficult military operation. Soviet forces are not well designed to undertake an opposed landing on a distant continent. The Australian peacetime order of battle includes 24 F-111 fighter-bombers, 75 FA-18 fighters on order, 20 P-3 ORION ASW aircraft, and six OBERON-class submarines, all of which are to be equipped with the HARPOON stand-off missile. The USSR would not only need to be capable of achieving local air superiority, but it would also need to overcome considerable logistic problems, e.g., to supply about 150 tons of fuel and 200-250 tons of water for each 10,000 men every day.[10] This would require the continuous support of a large tonnage of ships and transport aircraft which, because of the long distances they would have to travel, would be vulnerable to interdiction. It would be unrealistic to imagine that the USSR would attempt such a futile mission.

Invading New Zealand or one of the island states would be an easier proposition, but the Soviet Union would first need to secure its western flank against an attack from joint Australian and U.S. forces, as well as from American attacks along the vulnerable lines of its communication extending from the Sea of Japan or the South China Sea some 4,000 to 5,000 nautical miles.

Short of invasion, Soviet strategy in wartime could involve blockading or mining the narrow straits of Southeast Asia to Western shipping and attacking convoys enroute from the Persian Gulf and Australia to Japan and America. Such a strategy would involve the ANZUS (Australia, New Zealand, United States) powers, under the terms of the Radford-Collins Agreement, in routing shipping south about Australia and then north through the central Pacific to Japan and the west coast of the United States. This would complicate Soviet submarine operations, forcing them to take place in wide open ocean areas at great distances from home bases. The USSR could not count on maintaining naval or air bases in Vietnam, which would be highly vulnerable to U.S. aircraft carrier or bomber attacks from the U.S. bases in the Philippines or Guam. It would be easier for the Soviet forces to destroy Western oil or strategic non-fuel mineral supplies at source, for example by missile or bomber attacks on the Middle East oilfields, or at focal points in the Sea of Japan, or at unloading facilities at Japanese ports.

Australia and New Zealand are also much better placed than most other countries to sustain their national economies, even if at a substantially reduced standard of living, in the event of global war. Together, they are practically self-sufficient in food, energy, and most raw materials, and those essential goods that they presently import (such as lubricating oils) could be stockpiled in the warning time leading up to war. However, essential industrial machinery, transport equipment, and spare parts for their defense forces have to be imported and would be subject to a Soviet campaign of interdiction. Some protection against these problems could be derived from a conscious joint policy of building up stocks of essential imports and expediting capital replacement programs.[11] So long as Australia and New Zealand remained free from nuclear attack on the main population centers, it would be possible to conceive the restoration of their economies which could provide an adequate, if considerably reduced, standard of living. The islands of Oceania, which depend greatly on imports, would not survive so well, and Australia and New Zealand would probably have to share with them the economic means for survival. The total population of Oceania is about five million, three million of whom live in Papua New Guinea.

Other than these major contingencies involving global war, it is conceivable that Soviet strategy might include challenging Australian and New Zealand territorial claims in Antarctica, off-shore fishing resources in the region, or seabed mineral or energy rights with military force. But the USSR is a resource-rich country and any such military operations that it might mount in this remote region would be very vulnerable to counter-action by ANZUS forces.

118

Soviet Peacetime Strategic Interests in the Region

Short of the use of military force, the USSR has a range of strategic, political, and economic interests in the region. The Soviet Union is attracted to the prospect of low-risk advances that can bolster its image as a global power and, in that context, it constantly probes for opportunities. The decolonization process in Oceania and the coming to power of socialist governments in Australia and New Zealand have attracted Soviet attention. But it is worthwhile at the outset to emphasize the lack of contact and the continuing impact of distance which mark the USSR's relations with this region.

In the Soviet perception, Australia and New Zealand are tied directly into the Western alliance system and the islands of the Southwest Pacific are Western-inclined and generally suspicious of Soviet intentions. The ANZUS Treaty aligns Australia and New Zealand closely with the USSR's only superpower rival, the United States. Papua New Guinea, the major island state of Oceania, has friendly relations with Australia, including a strong defense relationship. The other Pacific island states, including independent nations such as Tonga, Fiji, and Western Samoa, are deeply religious, strongly anti-communist, and depend on the metropolitan countries for economic and security assistance, as well as for practically all their trade and investment. Moreover, the Soviet Union has been almost completely denied access to Oceania by a coordinated ANZUS policy.

The importance of ANZUS to the USSR needs to be clearly understood. Unlike NATO, ANZUS does not directly threaten the national security of the Soviet homeland with military attack. But the role of North West Cape, Pine Gap, and Nurrungar suggests that it is in the Soviet Union's interests to see these U.S. bases removed from Australia through political pressure. Moreover, Moscow would like to see the United States prevented from using port and air facilities in the region for its surface warships and military aircraft. As the following quotation indicates, Soviet bloc propaganda seeks to influence the denial of such facilities to America by frequently pointing out that it is only the presence of U.S. military forces in Australia and New Zealand that would make them possible targets for a Soviet nuclear attack:

> The presence of the bases automatically makes Australians hostages of the White House's adventurist course . . . . This alone turns Australia into a target for a retaliatory nuclear strike.[12]

Since the coming to power in 1984 of a Labor government in New Zealand that is committed to refusing visits to New Zealand ports by U.S. nuclear warships, the Soviet media has been full of gloating references to the prospect of the collapse of the ANZUS Treaty, e.g.:

If this idea is put into practice, it will mean an end to the aggresive ANZUS bloc.[13]

The demise of the ANZUS Treaty, or even severe political tensions within it, would have several important strategic benefits for the Soviet Union. First, Australia and New Zealand are counted among the close allies of the United States and any unraveling of that alliance system would benefit Soviet global competition with America. By the term "close allies" we mean that group of countries, which also includes Britain and Canada, that have a special relationship arising from their joint wartime experience. This includes the sharing of highly classified intelligence, defense science and technology, and access to sophisticated U.S. weapons systems. The USSR fears not only the military, economic, and technological strength of the United States but also the combined weight of the Western Alliance. Any breakdown of ANZUS would represent a major advance for the Soviet cause.

Second, as the quotations above show, the USSR expects any political disagreement between New Zealand and the United States over the issue of port calls by nuclear warships to have a negative effect on Australia's relations with America. The USSR would welcome this because of the key role that the three joint facilities at Pine Gap, Nurrungar, and North West Cape play in U. S. nuclear strategy. In addition, although port calls by U.S. warships to New Zealand and Australia are not vital in strategic terms, there is a possibility that refusing such visits could cause what _Izvestiya_ calls "a chain reaction"[14] with other such allies both in Asia (for example, the Philippines, and Japan) and in Europe (for example, Norway and Denmark).

The Soviet Union's interest in a nuclear-free zone in the South Pacific can also be seen in the context of wanting American warships and military aircraft excluded from the territories of close U.S. allies. Australia and some of the islands of Oceania want a South Pacific nuclear-free zone to allow for the transit of nuclear-powered warships through the region. The USSR is in favor of what it calls "a real nuclear weapon-free zone"[15] because it has no requirement to deploy its surface warships or submarines in the region in peacetime. Moreover, Moscow wants French nuclear testing excluded from the Southwest Pacific because France might find it difficult to find an alternative acceptable site, and this would slow down the development of French nuclear weapons.

Moscow has a number of more general strategic concerns with the military relations that ANZUS has with the ASEAN countries, and with Japan. Soviet commentators allege that the ANZUS countries are seeking to create a "Pacific Pact" or an "Asian NATO" which would include ASEAN in a united tripartite front with the United States, Japan, and West Europe to oppose the Soviet Union.[16] Japan is often given a central role in these schemes, and the ANZUS powers are said to be drawing Japan into a "JANZUS" treaty. Also the Japanese and Australian concept of a Pacific community, which would seek to strengthen economic inter-dependence among Pacific countries, is perceived in Moscow as "a closed military-political grouping along the lines of NATO."[17]

These Soviet attitudes reflect a worry that it is being outflanked in the Pacific by the superior economic power of the West and that important developing countries, such as China and the ASEAN group, are being drawn into this process. With regard to ASEAN, for example, the USSR apparently believes that these countries are being lured by the prospect of economic privileges with the ANZUS countries and that the "idea is not to single out the military aspect of the projected grouping for the time being."[18]

Soviet Political Interests in the Region

Within Australia, New Zealand, and the island states of Oceania the USSR does not have any potent weapons of political leverage. In Australia, for example, the Soviet Union has almost no influential lobby to speak of: not only does it not enjoy any basic support in the major Australian political parties, its activities are generally suspect even within the fragmented Australian communist movement.[19] Moscow recognizes two communist parties in Australia, the Communist Party of Australia and the Socialist Party of Australia, but their combined membership is less than 2,000, and they hold no seats in the Parliament.[20]

In New Zealand a similar situation exists with the Moscow-recognized parties (the Communist Party of New Zealand and the Socialist Unity Party) having only some 215 members and no Parliamentary representation. The combined vote of all such leftist parties in New Zealand is only 0.5 per cent of the total vote.[21]

Pro-Soviet communists do have key influence in New Zealand's important transport, processing, and building industries, although nowhere is their influence unchallenged or unrestricted. According to the Chief Ombudsman, Sir Guy Powles, the major threat to New Zealand's security is from the activities of foreign intelligence officers, specifically those from the USSR, rather than from local subversive organizations.[22]

In Oceania, there are no communist parties and Marxism is not an attractive philosophy in island states where Christianity is deeply entrenched. In contrast to the experience of post-colonial societies in Africa and Asia, force has not been used in the Southwest Pacific countries to remove a government, and there have been no military coups and there are no one-party states.[23]

Moscow will probably continue to work slowly to improve its presently minimal political position in the region, so as not to alarm the island nations. But the Soviet Union's political and strategic interests are seen to be in basic opposition to those of most countries in the region. In the last decade, for example, there has been an apparent growth of concern in Australian public attitudes about Soviet international policies and behavior. Almost 40 percent of Australians now think that the USSR is a threat to their country, up from 16 percent in 1978.[24] In contrast, Australia's security treaty with the United States is supported by almost three-quarters of all Australians.

There are some areas where Soviet and regional political interests coincide. Both Australia and New Zealand have an interest in seeing the USSR continue to be a member of the Antarctic treaty system, which for nearly a quarter of a century has ensured that this continent does not become an area of military competition. Cooperation over Antarctica has been maintained during the otherwise strained period of relations with the USSR since the December 1979 invasion of Afghanistan. This shared concern is an important one, particularly as interest is rising in the exploitation of the resources of Antarctica.

The USSR has the largest number of personnel of any nation operating stations in Antarctica, and it has growing interests in the krill and fish resources of the area, including those near Kerguelen Island, 2,000 nautical miles to the southwest of Australia. Australia and New Zealand claim about half of the continent, but they lack the military capacity to enforce their claims. Political, as distinct from military, solutions are to be expected from any disputes with the USSR involving Australian or New Zealand interests in the Antarctic region.

Another problem for Moscow is that often its political presence has been used by island leaders to raise the spectre of the Soviet threat. Suggestions that Tonga will allow the USSR to construct an airstrip or that Vanuatu may "throw open its ports to Soviet warships"[25] are guaranteed to make newspaper headlines in Australia and New Zealand. The latter allegation caused the Soviet Embassy in Canberra to deny that the USSR was asking any Pacific island country to allow its warships in.[26] Playing the "Soviet card" has become something of a South Pacific pastime: in 1982, Prime Minister Solomon Mamaloni of the Solomon Islands talked about approaching the USSR for aid, but his interest happened to coincide with his conviction that Australia was being obstinate in not providing the Solomons with a fast patrol boat of the type used by the Royal Australian Navy.[27]

122

A similar situation arose in 1981, when the Soviet Union offered a research ship to carry out hydrographic surveys in and around the waters of the Solomon Islands and Vanuatu. At a meeting of the South Pacific Forum, thirteen South Pacific nations unanimously agreed to reject all Soviet offers of aid on the grounds that it would soon lead to the Soviet Union establishing an undesirable foothold in the region. The then Prime Minister of the Solomon Islands, Sir Peter Kenilorea, said he did not want any Soviet involvement in the South Pacific as it would soon lead to a political and possibly a military presence.[28] The United States, Australia, and New Zealand agreed to carry our hydrographic research in the region. In a later development, the Soviet representative at the annual session of the United Nations body ESCAP (Economic and Social Commission for Asia and the Pacific) in Bangkok attempted to have read into the minutes the fact that oceanographic data collected by the Soviet hydrographic vessel Kallisto had been made available to ESCAP's committee on offshore areas. This met immediate resistance from the Papua New Guinea and Solomon Islands delegations who protested that they had not been informed of the Kallisto's research activities.[29]

Thus far then the coordinated policies of the ANZUS partners and the countries of the South Pacific Forum have been successful in denying the Soviet Union a major political foothold in the region. They are anxious to avoid a situation arising in Oceania comparable to that in the Indian Ocean where Soviet offers of aid with the fishing industry and visits by hydrographic vessels (both of which can have intelligence collection capabilities) have developed into port calls by warships.

Although the USSR has been unsuccessful so far in finding any friends in the region it will probe for opportunities. Even though Oceania is not an unstable part of the world there are some situations that will require close monitoring in case the USSR tries to insert itself. There have been allegations by Prime Minister Ratu Sir Kamisese Mara of Soviet interference in the Fijian elections in 1982, but these claims were later withdrawn by the ruling Alliance Party in evidence before a Royal Commission.[30] More likely areas of Soviet attention are the French colonies, New Caledonia and French Polynesia. France's reluctance to grant independence to New Caledonia is already forcing the Kanak Liberation, the Melanesian-based independence movement, to consider the possibility of Libyan assistance. This would no doubt suit the Soviet Union's purposes of fostering instability. New Caledonia lies less than 750 nautical miles off Australia's east coast, and it is a similar distance from New Zealand. It is an important producer of nickel. Neither Australia nor New Zealand would welcome Libyan interference, and it seems likely that other Pacific states, including Melanesian countries such as Papua New Guinea, will seek to dissuade the Kanaks from this course, which would be seen as contrary to "the Pacific Way" of doing things.

Papua New Guinea is another country that Moscow might seek to penetrate because it is the largest, and potentially most influential country, in Oceania. There are separatist tendencies in some parts of the country -- for example, Bougainville -- and Papua New Guinea faces difficult economic problems. But without a resident mission there and in the absence of close economic ties (see below), there seems to be little opportunity for direct Soviet interference. In any case, Soviet interests are probably more closely engaged in redeveloping friendly relations with Indonesia, which it sees as the dominant country in ASEAN and virulently anti-Chinese. Moscow is also likely to be attracted by political instability in the Philippines where the prospect of the loss of U.S. influence is much more significant than any advances the USSR could make in Papua New Guinea.

Soviet Economic Interests in the Region

The Soviet Union is a significant trade partner of both Australia and New Zealand. Trade turnover has more than doubled in the last seven years and is now worth about $US1,200 million annually. This is not a large amount, and it is much less than the USSR's trade with Argentina, for example, and only about one-tenth of Soviet trade turnover with Hungary. In regional terms, however, Soviet trade with Australia and New Zealand is larger than that with the ASEAN countries as a group. The USSR's trade with the Pacific islands is so small that it is not recorded in official Soviet trade statistics. As a rule, what trade there is, in such commodities as copra, coffee, cocoa and tea, is conducted either through third countries or is purchased by the USSR on world markets.[31]

From a Soviet perspective, trade with Australia and New Zealand has always been heavily in favor of these countries, and it shows no sign of moving to a more even balance. In 1982, the ratio was 35 to 1 against the USSR. From these two countries, the USSR imports raw materials, especially wool, and foodstuffs, such as wheat, butter, meat, sugar, and fish, that it requires because of deficiencies in its own economic system. Australia and New Zealand, on the other hand, are advanced nations that have little demand for the sort of industrial products that the USSR produces. Soviet goods do not compete well in terms of quality compared with imports from Japan, the United States, and West Europe, and it is easier and safer to buy from these traditional suppliers. If Australia and New Zealand were not available as suppliers of textile raw materials and foodstuffs, Moscow would presumably direct its purchases elsewhere, for example, Uruguay, Argentina, Canada, the

124

United States, or Brazil. The Soviet Union buys what it wants, when it wants, at prices which it finds acceptable. Moscow is not doing Australia or New Zealand a favor when it chooses to buy their wool or meat.[32]

From the point of view of Australia and New Zealand, trade with the Soviet Union is rather more important. The USSR is New Zealand's fifth or sixth largest export market. It has been consistently one of New Zealand's best customers for carpet wool, and currently it ranks third after Japan and Britain. It has also emerged as New Zealand's sixth largest customer for meat, and the Soviet Union has become particularly important to the New Zealand mutton industry. Mutton is not a meat that is very easy to dispose of on other world markets, and the USSR now takes almost half of New Zealand's exports. Soviet meat purchases are characterized by considerable fluctuations due to such factors as the success or failure of the USSR's grain harvest and decisions whether to slaughter domestic animals. The USSR seems to have switched some of its meat trade to Argentina, which is now the largest supplier of frozen meat to the USSR, and France is also providing competition to New Zealand. The impact of these variations on the New Zealand sheep meat producers is significant, and Moscow would be aware that its continuing access to New Zealand fish resources could be dependent on more stable orders for mutton. Butter and milk powder sales to the USSR have also become important recently, and this assists the New Zealand dairy industry at a time when these products are generally in surplus supply on world markets. The USSR is New Zealand's second largest butter market, but sales are on an ad hoc basis, varying with domestic shortages in the Soviet Union. Thus there are influential sectors in the New Zealand farming industry that would not want to see the Soviet market jeopardized for political purposes.

Trade with the USSR is not quite so significant in overall terms to Australia. While exports of wool and wheat are important (the USSR is normally Australia's second largest wool customer after Japan and the second largest wheat purchaser after Egypt), wheat purchases are erratic. The Soviet Union purchases about 125,000 tons of wool a year on world markets, and almost half of this comes from Australia, which is the world's premier grower of fine wool for the textile industry. The USSR could conceivably manipulate the Australian wool industry by deliberately affecting auction prices.

The USSR has the largest fishing fleet in the world. The declaration by many countries, especially in the North Pacific, of 200-mile fishing zones has encouraged an increase in Soviet distant fishing operations. Fish provides 15 percent of the animal protein in the Soviet diet, and the consumption of fish has more than doubled in the USSR in the last 20 years. The Soviet Union has been

125

particularly concerned to establish a base for its fishing fleet in the South Pacific, which operates at a distance of some 6,000 nautical miles (more than 11,000 kilometers) from headquarters at Vladivostok. The main area for fishing is in areas adjacent to New Zealand and in the Fiji-Kiribati region. Port calls are made for refueling, provisioning, and crew recreation in Fiji and New Zealand. In the past, fuel and logistics support had to be provided by vessels of the Soviet Merchant Marine. The USSR has an extensive fisheries research program in the South Pacific that it has tried to use as a means of gaining access to the island states. But, in 1979, the South Pacific Forum established a regional fisheries agency which should serve to curtail Soviet activities.

The Soviet Union has access to only one permanent fishing base, and that is in New Zealand where the activities of Soviet trawlers can be strictly controlled and monitored. About 20 to 30 Soviet fishing vessels operate at any one time in New Zealand waters and up to another three vessels operate in tropical waters of the South Pacific. At present, the USSR gets less than 2 percent of its annual fish catch from this part of the world, but this accounts for about one-third of all fish caught in New Zealand waters.[33]

Access to fishing facilities in New Zealand might serve to reduce the pressure on the Soviet Union to involve itself elsewhere in the region. The cold waters of New Zealand are more productive, and the USSR has little experience of long-line fishing for tuna in tropical waters, which is the main fish resource of the island states.

It may, however, be overly sanguine to expect that Moscow might not press for access to fishing ports elsewhere in the Pacific. Although the Soviet Union obviously has the right to discuss trade and fishing agreements with island nations, it should be an Australian, New Zealand, and U.S. policy to develop measures which give the island states no reason to consider turning to the USSR for such assistance. This could give Moscow undue political and economic influence in the region.

The Soviet Union has the world's largest oceanographic research program, and it has been active in the South Pacific since 1957. Much of its research centers on the ocean environment, including studies of the ocean bottom, physical and chemical properties of seawater, oceanic currents and atmospheric processes over the sea, the formation of biological products in the oceans, and "the possibilities to influence marine biosystems to increase their productivity."[34] The Soviet Union probably knows more about the oceanography of the South Pacific than any other country.[35] Soviet hydrographic ships, some of which are naval-manned and subordinate to the Soviet Navy, have been surveying the southern oceans for over twenty-five years. They include such vessels as the <u>Vitiaz,</u> <u>Dimitry Mendeleev</u>, <u>Professor Bogorov</u>, and the <u>Kallisto</u>. The latter ship, for example, is operated by the Scientific Research Institute

126

from Sakhalin, and it has the ability to conduct bathymetric and seismic operations, to determine the existence of commercially exploitable minerals, and to collect fishing data.

Some of this data has potential military utility. Such a detailed knowledge of the ocean characteristics could be useful for future submarine operations. It has been noted in the past that some Soviet hydrographic vessels seemed to have a particular interest in the deep-water trench that extends northward from New Zealand to Tonga and Western Samoa. Contrary to the views of some commentators,[36] the Soviet Union does <u>not</u> have any compelling reasons to deploy its strategic submarines to the South Pacific, but it could conceivably be preparing for wartime contingencies for operations by hunter-killer submarines. Some Soviet hydrographic ships that have operated in the region have been accompanied by a "research" submarine.

The USSR carries out regular missile testing of SLBMs and ICBMs in the north of the region, generally between the Line and northern Cook Islands. A land-based telemetry tracking station in the region would be convenient, but the USSR is unlikely to get one. Seaborne instruments on Soviet electronic intelligence ships seem to operate perfectly well for the Soviet Union's military needs.

Policy Implications for Regional Security

This discussion has analyzed the Soviet Union's political, economic, and strategic interests in the region, and it concludes that the Soviet Union has little influence. Moscow perceives Australia, New Zealand, and the island states of Oceania as distant countries closely aligned with the United States and Western interests and dominated by generally unfriendly attitudes toward the Soviet Union. The USSR does not have much political influence in this region, its strategic interests are few, and its economic activities are relatively modest. Moreover, as Gregory Fry points out, Australia and New Zealand, in view of their crucial role of providing regional finances, are in a position to influence policies toward the USSR in subtle ways.[37] ANZUS strategy has been successful in coordinating the policies of Australia, New Zealand, and the United States so as to exclude the Soviet Union from the region. The Soviet Union's activities are restricted to trade and diplomatic relations with Australia and New Zealand and little more than the movement of its fishing fleet, research vessels, merchant ships, and passenger liners through the South Pacific. The USSR has had only limited impact on the islands of Oceania.

The question remains, what are the prospects of an increase in the Soviet presence in this region? There are few possibilities for a major breakthrough in the trade area. Soviet offers to build hydroelectric dams or assist with port development in Australia or New Zealand are unlikely to receive any encouragement, and Aeroflot is highly unlikely to gain landing rights in either of these countries. Any increase in two-way trade that does occur will be modest unless the USSR has a particular need for larger imports of Australian and New Zealand food or wool because of domestic shortfalls.

The Soviet Union will continue to pursue its fishing interests in the region. It will seek to use its scientific and technical knowledge to entice island states into joint fishing ventures. Imports of fish account for as much as 10 to 15 per cent of the total imports of countries such as Fiji, Solomon Islands, Papua New Guinea, Tonga, and Vanuatu, and joint venture fishing arrangements with the Soviets could save large amounts of foreign exchange. But Soviet experience is more in the area of cold water fishing and, in any case, it has a poor reputation for over-fishing the resources of other Third World countries such as Mauritius, Angola, and Mozambique that cannot properly police their fishing zones.

Politically, the USSR's involvement in the region will almost inevitably increase from its present minimum. Sooner or later, the Soviet Union will probably be successful in establishing resident missions in some of the larger island states, such as Papua New Guinea and Fiji. There are not many trouble spots in the region that Moscow can seek to exploit because "the Pacific Way" is to settle differences more by conciliation than by confrontation. Nevertheless, the situation in New Caledonia will require close monitoring to avert any possible Soviet or associated interference, such as from Libya. Much will depend on Australia and New Zealand being able to provide genuine assistance to facilitate the emergence of effective independent nations in both New Caledonia and French Polynesia and to assist the process of nation-building which has so recently commenced elsewhere in the South Pacific.

Strangely enough, given the low priority of this region for Soviet strategic interests, one of the most hopeful developments for the USSR, which could have global repercussions, has been none of its own making. If New Zealand's attitude concerning U.S. nuclear warship visits cannot be resolved amicably within the framework of the ANZUS alliance, then the prospect of a break-up of the ANZUS Treaty would be of enormous benefit to the USSR's world-wide interests. Clearly, the solution to this disagreement lies with some sort of compromise that accommodates both U.S. and New Zealand interests without threatening the stability of the region. Nothing would be more welcome in Moscow than the dissolution of ANZUS, involving as it does such close allies of Washington.

In the 1990s or beyond, the Soviet Union will most likely deploy warships to the South Pacific. There is no strategic imperative to do so, but the USSR now has global naval interests and a desire, as the new superpower, to show the flag. It has steadily expanded its naval presence over the last twenty years from the Mediterranean and the Indian Ocean to the west coast of Africa and the South China Sea. It seems logical to expect that, if for no other reason than familiarization with all ocean areas, Soviet surface warships may one day pass through the region. As for Soviet submarines, the new generation of quieter, longer range boats (such as the SIERRA and MIKE-class) are likely to patrol in more distant waters looking for weaknesses in Western anti-submarine defenses. The ANZUS partners will need to be particularly alert to this possibilty because of its implications for wartime contingencies.

Overall, the appropriate Western response to any heightened Soviet involvement in this region is to step up those policies of close consultation and collaboration which have been so successful in the past in preventing regional countries from moving too close to the USSR. For example, in the area of surveillance and enforcement of 200-mile exclusive economic zones there is a need for a cooperative regional approach -- especially as the island states are unable to acquire significant military forces of their own. At the 1983 South Pacific Forum meeting, the Australian government offered, under the defense cooperation program, to design and build a South Pacific patrol boat to meet the needs of the island states for maritime surveillance. And the Chief of Air Force Development visited the Solomon Islands, Vanuatu, Fiji, Tonga and Western Samoa in September 1983 to discuss how Australian P-3 ORION training flights in the region could assist countries with maritime surveillance of their local waters. Under these circumstances, and given Australian and New Zealand monitoring capabilities, it seems unlikely that the USSR would be willing deliberately to challenge the national security of island countries in its pursuit of fish.

In summary, Soviet penetration of this region on any scale is likely to remain a potential rather than a realized threat in the remainder of the 1980s. Moscow is unlikely to challenge established American positions in the South Pacific, where there could be a risk of confrontation in a part of the world where the ANZUS partners are clearly the dominant powers and where the projection of Soviet forces would be vulnerable. The Soviet Union's military presence in Vietnam has served to strengthen regional resolve to prevent any further Soviet military encroachments south into the ANZUS area. In any case, Soviet strategy against this part of the world will be constantly overshadowed by their more important concerns to the north, and their policies toward the South Pacific are likely to remain fairly low key. In the Soviet view, this region is likely to continue to be "an ANZUS lake" in the foreseeable future.

129

NOTES

1. See Dibb, Paul, "The Interests of the Soviet Union in the Region: Implications for Regional Security," International Security in the Southeast Asian and Southwest Pacific Region, Miller, T.B., ed., (St. Lucia: University of Queensland Press, 1983), p. 52.

2. Ibid. pp. 54-55 and McGwire, Michael, Soviet Military Objectives, (Washington, D.C.: The Brookings Institute, 1984, unpublished), p. 25.

3. Speech by the Minister for Foreign Affairs, Mr. W. G. Hayden, Australia and Asia: Options and Opportunities, (Sydney, October 16, 1984), p. 9.

4. Ball, Desmond, and R. H. Mathams, "The Nuclear Threat to Australia," Australia and Nuclear War, Denborough, Michael, ed., (Canberra: Croom Helm Australia, 1983), p. 41.

5. Ibid., pp. 41-42.

6. Joint Parliamentary Committee on Foreign Affairs and Defence, "Threats to Australia's Security -- Their Nature and Probability," (Canberra: Australian Government Publishing Service, 1981), pp. 16-17.

7. Ibid.

8. The question of the invasion of Australia was intensively studied by Japan during 1942. In a General Outline of Policy on Future War Guidance, agreed on at an Imperial General Headquarters Army/Navy liaison conference on March 7, 1942, invasion of Australia was rejected inter alia because it would require the main body of the Combined Fleet and an infantry force of 12 divisions. The shipping required for the Army alone would amount to 1.5 million tons. The progress of invasion might require the Army to make additional commitments of large strengths. Takushiro, Hattori, Dai To-A Senso Zenshi, (Tokyo, 1983, Part III), p. 292.

9. "Threats to Australia's Security - Their Nature and Probability," Op. cit., p. 31.

10. Ibid., p. 32.

11. Coombs, H.C., "The Economic and Social Impact of Nuclear War for Australia and its Region," Denborough, Michael, ed., Op. cit., p. 122.

12. Izvestiya, December 2, 1983, p. 4.

13. Moscow Domestic Service, 1645 GMT, July 16, 1984 (FBIS Daily Report on the Soviet Union, July 17, 1984, page E3).

14. Izvestiya, July 25, 1984, p. 5.

15. Moscow TASS in English, 1414 GMT, August 29, 1983 (FBIS Daily Report on the Soviet Union, August 30, 1983, page E1).

16. Krasnaya Zvezda, May 2, 1984, p. 3 and Izvestiya, July 25, 1984, p. 5.

17. Krasnaya Zvezda, August 8, 1984, p. 3.

130

18. _Izvestiya_, July 25, 1984, p. 5.

19. Bowan, John, "Australia's Relations with the Soviet Bloc," in _Australia's External Relations in the 1980s_, Dibb, Paul, ed., (Canberra: Croom Helm Australia, 1983), p. 166.

20. Starr, Richard F., "Check List of Communist Parties in 1983," _Problems of Communism_, March-April 1984, p. 44.

21. _Ibid._, p. 45.

22. Powles, Guy, "Internal Security in New Zealand," Erik Olssen and Bill Webb, eds., _New Zealand Foreign Policy and Defence_, (Dunedin: University of Otago, 1977), pp. 123-4.

23. Fry, Greg, "Succession of Government in the Post-Colonial States of the South Pacific: New Support for Constitutionalism?" _Politics_, May 1983, p. 56.

24. Morgan Gallup poll in _The Bulletin_, July 12, 1983, p. 68.

25. _The Australian_, October 20, 1982.

26. _Ibid._

27. _Sydney Morning Herald_, October 21, 1982.

28. _The Age_, August 12, 1981.

29. _Pacific Islands Monthly_, July 1983.

30. _Pacific Islands Monthly_, September 1983.

31. Tumarkin, D.D., "USSR - The Unknown Northern Neighbor," in _Foreign Forces in Pacific Politics_, Crocombe, R., and A. Ali, eds., (Fiji: University of the South Pacific, 1983), p. 148.

32. Gustafson, Barry, "New Zealand and the Soviet Union," in Olssen, Erik, and Bill Webb, eds., _Op. cit._, p. 115.

33. Herr, Richard A., "Strategy and Security: the choices are few," Crocombe R., and A. Ali, eds., _Op. cit._, p. 298. The main species caught are blue whiting, orao dory, and squid.

34. Tumarkin, D.D., _Op. cit._, pp. 147-8.

35. See, for example, _Atlas Okeanov-Tihii Okean_, Naval Fleet, Ministry of Defense, Moscow 1974. This 300-page atlas contains the most detailed published information available about the ocean floor, climate, hydrology, hydrochemistry, and biogeography of the Pacific Ocean.

36. See Herr, Richard A., _Op. cit._, p. 297.

37. Fry, Gregory E., "Regionalism and International Politics of the South Pacific," _Public Affairs_, Fall 1981, p. 481.

Chapter 16

GROWING SOVIET INTEREST IN SOUTH ASIA

Stephen P. Cohen

Introduction

Twenty-five years ago, there was virtually no support for the Soviet Union in South Asia except for the pro-Soviet wing of the Communist Party of India (CPI) and a few ideological supporters in the Indian Congress Party.[1] The Communist Party of Pakistan was outlawed, and in any case it had a small following. Soviet influence in Afghanistan was competitive but marginal (even then the local communist party was sharply divided),[2] and there was no Soviet presence in Nepal and Ceylon. The USSR was about to enter into a major arms deal with India, but Indian MiGs did not fly until 1964, and Indian defense planners had largely turned to the West after their border war with the People's Republic of China (PRC) in 1962. Indeed, American and British Commonwealth air forces participated in joint exercises with their Indian Air Force counterparts, India adopted some of the McNamara innovations in defense planning, and several hundred U.S. military personnel were stationed in India until 1965.[3] A large U.S. civilian and military presence remained in Pakistan until 1965; Pakistan then liked to term itself the "most allied of allies," with strong ties to the Central Treaty Organization (CENTO), and to the South East Asia Treaty Organization (SEATO), and a bilateral U.S. military assistance treaty.

By 1985, the Soviet Union had planted itself firmly, and perhaps permanently, in devastated Afghanistan. It had cordial relations with Pakistan even as Moscow regularly accused that state of aiding "insurgents" in Afghanistan. Soviet economic projects in Pakistan, including a steel mill in Karachi, were on schedule. The Soviet presence in Nepal, Sri Lanka, and Bangladesh remained minimal, but that certainly was not the case in India, which had become closely linked to the Soviet economy and defense establishment through massive purchases of weapons, often bartered for Indian-made consumer goods. The Indian Air Force was a display

132

case of recent Soviet technology, the vessels of the Navy were more than half Soviet or Polish in origin, and the Indian Army was newly dependent upon the Soviet Union for armor. This was the situation, one might add, twenty-five years after a program of defense self-reliance was begun by V. K. Krishna Menon and Jawaharlal Nehru.

Does the above picture represent a steady expansion of Soviet influence in South Asia over the past twenty-five years? Is there any substance to the Soviet boast just over twenty years ago that two billion people would be living under communism by 1980?[4] With the significant exception of Afghanistan, on its way to becoming a Soviet Central Asian republic in all but name, it does not.[5] Soviet influence was greater in South Asia in 1966-1971, when the United States had virtually withdrawn from the region. The USSR presided over the Tashkent meeting which formally ended the 1965 Indo-Pakistan war (and received American blessing). The USSR supplied weapons to both India and Pakistan in 1968, and, after the Indo-Soviet Treaty of Peace, Friendship, and Cooperation of 1971, it greatly increased its weapons supplies to India. Some have argued that it was at this point that Moscow realized the significance of its Far Eastern military buildup, which was used to deter China from entering the 1971 conflict on the side of Pakistan.[6]

The Soviet Union also floated its regional security treaty proposal during this period. This proposal was given serious consideration in New Delhi, although ultimately rejected. However, Moscow failed, as had London and Washington earlier, to unite the two major South Asian states into a de facto alliance that might serve broader interests. And, of course, communist ideology remains unattractive to the South Asian states, most of all to Afghanistan, where it is sustained only by a massive Soviet military presence. The present situation is not a case of more or less Soviet influence than in 1960, or 1965, or even 1970. It is a different kind of influence: more brutal, more direct, far more costly, but fixed upon the same goals.

With regard to China, the Soviet Union found it very troubling to see another major communist power exercising an independent diplomacy along the Soviet periphery, even if it was a diplomacy aimed at easing pressure on China itself by strengthening states with a common strategic interest.[7] For Moscow, China alone, or China plus Pakistan, did not pose a vital threat.[8] However, China in combination with a large industrial power could pose such a threat.

The prospect of a China-U.S.-Pakistan relationship must be seen in this broader context: not only would it strengthen an unfriendly (albeit not hostile) state that can embarrass Moscow in Afghanistan; it is a potential link in a border security system which would be an effective counter to Soviet power. The direct link between China and Pakistan was particularly galling; this allowed direct passage between Xinjiang and Gilgit and traversed the

133

Karakorams only a few miles from Afghanistan's Wakhan corridor. This desolate Afghan area was the meeting place of four historic empires (British Indian, Persian, Russian, and Chinese). Soviet leaders must regard it as having great symbolic and strategic value, as they occupied it simultaneously with their capture of Kabul and other major Afghan cities.

Compared with Soviet sensitivity to China, Moscow's growing interest in the Indian Ocean is secondary.[9] The Soviet Union remains a land-based state, aware of, and excessively fearful of the diversity on its northern, southern, and eastern borders, along the seventy-five percent of its territory that lies in Asia.[10]

The structure of Soviet involvement and commitment in South Asia could change because of three possible developments. First, if their relations improved, neither Peking nor Moscow would have as great an incentive to support what they believe to be their regional surrogates, Pakistan and India. Such normalization is improbable.[11] Somewhat more probable are two other developments.

The second possible development involves Soviet interests in Iran and the Persian Gulf. Should the gulf's politics become more unstable, some Soviet strategists might argue that a warmer relationship with Pakistan might pay considerable dividends in a region where there already is a major Pakistani military presence, even at the cost of strained relations with India. For Moscow the calculation would focus on the relative value of India vis-a-vis China, versus the relative value of Pakistan vis-a-vis the gulf and Afghanistan. Such a closer Soviet-Pakistan relationship might just detach Pakistan from Chinese and American influence as well. The present Pakistani leadership is unlikely to subscribe to such a policy, but there are those in the political community, and even within the military, who have argued for closer ties to Moscow.[12]

The third alternative to the present structure in South Asia would be an increase in regional cooperation, free from Soviet control. Were India to conclude that closer ties to Pakistan lessened its need for Soviet arms; and that its own power was more than sufficient to enable it to negotiate on an equal basis with China, it might "do a deal" with both antagonists and emerge as a powerful regional leader, free from the stigma of its Soviet connection.

To summarize: Soviet interests in South Asia are largely indirect, and derived from its more important conflict with the PRC. India is one of the few countries with a live border with China, and could be vitally important to the Soviet Union in case of a major conflict with the PRC.[13] There is no evidence that the Indians have agreed to such a role (and Moscow must wonder how useful the Indians would actually be in such a crisis). But only India and Vietnam have the capacity and motivation to assist the USSR in balancing China. Strengthening these states does not threaten any established Soviet position in South or Southeast Asia.[14]

134

The Sovietization of Afghanistan may take a very long time -- indeed, it may never be completed. Moscow has found the Afghans to be a much tougher foe than they expected. From a military perspective, the gradual increase in Soviet troops in Afghanistan to about 150,000 by the end of 1984, and the adoption of large-scale search and destroy missions aimed at the destruction of crops, represents a slight change in Soviet tactics. But this is matched by the gradual improvement in Afghan tactics, weapons, and greater coordination between different guerrilla groups. The war, after over five years, remains a more violent stalemate with no sign that either side will bend, let alone yield and negotiate.[15]

While the military and political battles continue, the Kremlin will take whatever benefits it can from Afghanistan. Natural gas and minerals resources are promising, and balance some of the costs of war and occupation. So would be the use of Afghan territory by military forces which are oriented towards the gulf, the Indian Ocean, or further afield. These, however, are the prerequisites of imperialism, not, in this case, its cause.

Soviet Impact on South Asia

When the Soviet Union invaded Afghanistan, its role in the rest of South Asia was at low ebb. While the Janata government (1977-1980) in India had negotiated a major arms deal with Moscow, it preferred Western weapons when they were available. The dominant strategic issue in the region was India's growing military power vis-a-vis Pakistan, not an anticipated Soviet invasion. The invasion took all South Asians by surprise, although leaders in Islamabad were warning visitors in April 1978 that the coup was irreversible and that the Soviet Union had achieved a foothold in the subcontinent.

Pakistan had earlier responded to India's growing military power by embarking upon a covert nuclear program.[16] Yet its chief concerns were with domestic order, as the military regime led by Zia ul-Haq had not yet stabilized. But Islamabad acknowledged India's conventional military dominance, and it had adjusted its own strategy along more defensive lines, as all three of the Indian services had begun to embrace a more offensive-minded approach.

At the general level, the Soviet invasion of Afghanistan has not caused any serious change in relations among the states of South Asia -- excepting, of course, between Afghanistan and the rest. Afghanistan has not been invited to join the South Asian Regional Council (SARC), and all South Asian states, including India, called for the withdrawal of at least "foreign" forces from Afghanistan.

However, the Soviet presence in Afghanistan has jolted the "balanced imbalance" between India and Pakistan. Some had hoped that the Soviet presence would bring the two states closer together, but it has not. Yet, they have not been driven into war. India has not threatened Pakistan, but it has complained loudly and frequently about Pakistan's efforts to rearm itself. Pakistanis recognize that the Indians could have done worse, but some have recently predicted an Indian escalation of pressure against them, and they remain suspicious of India, just as they remain apprehensive about the prospects of increased Soviet pressure from the West.[17]

Pakistan's Soviet Threat

Pakistan is currently a state with a three-front security problem. The threat from India originated in the partition of British India in 1947. It has been extended vertically and horizontally as the Indians have developed their military infrastructure in Rajasthan and have acquired aircraft (the British Jaguar) that can reach every corner of Pakistan.

The second threat is internal: Pakistan has major dissident groups and regions, most notably Sind and Baluchistan, and the military regime of General Zia remains less than popular. Paradoxically, the most recent threat, from Moscow through its Afghan clients, is also the oldest. It is the latest manifestation of a very old "great game" of imperial expansion, a game that began in the nineteenth century but which had virtually disappeared from public consciousness for some twenty-five years.[18] Pakistan has found itself in the unenviable position of the boy who cried wolf often without much conviction -- but the wolf has arrived.

The gravest threat to Pakistan is not from a single source but from a combination of external and internal sources. Foreign support for dissidents and Soviet or Indian forces acting in concert would present an overwhelming military problem. While Pakistan has a large and well-trained military, Indian forces are much bigger, and the Soviet forces theoretically have an unlimited potential.

This image of Pakistan threatened on both fronts, and at home, has led many observers to conclude that its military situation is hopeless. Before the Soviet invasion of Afghanistan, Indians had expected Pakistan to recognize its permanent inferiority and fit itself into an Indian-dominated system of regional security.[19]

Many Pakistanis felt that they had fallen behind India in conventional arms, which led Prime Minister Zulfikar Ali Bhutto to begin a covert nuclear program. When the Soviet forces moved into Afghanistan, Pakistan's strategic vulnerability was again stressed by outside observers. They opposed military support for Pakistan on the grounds that it might provoke Moscow to foment rebellion in Baluchistan. Many Pakistani civilians (and some in the military) threw up their hands at the prospect of resistance, and they urged a policy of conciliation with the Soviet Union and even India.

136

Further, Pakistan continues to be criticized for failing to move more of its forces to the Durand Line, a line demarcating the Indo-Afghan frontier, negotiated by Sir Mortimer Durand in 1893. Instead, Pakistan keeps its forces across the border from India.

This force concentration on the border with India is taken as evidence that Pakistan does not take the Soviet threat seriously, and is using its American aid to build up its capacity against India. A careful analysis of the actual terrain involved, the level of Soviet forces presently in Afghanistan, and the historical precedents would indicate that Pakistan's military situation is not as desperate as the above suggests, and that the impact of the Soviet occupation of Afghanistan on Pakistan has been miscalculated.

First, the Soviet force levels in Afghanistan are barely adequate to control the major cities and only intermittently control major road routes. Soviet/Afghan airpower ranges unopposed over Afghanistan, but it would meet a technological equal in the Pakistani Air Force. Some idea of the increase in Soviet forces necessary to pose a major threat to Pakistan can be gained from calculations of the defensibility of the North West Frontier and Baluchistan. The British estimated that a joint Afghan-Soviet invasion force would be required to pose a threat to India, and that it could be met with an Indian force of about the same size (five divisions) as Pakistan now has deployed along the Durand Line.[20]

Second, the combat record of the Pakistan Army is such that the Soviet forces could expect a stiff battle. The Pakistan Army may be the best army that never won a war. Its performance in the invasion of India in 1965 was excessively zealous, it fought well in East Pakistan (even though demoralized and often ineptly led), and there is no evidence -- despite a great deal of insinuation -- that its involvement in politics since 1977 has hurt its fighting spirit.

Third, a direct Soviet attack on Pakistan would raise the prospect of American, Chinese, and other support. A Soviet buildup of ground forces would give these and other countries sufficient opportunity to coordinate their assistance.

The Soviet military threat to Pakistan has been exaggerated. Pakistan has sustained its precarious security with a modest increase in its forces. What has dramatically changed is the prospects for a two-front war, with Soviet and Indian pressure applied at the same time, overwhelming Pakistan's defenses. Pakistan's reserves for the Rajasthan/Sind front are the same troops that are deployed against the Soviet/Afghan forces in Baluchistan. If these reserves were frozen in place, Pakistan would be at a severe disadvantage. If one includes the prospect of internal disorder, then Pakistan's situation could become desperate. The critical question becomes, therefore, not whether the USSR threatens Pakistan, but whether joint pressure is applied by the USSR and India.

137

India's Likely Future Behavior

The Soviet invasion of Afghanistan came as a considerable surprise to India, which had not been told in advance of Soviet intentions. Compounding India's embarrassment, the first public statement on the problem by the new government of Indira Gandhi had to be retracted. India's polite and private suggestions to Moscow that it withdraw were ignored. In any case, the Indira Gandhi government was more concerned with the indirect consequences of the Soviet invasion than the direct. It launched a vehement campaign against U.S. military support of Pakistan, lobbying intensively (and with some effectiveness) in Washington. The Indian military had embraced a first-strike (or pre-emptive strike) military doctrine over the 1970s, and it had drawn selectively on the Soviet Union to fill in gaps in its inventory. The Soviet invasion had, indirectly, not only aided Pakistan's rearmament but put India in an humiliating position vis-a-vis the Soviets.

The paradox of increasing Indian dependence upon Moscow at the moment when the USSR entered South Asia as a military power is explained as a manifestation of India's client status or as an indication of a long-range plan in which both countries will join forces and swallow up Pakistan. These suspicions are, of course, stressed by those U.S. congressmen and Pakistani strategists who have decried Indo-Soviet collusion for years.[21] If either of these arguments is correct -- if India is a client of Moscow's, or if Indian interests parallel Moscow's -- then the situation in South Asia is grave, indeed. Ultimately, we could expect the joint pressure of these two states to overwhelm Pakistan, and it is unlikely that Pakistan's distant friends could do much about it. Moscow would obtain a foothold in Pakistan itself either directly, or through client states along the Afghan border. Finally, the alleged Soviet "dream" of a warm-water port would be fulfilled, as these client states knuckle under to Soviet demands. For the following reasons, however, these arguments do not seem plausible, and it is very unlikely that India will join with the Soviet Union in pressuring Pakistan or risk a solo attack on Pakistan.

First, Pakistan is an irritant to India but does not pose a vital threat. Second, the Indian armed forces are themselves temporarily vulnerable. Many of the indigenously built weapons systems are no longer modern, and the Indian defense industry is incapable of producing adequate replacements. Thus, India has had to turn abroad for wholesale renewal of its aging armor force and many aircraft types. Third, the alleged Soviet "connection" is problematic. There are several possible cases: Moscow could ask India for assistance against Pakistan; India could ask the Soviets for assistance should they decide to rectify the Kashmir border or otherwise pressure Pakistan; and both, for different motives, could

138

agree on a joint strategy of pressure. However, the likely Indian calculation in each of these cases probably suggests caution.

A Soviet request for Indian assistance (or, as some would put it, a request that India act on behalf of the Soviet Union) would be analyzed carefully in New Delhi in terms of likely Indian gains and losses. Any kind of Indian pressure on Pakistan runs the risk of Pakistani air retaliation, ground warfare, and foreign involvement. India would want to make certain that an initial attack on Pakistan would quickly end the war, with Indian objectives achieved.

Furthermore, a joint Indo-Soviet operation, even if successful, provides no guarantee against future clashes with the Soviet Union along their new border. Would this border be drawn at the Hindu Kush, the Durand Line, or the Indus? Would several post-Pakistani states emerge? Which of these would become Soviet, Chinese, or Indian clients? What would India do if one of its clients were to become entangled with a Soviet client constructed out of the old Pakistan? In any such conflict, or in a heightened conflict with China, good relations with the United States would be essential, but these would not survive a joint Indo-Soviet operation against Pakistan. India might be tempted to join with the Soviet Union in attacking Pakistan in a situation which paralleled 1970, when Pakistan itself was in a state of civil war and millions of refugees had fled to India. India's intervention was rapid and decisive, and a pro-Indian government was put in power in the new state of Bangladesh. While Indians today are concerned about the modest growth of Pakistani power, informed Indian strategists recognize that while a weak Pakistan suits Indian interests, a broken Pakistan does not, because of the presence of Soviet forces a mere two hundred and fifty miles from Indian territory.

Our own view, discussed above, is that Pakistan's ability to resist Soviet pressure is greater than most observers have imagined. Just as a number of predictions concerning Pakistan's imminent disintegration have not been borne out, it may be that expectations concerning Pakistan's military weaknesses will be revised. New Delhi may yet reconsider its strategy of dominance, which has been disrupted by modest additions to Pakistan's weapons in the hands of its armed forces. Indian regional dominance may yet be achieved through a sharing of the military burden of regional defense. The alternative for India is to engage in an arms race propelled by the actions of its own major arms supplier, the Soviet Union.

Concluding Comments

This essay has discussed extreme cases. These are important to consider, if only to show that they are not imminent. The real threat to Pakistan from the Soviet Union lies at a lower level than an all-out attack. A joint Indo-Soviet attack is even less likely. Pakistan's capacity to meet such threats -- or at least compel an attacker greatly to increase the level of force required for success -- is greater than most observers have recognized. Even Pakistanis tend to exaggerate their security dilemma. The gloom that pervaded the conference rooms of Pakistani strategists five years ago was unnecessary: Pakistan remains a powerful, united state with an effective military establishment. It has no hope of winning against a concerted or long-term threat, but short of that it is more capable of protecting itself than most observers thought five years ago. This conclusion has several implications for the future of South Asia, and the Soviet presence in Afghanistan:

o   The Soviet forces entered Afghanistan because of a combination of hubris and ignorance, and, above all, to ensure that an ally on the USSR's border would not fall.

o   Soviet expansionism, at least in South Asia, has been a function of the weakness of individual states. Even if the Soviet Union's ambitions were unlimited, its expansion could only march with opportunity, and the opportunities for a move in the direction of Pakistan are less than many have thought.

o   The likelihood of Pakistan's continued low-level tacit support for the Afghan resistance fighters, the mujaheddin, is very good. It is difficult for Moscow to stop mujaheddin activity, and it would require a great degree of pressure to get Pakistan to stop its support.

o   It is unlikely that India will join with the Soviet Union in pressuring Pakistan, or that it will launch an attack upon Pakistan by itself.

o   The old conflict between India and Pakistan still blocks a coordinated regional response to the Soviet occupation of Afghanistan. India missed its moment in 1980-1981, but that was not necessarily the last chance. If a joint regional response could be forged, then serious diplomatic and even military pressure could be put on the USSR, along with a concerted plan that could ease out the Soviet forces with Moscow's dignity intact.

This paper was completed before the assassination of Indian Prime Minister Indira Gandhi, on October 31, 1984.

140

NOTES

1. For an excellent compilation of views on the Soviet role in South, East, and Southeast Asia see: The Soviet Role in Asia, Hearings before the Subcommittees on Europe and the Middle East and on Asian and Pacific Affairs, U.S. House of Representatives, Committee on Foreign Affairs, 98th Congress, July-August, 1983. See also Zagoria, Donald S., ed., Soviet Policy in East Asia (New Haven: Yale University Press, 1982).

2. For a survey of the communist parties of Afghanistan see Arnold, Anthony, Afghanistan's Two Party Communism: Parcham and Khalq (Stanford: Hoover Institution Press, 1983).

3. See the Indian note in Foreign Affairs Record (New Delhi), November, 1963, pp. 264-265.

4. Strumilin, S., "The World 20 Years from Now," Kommunist, No. 13 (September 1961), pp. 25-36, Current Digest of the Soviet Press, Vol. 13, no. 38 (October 18, 1961), pp. 3-7.

5. For an excellent overall assessment of the net gains and losses of Soviet influence in Asia, and South Asia in particular, see Thornton, Thomas P., prepared statement and testimony, The Soviet Role in Asia, pp. 3-27, 98th Congress.

6. See Gelman, Harry, "Soviet Policy Toward China: The Contending Perspectives in Moscow," Soviet Role in Asia, p. 353.

7. See Pollack, Jonathan, The Lessons of Coalition Politics: Sino-American Security Relations (Santa Monica: Rand Corporation, 1984).

8. Stephan, John J., "Asia in the Soviet Conception," Zagoria, Donald S., ed., Op. cit., p. 40.

9. For an excellent survey, see Andersen, Walter K., "Soviets in the Indian Ocean: Much Ado About Something -- But What," Asian Survey, Vol. 24, No. 9 (September 1984), pp. 910-930.

10. About a third of Asia is in the Soviet Union. The Soviet leaders are more aware of the myth of the unity of Asia than many in the West, since their own "Asian" territories are quite diverse. For a discussion of Soviet national pluralism see Connor, Walker, The National Question in Marxist Leninist Theory and Strategy (Princeton: Princeton University Press, 1984), and Stephan, Op. cit., p. 31.

11. Two recent collections, that by Zagoria, and the hearings, The Soviet Role in Asia, present a wide range of views on this issue, as well as on Soviet goals in Asia, which include "equality," "hegemony," "world socialism," a "security glacis," and "defensive." See especially the articles and testimony by Thornton, Kelly, Brown, Zagoria, and Langer.

12. The author has met a number of Pakistani army officers who, in frustration at the perceived failure of the United States to support Pakistan, have speculated that "perhaps we should turn to

the Soviets." Such views have receded since the Soviet invasion of Afghanistan but they are held more widely among dissident Pakistani civilians.

13. Edward Luttwak's scenario of a Soviet attack on the PRC is indirectly verified by the amount of Soviet equipment pouring into India. See Luttwak, The Grand Strategy of the Soviet Union (New York: St. Martin's Press, 1983).

14. Pakistan, now a close friend of China, has a negative importance for the USSR. Moscow was as eager to undercut Chinese influence there in the 1970s as it was once eager to undercut American influence in Pakistan. However, the prospect of an extended occupation of Afghanistan and Pakistan's good ties to the Islamic world are factors that have nothing to do with the United States or China, and might yet prompt a change in Soviet policy.

15. The best overview of the Soviet involvement in Afghanistan is in Bradsher, Henry S., Afghanistan and the Soviet Union (Durham: Duke University Press, 1983). It should be noted that as a result of the Soviet invasion, about a quarter of the Afghan population are either dead or live as refugees in Pakistan (almost three million) or Iran (almost one million). Askari-Rizvi, Dr. Hasan, "Afghan Refugees in Pakistan: Influx, Humanitarian Assistance, and Implications," Pakistan Horizon Vol. 36, no. 1 (1984), pp. 40-61. See also Amin, Tahir, "Afghan Resistance: Past, Present, and Future," Asian Survey, Vol. 24, no. 4 (April 1984) pp. 373-391; and Allan, Pierre, and Albert A. Stahel, "Tribal Guerilla Warfare Against a Colonial Power: Analyzing the War in Afghanistan," Journal of Conflict Resolution, (December 1983).

16. The prospect of a Pakistani nuclear weapon is discussed in Cohen, Stephen P., The Pakistan Army (Berkeley: University of California Press, 1984), pp. 152 ff.

17. For views by the leading Pakistani advocate of normalization between India and Pakistan, see Akram, A.I. (Gen., Ret.), Make Peace, Not War (Islamabad: Institute of Regional Studies, 1982). A critique of Akram's views can be found in "India's Military Ascendancy," by "Cassandra," The Muslim (Islamabad), April 15, 16, 1983.

18. See Hauner, Milan, "The Last Great Game," Middle East Journal, Vol. 38, no. 1, Winter, 1984, 72-84, and Canfield, Robert L., "Soviet Gambit in Central Asia," Journal of South Asia and Middle Eastern Studies, Vol. VI, no. 1 (Fall 1981), pp. 10-30 for two perceptive surveys of the historical significance of the Soviet move to Afghanistan.

19. The most comprehensive statement of Indian strategic goals is in an "Address" forty-three pages long by the then Indian Defense Minister, C. Subramaniam, "India's Defense Strategy in the New Decade," delivered in late 1979. Another comprehensive and

142

authoritative summary of Indian strategic objectives is in Bajpai, K.S., ed., India's Security (New Delhi: Lancer's, 1983).

20. The British developed several plans from 1926 onward, most of them assuming joint Afghan-Soviet military action. They steadily scaled down their own plans, from a pre-emptive invasion of Afghanistan to a simple defensive deployment along the Durand Line. This would have required only five or six divisions, plus air superiority. See Historical Section (India and Pakistan), Official History of the Indian Armed Forces in the Second World War, Defense of India: Policy and Plans (N.P.: combined Inter-Services Historical Section, distributed by Orient Longmans, 1963), pp. 23, 39.

21. "Indian-Pakistan Tension Causes Concern to U.S.," New York Times September 15, 1984. Two senators indicate that Mrs. Gandhi had been advised to attack Pakistani nuclear facilities.

Chapter 17

SOVIET INROADS TO THE PERSIAN GULF STATES

Roger E. Kanet and Sumit Ganguly

Ever since the mid-1950s, when Nikita Khrushchev initiated a policy of expanded involvement in the Third World, the region of Southwest Asia has been high on the list of Soviet regional priorities. The strategic location of the area -- adjacent to the southern boundaries of the USSR as well as the Middle East and the Persian Gulf region -- and the Soviet concern about the concentration of U.S. political and military influence in the entire area have been among the most important long-term determinants of Soviet policy. During the past two decades concerns about the possible extension of Chinese influence into the area, as well as the critical importance of Persian gulf petroleum resources for Western nations, have added to the attractiveness of this part of the world for Soviet meddling, or at least influence-peddling.[1]

The corollary of the Soviet attempt to preclude the establishment of influence in the region by one of the two major opponents of the USSR has been the desire to create a Soviet-oriented grouping of Southwest Asian states. The unsuccessful attempts in the late 1960s and early 1970s to generate support for an Asian collective security system centered on Moscow provide evidence of this objective.

In addition to the broad goal of a Soviet-oriented bloc of states along the southern borders of the USSR, Soviet leaders have also been interested in military-security and economic benefits that they might gain from closer contact with the countries of the region. Until the invasion and occupation of Afghanistan in late 1979, however, the Soviet leaders made little headway in turning their economic, military, and political involvement into an active military presence similar to what they were able to acquire in places such as Egypt (until 1972), Somalia (until 1977), and elsewhere in Africa and Asia.

Overall, Soviet policy in Southwest Asia and the gulf region has been an integral part of Soviet activities in the Third World

144

more generally and has, over time, been closely related to Soviet initiatives in the Middle East and other portions of Asia. The primary motivating factor in Soviet policy has been the global competition with the United States and its allies and the desire to strengthen the overall security capabilities of the Soviet state, while at the same time undermining the long-term interests of the Western states.

Soviet Aim in Afghanistan

The primary objectives of Soviet support for the Communist Saur Revolution of April 1978 and of the invasion in late December 1979, which occurred after the Taraki and Amin regimes had proven incapable of generating even the most modest popular support for their brand of communist revolution, concerned the maintenance and strengthening of Soviet influence, even control, in a country considered vitally important for long-term Soviet interests.[2] Such factors as the strategic benefits to be obtained by the occupation of Afghanistan by what is now well over 100,000 Soviet troops were related to the fear that an anti-Soviet regime might come to power in Afghanistan and eventually provide the United States with opportunities for influence in the region.

It is true -- and obviously of major significance for the interests of the United States and its allies -- that one of the consequences of the Soviet invasion was the extension of Soviet military power closer to the oilfields of the Persian Gulf. The continuing Soviet effort to consolidate its military and political domination in Afghanistan has most recently been coupled with diplomatic efforts aimed at "normalizing" relations with a number of important Persian Gulf states, especially with the State of Kuwait and the Kingdom of Saudi Arabia.

Current Soviet policy in Afghanistan is oriented -- as was Soviet policy in East Europe in the earlier post-1945 period -- toward the creation of a stable communist regime dependent upon and dominated by the USSR. Such a regime would provide Moscow with a number of visible benefits.

First of all, the possibility of the development of a hostile Afghan government allied with China or the West on the southern borders of the Soviet Union would be eliminated. Closely related to this is the fact that a stable and communist Afghanistan would provide the USSR with an effective buffer in the south and, moreover, would provide opportunities for influencing governments in the region -- in particular those of Pakistan, Iran, and the Persian Gulf states.

Other factors that favor the continued Soviet efforts to "pacify" Afghanistan as a dependent communist state include the successful experience of the pacification of Central Asia by the Soviet government in the 1920s, commitments to the Afghan Communist party (the People's Democratic Party of Afghanistan, or PDPA), the unwillingness of the Soviet leadership to back down on such commitments, and the evidence that the successful creation of a communist regime in Afghanistan would provide for the continuing vitality of the claimed inevitability of Marxism-Leninism as the single global social system of the future.

Although the Soviet Union has been sporadically involved in United Nations-sponsored negotiations concerning the future of Afghanistan, it is clear that no successful agreement can be expected to emanate from these talks that would result in a Soviet military withdrawal and the establishment of a truly autonomous Afghan government. The major escalation of Soviet military operations in Afghanistan during 1985 provides clear evidence that the USSR is in Afghanistan to stay and that it is willing to expend the resources necessary to remain.

The costs that Moscow has incurred in Afghanistan during the course of the past five years have been quite high, but definitely not of an order that would result in a reconsideration of basic Soviet policy. From Moscow's perspective, the inevitability of the collapse of the PDPA regime in Kabul, were Soviet troops to be withdrawn, would bring with it costs far higher than those of continuing the military occupation and "pacification" of the country. Although Soviet casualties have risen during the past two years as the level of fighting has escalated, they continue to remain relatively low.

The Persian Gulf, the Soviet Union, and Western Interests

Although the Soviet Union has clearly extended its military capabilities in Southwest Asia as a result of the invasion and occupation of Afghanistan -- a factor which enhances its potential for expanding its role in the Persian Gulf region -- Moscow has yet to employ its capabilities effectively as an instrument of influence in the key gulf states.

Before turning to a discussion of Soviet efforts to establish a presence and extend influence in the region, it is important to examine the importance of the gulf for the interests of the United States, Japan, and their European allies.

Unlike U.S. interest in West Europe, which stems from long-standing links of culture and history and more recent concerns about markets, U.S. interests in the Persian Gulf stem from lesser objectives. Here the United States is primarily interested in ensuring continued access to the petroleum resources of the region and also in the recently-expanding markets which have been created through oil revenues.

146

The major interest that Japan and the other states of East Asia share with the United States -- as far as the Persian Gulf is concerned -- is twofold:

First, an uninterrupted access to the petroleum reserves of the region, and

Second, access to the markets of the region.

Given these interests, the key question that arises is how they may be undermined if the Soviet Union were to make encroachments in the direction of the gulf. Broadly speaking, there are two dominant schools of thought about Soviet interests in the Persian Gulf. One view holds that the Soviet Union is interested in expanding toward the gulf as part of the historic Russian drive to acquire warm-water ports. This view is perhaps best expressed by W. Scott Thompson, who argues:

My working assumption is that it is basic Soviet strategy to reach the warm waters of the Indian Ocean .... There need be no "master plan" for this assumption to be seen as reasonable. Moscow would understandably like to break out of what, at one period, it surely saw as its encirclement. Its cultivation of good relations with India, its occupations of parts of Iran thrice in this century, its invasion of Afghanistan, its treaty of friendship with Iraq, and its attempts to be the balancer in the Iran-Iraq war are all, in part, manifestations of this general expansionist desire.[3]

It appears important to state that analysts who see the USSR seeking to expand its horizons in the direction of the gulf also see a generally expansionist drive underlying Soviet global strategy as a whole. In contrast to the view taken by Thompson, we find a markedly divergent view of Soviet interests and objectives expressed by R. L. McLaurin, another scholar working on Soviet policy in the region:

The Persian Gulf has not, however, been a Soviet neighbor, either recently or in the distant past. The Gulf was of virtually no importance to Russia for centuries. Where would Russian warm-water ports in the Gulf have traded? And with what? Russia's internal lines of communication in areas closest to the Gulf were not highly developed. Certainly a Russian naval force permanently stationed in the Gulf was unthinkable but would not have been unsinkable: the Strait of Hormuz would have left such a fleet bottled up, without logistic support, and cut off from major bodies of water.[4]

The approach that we adopt in assessing Soviet interests and objectives in the region of the Persian Gulf falls in between the two views spelled out above. We believe that the Kremlin has multiple goals in the region and is not necessarily on an inexorably expansionist path towards the warm waters of the Indian Ocean. What then, are the Soviet interests in the region? In our view, they include (not necessarily in a sequential or a hierarchical order):

o   to the extent possible, reducing Western influence, in particular that of the United States, in the area;

o   expanding Soviet influence in the region;

o   obtaining access to the resources of the region through the presence of friendly governments (which are preferably also at least professedly Marxist);

o   ensuring Soviet security interests.

It is quite obvious that our enumeration of Soviet interests and objectives suggests that they are intrinsically linked with one another and can only be separated for analytical purposes. For example, if the USSR succeeds in ensuring that particular states or sets of states have regimes that are not hostile to Soviet interests and keep their distance from the West, other Soviet concerns (such as security interests) would probably also be enhanced.

Soviet Concerns in the Middle East

Soviet influence waned in the Persian Gulf region in general and Iran in particular through the 1950s, as the United States increasingly made inroads into this region. Specifically, in Iran the government of Mohammed Mossadegh was overthrown with the tacit approval of the United States, after he nationalized the foreign oil companies.[5]   More broadly, the United States succeeded in establishing an entire network of military alliances from the Far East to the Middle East, including the South East Asia Treaty Organization (SEATO) and the Central Treaty Organization (CENTO), which sought to contain the expansion of Soviet power.

Although these alliances would eventually unravel because differences among their members proved to be greater than the fear of a common enemy, from the Soviet standpoint they represented encirclement.   One primary goal of Soviet policy from the mid-1950s on was the dissolution of these U.S.-centered alliances.   In fact, even prior to the consolidation of the Western alliance system, the USSR initiated major efforts to break through this network.

148

The USSR began to make tenuous inroads into the Middle East through its support of Gamal Abdul Nasser of Egypt and the various governments that ruled Syria in the 1950s. What influence Moscow was able to garner in the Middle East in the late 1950s remained confined to the northern and western section of the region and did not extend into the resource-rich Persian Gulf area. In fact, it was not until a coup in Iraq in 1958 removed the pro-Western government that the USSR was provided with its initial opportunity to establish contacts with one of the Persian Gulf states.

In the wake of the coup that brought Qasim to power, Iraq withdrew from the Baghdad Pact and also abrogated the 1955 Anglo-Iraqi treaty. Despite the anti-Western character of the new Iraqi regime, Moscow quickly realized that the Iraqi communists were not permitted to operate openly in the country and instructed them to subordinate their interests to those of a strong, nationalist ruler. While the Soviet Union was none too happy with Qasim's domestic policies, it nevertheless continued to support him with both economic and military aid.[6]

This Soviet willingness to sacrifice ideological goals to achieve other interests -- in this case the denial of Western influence -- was hardly exceptional. The USSR repeatedly has demonstrated that it is willing to overlook the ideological coloration of many of its prospective clients in order to promote goals deemed to be more important for Soviet interests.

This pragmatism paid off, and with the Ba'ath coup in 1963 Moscow was able to improve its standing in Iraq. The major boost to Soviet interests, however, came in the aftermath of the 1967 Arab-Israeli conflict when Iraq broke its ties with a number of Western states, notably the United States, the United Kingdom, and West Germany. It is important to point out, lest we make the wrong inference, that while the breaking of diplomatic relations with the Western nations redounded to the benefit of Moscow, the underlying reasons for the break had little to do with Soviet influence in Iraqi politics. Thus, it was a convergence of interests that served to bring Iraq and the USSR together rather than the Soviet ability to make Iraq carry out its dictates.

In the late 1960s and the early 1970s, as the Iraqis sought to expand their influence in the Persian Gulf (particularly after Nasser's death in 1970), they found further common ground with the USSR. For it was about this time that the Kremlin was despairing about the utility of providing foreign economic aid and was increasingly relying on arms sales.[7] This shift in policy coincided with Iraqi needs, particularly in light of the fact that the Iraqis had severed relations with the Western nations, except France, which were in the position to supply them with arms. Furthermore, owing to its intransigence towards the Western states, Iraq encountered various difficulties with the Western oil companies. This in turn

149

provided the USSR with the opportunity to extend technical help to the Iraqis for their petroleum industry.

Despite the involvement of the USSR in the Iraqi oil industry (particularly after the oil embargo of 1973) and the continued sale of weaponry to Iraq, both to satisfy its regional aspirations and to curb the activities of the Kurdish rebels, Moscow's ability to influence Iraqi foreign policy remained limited. Thus, despite Soviet pressure to endorse various peace plans for the Middle East, the Iraqis remained aloof. Furthermore, after initial collaboration with domestic communists, Iraqi President Saddam Hussein dealt with them in a rather ruthless fashion and, though Moscow protested, it appeared unable to do much to change Hussein's behavior.

Two Yemeni Republics

If Moscow fared none-too-well in its relations with a gulf state widely considered to be a quasi-client state, how has it fared with other states in the gulf since its initial forays into the region? Moscow's interest in the two Yemeni Republics dates back to the early 1960s. Following the military coup in North Yemen in 1962 Moscow sought to maintain its early friendly relations with the strategically-located state. By 1964 Kremlin leaders had signed a treaty of friendship and economic and technical cooperation which provided the North Yemenis a loan of 65 million rubles.[8] Soviet activities in North Yemen continued to expand until the overthrow of President Sallal in 1967. This led to direct Soviet military involvement on behalf of the new regime, although the USSR was inhibited from expanding its military role in the conflict after U.S. warnings to refrain from such activity.[9]

As the civil war dragged on, the military rulers who had overthrown President Sallal sought to reduce their dependence on the USSR and made overtures towards the West and the Saudis. About the same time border clashes broke out with South Yemen, and Moscow tilted towards the latter with whom they had become involved following the departure of the British in 1967. However, Moscow was unwilling to forego completely the investment that it had made in North Yemen and attempted to maintain ties with South Yemen also.

Ultimately, it was in South Yemen that Moscow did succeed in establishing a firm toehold. The reasons for the Soviet success were twofold. First, the regime that replaced British rule was radical and leftist in character. Second, it was also desperately in need of resources for economic development. These two factors gave Moscow the opportunity of making headway into this underdeveloped nation. The major payoffs that have accrued to the USSR from its investments in South Yemen include access to air and naval base

150

facilities, particularly in Aden. Furthermore, owing to its cordial relations with South Yemen the USSR was able to provide support for the Dhofar rebellion in Oman.[10]

Limited Success in Iran, Saudi Arabia, and Kuwait

Despite a long-standing interest in Iran and certain cooperative arrangements that they worked out with the Shah, the Soviet leaders have been markedly unsuccessful in obtaining any degree of long-term influence or leverage over Iran's foreign or domestic policies. While Moscow may take delight and derive comfort from Ayatollah Khomeini's description of the United States as "the Great Satan," it is also acutely cognizant that the Iranian leadership is hardly sympathetic to Soviet interests in the region. Also, contrary to popular belief that Moscow stands to gain from the revolutionary pronouncements and proclivities of the Iranian regime, we would argue that -- in all likelihood -- the USSR has much to fear from the brand of revolution that the Ayatollah and his followers are interested in fomenting. Thus, while cautious about criticizing Khomeini in a direct fashion, Moscow has criticized the Khomeini regime's attempts to suppress the pro-Moscow Tudeh Party in Iran.[11]

Moscow's willingness to criticize the muzzling of the Tudeh party stems less from concern for the plight of the party (they remained silent when the Shah's SAVAK, the dreaded Iranian internal security force, wreaked havoc on the Tudeh and its members) than a simple recognition that it has little to lose by criticizing Iran. In a very clear sense this situation demonstrates the low ebb to the Soviet position in Iran. Certainly the situation is of concern to Moscow, which was early in recognizing the regime of Ayatollah Khomeini. In this regard, Moscow's response to the Iran-Iraq war is instructive. While Moscow has increasingly moved towards supporting Iraq in the conflict, it has sought to play its cards in such a fashion that it does not entirely vitiate its relations with the Iranians. In short, Moscow is apparently trying to hedge its bets on the outcome of that conflict.[12]

While unwilling to confront the United States directly, the Soviet Union is nevertheless seeking to expand its influence in the Southwest Asian region -- though, as we have noted, Soviet success has been quite limited. One key state which Moscow would like to court (or even help engineer an overthrow of its regime) is Saudi Arabia. Moscow has no diplomatic relations with the Saudis, and it appears highly unlikely that such a diplomatic breakthrough is on the horizon. The Saudi regime is a conservative monarchy and is strongly critical of atheistic communism. It has also banned the communist party in the country, thereby denying Moscow the opportunity of resorting to a form of informal penetration. Furthermore, the Saudis, in tacit cooperation with the United States, serve as a bulwark against revolution in the Persian Gulf. Given the nature of their regime, they are extremely concerned about revolutionary movements, whether they are of a secular or a religious character.

Apart from Saudi Arabia, the only other actor of any significance in the gulf is Kuwait. Moscow recently developed formal diplomatic ties with Kuwait, a country which the Soviet leaders had viewed as independent in name only at the time of its independence from the United Kingdom. Kuwait has sought to pursue a rather delicate foreign policy stance, refusing to align itself with either superpower. It has opposed the U.S.-sponsored Rapid Deployment Force and also the installation of American bases in the Persian Gulf. And, while commending the Soviet stand on the Arab-Israeli conflict, Kuwait has also made clear to Moscow that it wishes to minimize all superpower intrusion into the gulf.[13] Thus far the Kuwaitis have been reasonably successful in this strategy.

U.S. Interests Prevail

Given this analysis of Soviet behavior in the Persian Gulf area, we can contend that the USSR does not pose an imminent threat to the interests of the Western nations in general nor to East Asia in particular. Indeed, it appears that the major immediate problem in the gulf stems less from Soviet intrusions or possible Soviet interference with oil supplies than from the likelihood of instability emanating from the internal structure of the regimes of the area.

A major fact of life is the fundamentally unrepresentative character of the bulk of the regimes in the region. As these societies undergo modernization (brought about through petroluem-fueled development), many of the primordial ties of clan, tribe, and family will break down, thereby giving rise to the possibility of domestic instability.

One witnessed this to a degree in the Shah's Iran, where the changes brought about by industrialization, along with many resultant social and economic inequities coupled with the repressive nature of his rule, gave rise to a militant Islamic fundamentalism. Owing to the nature of the Saudi regime (despite the fact that its citizens enjoy one of the highest per capita incomes in the world), it is entirely possible that one may witness similar upheavals there. The possibility of such an upheaval has not been lost on the Iranian ruling clergy, which has periodically called for the overthrow of the present Saudi regime.

Furthermore, apart from the possibilities of domestic conflict and upheaval, there also remains the constant likelihood of

152

interstate conflict. This possibility exists largely because of a number of unresolved territorial disputes in the region which may yet culminate in war. These again may have detrimental consequences both for oil supplies and for markets in the region -- both of which are of considerable interest to the East Asian states, particularly Japan, and West Europe.

It appears that, while the Soviet Union does have both the motivation and the potential for mischief-making in the region; so far, Soviet activities have been limited, partly because of the inhospitable reception that Moscow has received from most of the regimes and partly because it does not possess the necessary instruments for influence. For example, the oil-rich states have almost uniformly shown a predilection for Western manufactured goods and Western capital equipment over those provided by the USSR. Apart from the constraints inherent to the region, Soviet activity has also been hobbled owing to the knowledge that this area is of vital concern to the United States and its allies and that blatant interference would bring about commensurate U.S. responses. Washington's resolve to protect its interests and those of its allies is evident from the U.S. force deployments, a fact that can hardly be lost on the Soviets.[14]

Moscow's Efforts Continue

For the foreseeable future, therefore, Moscow is most likely to continue to pursue policies aimed at supporting regional states in their conflicts with the West. Moscow's hope is to establish what it often refers to as "mutually beneficial relations" that can evolve into long-term stable relationships. In addition, Moscow is likely to continue to take advantage of instabilities that promise, in its view, to weaken or displace pro-Western political elites. All of this is part of what a group of French analysts of Soviet Third-World policy have referred to as "an oblique strategy" aimed at defeating the USSR's major opponents through an indirect strategy of gradually undermining their interests in the Third World.[15]

It is important to keep in mind, however, that even though the USSR has not proven particularly successful over the course of the past thirty years in turning political, economic, and military support for countries of the Persian Gulf region into an effective Soviet presence or into the Soviet ability to dictate developments in the region, the Soviet leadership has continued to expend resources for this purpose. Although direct Soviet extension of military power beyond the borders of Afghanistan is not likely, the Soviet military presence in Afghanistan -- in particular, should Moscow be successful in completing the pacification of the countryside -- would provide the Soviet leaders with the opportunity during a future crisis to bring military pressure to bear against either Pakistan or Iran. It is by no means unthinkable that in a post-Khomeini Iran the Soviet Union might provide clandestine support for elements of the Iranian population that opposed the continued domination by the fundamentalist clergy, or the domination of minority regions by the government in Teheran.

The Persian Gulf region is of vital importance for the economic well-being of West Europe and East Asia. So long as the USSR remains committed to an overall policy of attempting to undermine Western interests in this area -- as well as in other areas of the world -- the United States and its allies must be prepared to respond effectively. As we have argued, the Soviet leaders are far more likely to pursue policies aimed at supporting domestic instability in pro-Western states and at supporting states in the region in conflicts with the West, than to engage in direct military involvement in the region. However, the Soviet military presence in Afghanistan could not only provide a bridgehead from which to support unrest elsewhere, but this presence could also act as a form of intimidation to influence the decisions of political elites throughout the area.

154

NOTES

1. For discussion of the petroleum resource endowments in the region see Chubin, Shamram, ed., Security in the Persian Gulf: Domestic Political Factors (London: International Institute of Strategic Studies, 1981).

2. See Bradsher, Henry S., Afghanistan and the Soviet Union (Durham, NC: Duke Press Policy Studies, 1983).

3. Thompson, W. Scott, "The Persian Gulf and the Correlation of Forces," International Security, vol. 7, no. 1 (1982), p. 159.

4. McLaurin, Robert L., in Mohammed Mughisuddin, ed., Conflict and Cooperation in the Persian Gulf (New York: Praeger, 1977).

5. The best analysis of the U.S. role in the overthrow of the Mossadegh regime can be found in Rubin, Barry, Paved with Good Intentions (New York: Oxford University Press, 1980).

6. See Yodfat, Areh Y., The Soviet Union and the Arabian Peninsula (London: Croom Helm, 1983, p. 17).

7. See Kanet, Roger E., "Soviet Military Assistance to the Third World," Copper, John F., and Daniel S. Papp, eds., Communist Nations Military Assistance (Boulder, CO: Westview Press, 1983), pp. 39-71.

8. Yodfat, The Soviet Union, p. 3.

9. Ibid.

10. See Zalmay, Khalilzad, "Soviet Policies in West Asia and the Persian Gulf," in Kanet, Roger E., ed., Soviet Foreign Policy in the 1980s (New York: Praeger, 1982), p. 322.

11. Demchenko, Pavel, "Retribution Being Readied, Pravda, March 23, 1983, p. 5.

12. See Glukhov, Iurii, "Protracted War," Pravda, November 14, 1983, p. 5.

13. For an elaboration of this point see Yodfat, The Soviet Union, pp. 134-137. See also Martin, Lenore G., The Unstable Gulf (Lexington, MA: D.C. Heath, 1984), passim.

14. For a good enumeration and discussion of U.S. deployments in and around the region see Martin, Op. cit., p. 175.

15. L'URSS et le Tiers-Monde: Une Strategie Oblique (Paris: Fondation Pour les Etudes de Defense Nationale, Groupe d'etudes et de recherches sur la strategie Sovietique, 1984).

Chapter 18

OUTLOOK FOR THE PACIFIC BASIN

Part I: The American View

Richard M. Fairbanks, III

Soviet bellicosity in the conduct of its foreign policy with states of Asia and the Pacific Basin defies any reasonable explanation. That is a particularly troublesome observation when one considers the many recent positive developments which are evolving both on the continent of Asia and among the other states washed by the waters of the Pacific. This discussion highlights what is at stake for those who value and support freedom and prosperity in the Pacific Basin.

When one contemplates the possible evolution of this region over the next ten to fifteen years, those stakes are substantial and exciting for everyone concerned. Politically and economically, the prospects for the Pacific Basin are bright, despite the fact that this is one of the most heavily armed regions in the world. In Vietnam, Kampuchea (Cambodia), and Laos, some 1.1 million men are now under arms, while on the Korean peninsula there is a combined total of 1.5 million troops. In addition to 4.4 million men in uniform in the People's Republic of China (PRC) and Taiwan, approximately one-third to one-half of the USSR's ground forces -- some 53 divisions -- are garrisoned in the Soviet Far East. Soviet air power, both tactical and strategic, continues to grow; the Soviet Pacific Fleet is now the USSR's largest; and SS-20 missiles bring much of the population of the region within missile range.

Regional Stability

Despite these grim facts, the region enjoys a surprising degree of stability -- a stability which derives from a number of factors independent of the military balance of forces. Economic reality, in particular, has injected a dynamic counterweight into the regional equation. Maintenance of the dynamic stability which has resulted will require a clear appreciation for the forces at work in this

156

region. Most importantly, it calls for a recognition of the fact that cooperation among like-minded states in the region, particularly those which share the common goals of peace and regional development, is indispensable. The reality is that broad Pacific economic cooperation now exists and is growing at an accelerating pace. Political maturation and economic expansion have set in motion a dynamic process which already is transforming the Pacific Basin into one of the most productive regions of the world.

The Pacific Ocean, all 64 million square miles of it, is by far the largest body of water on the planet. The littoral states of the Pacific include some 33 nations that represent about 60 percent of the world's population. They contain the largest country in the world in area, the largest in population, the two greatest military powers, and the three top economies. The diversity of cultures and history are vast. About a third of the world's languages are spoken there. (In fact, over 700 languages are spoken in tiny Papua New Guinea, a country with a population one-fifth of Tokyo's.)

Trade with Pacific Basin States

Japan, one of the most remarkable success stories in modern times, is a valued friend and ally, and our largest overseas trading partner. Over the past decade, the countries of East Asia and the Pacific have become major trading partners of the United States, and they have now overtaken our traditional trading partners in Europe. In 1983, U.S. trans-Pacific trade was 25 percent -- or $226 billion -- larger than our trade with Europe. Of our twenty largest overseas customers, seven are in the East Asia and Pacific region.

For the first half of this century, total world trade by the United States (imports and exports) amounted to less than 4 percent of our Gross National Product (GNP). By 1959, it had grown to somewhat less than 6 percent; but in the past 25 years it has almost tripled to 17 percent of our GNP. If present rates of growth continue, foreign trade will, by the year 2000, amount to more than 25 percent of the U.S. GNP -- or approximately Japan's current percentage. By any measure, those are significant figures, and it goes without saying that as trade continues to grow as a component in our national economy, trade policy looms increasingly large in U.S. foreign policy. The interrelationship between foreign trade and foreign policy is nowhere clearer than in the Pacific, where prosperity has been achieved through aggressive export promotion. Restrictions on trading opportunities overseas can thus have a very direct bearing on vital national interests. As trade and economic interaction grow, so does the potential for controversy and friction.

As mentioned earlier, total U.S. trade with East Asia and the Pacific surpasses U.S. trade with any other region of the world. In addition, the East Asia and Pacific share of total U.S. trade is rising. In 1982, U.S. trade with East Asia and the Pacific was $126.5 billion, or 27.7 percent of total U.S. trade. In 1983, U.S. trade with East Asia and the Pacific was $136.7 billion -- almost 30 percent of total U.S. trade. In 1982, trade with the Pacific was less severely affected by recession than trade with countries in most other regions: while total U.S. world trade declined more than 5 percent, that with East Asia and the Pacific was off less than 1 percent. In 1983, total U.S. world trade rose .5 percent, while trade with this region grew 8 percent.

In 1983 United States exports to the East Asia and Pacific region were 26 percent of total U.S. exports; imports from the area were 33 percent of total imports. Japan alone accounted for almost 14 percent of total U.S. trade.

ASEAN's Success

The six countries (Brunei, Indonesia, Malaysia, the Philippines, Singapore, and Thailand) that constitute the Association of South East Asian Nations (ASEAN) are of growing importance to the United States. Taken together, the ASEAN countries are now America's fourth largest trading partner behind only Canada, Japan, and (within $5 billion of) Mexico. U.S. trade with ASEAN grew almost 10 percent in 1983 over 1982, and ASEAN bought almost $10 billion of American goods -- 5 percent of total U.S. exports.

The United States depends on East Asia and the Pacific for raw materials and other products vital to the U.S. economy: more than 90 percent of the natural rubber, and large amounts of imported wool, tin, meat, tropical lumber, bauxite, and sugar. ASEAN countries are important suppliers of raw materials. Indonesia for example provides nearly 10 percent of U.S. oil imports. On the other hand Japan, Korea, Taiwan, and Hong Kong import vast amounts of U.S.-produced food and raw materials (including some 62 percent of timber shipped from U.S. ports) as well as machinery, equipment, and other finished products.

In general, the cause of increased U.S. attention to the Pacific is the recognition of our growing economic links; the political opportunity for increased exchange with dynamic countries sharing many of our values; and, the strategic reality of the geopolitical importance of the region. And the purpose of our increased attention to the region is to improve America's relationships with other countries of the Pacific at all levels -- governmental, business, cultural, and educational. A process of more regularized contact and communication of ideas will aid in avoiding and resolving differences which may arise. This is particularly true in the trade field. The better we understand the needs and goals of our

158

Pacific partners, and the better we can make them understand U.S. policies and objectives, then the better we will be equipped to search out avenues for agreement, cooperation, and compromise.

Increasingly, regional issues have arisen which are multilateral, and these cannot be solved by purely bilateral means. Various mechanisms have been created to provide a greater voice for smaller countries in regional affairs and a means for dealing with multilateral problems. ASEAN is an example of such a regional mechanism which can provide the kernel of multilateral cooperation in the Pacific.

ASEAN is a still unfolding success story that tends to be overshadowed by the achievements of Japan, Korea, and Taiwan. ASEAN was formed in 1967 during a period of turmoil in Southeast Asia. Its goals are to strengthen cohesion and self-reliance and to promote regional economic, social, and cultural development. ASEAN developed slowly, in part because of the diverse political, cultural, and historical backgrounds of its member countries and their competitive economies. Cohesion was strengthened following the first summit conference of ASEAN leaders in 1976. At the same time, ASEAN began a series of dialogues with the foreign ministers of Japan, Australia, New Zealand, Canada, the European Community, and since 1977, the United States.

U.S.-USSR Policy Trends

In late 1983, U.S. Secretary of State George Shultz asked this commentator to undertake a review of U.S. policy regarding the Pacific Basin. We recognize that the private sector has led the way and will continue to do so, in creating a sense of Pacific community built on trade and economic progress. Our task in government is to support and strengthen that process. In response to the secretary's request, a series of meetings and conversations were held with governmental, academic, and business leaders throughout the Pacific. These discussions led to a number of conclusions.

First, as noted earlier, a sense of Pacific cooperation exists today at the private sector level -- particularly among economists, academics, and other experts. Second, the choice of governments is to determine what they should do to support and deepen this spirit. Third, we must ask ourselves what are we growing toward? Clearly we are not moving toward something like the European community, massive new bureaucratic arrangements, or super-sovereignty. What will emerge here will be uniquely Pacific and achieved by consensus. Fourth, we must ask, does this matter? In a word, is this movement toward increased cooperation in the Pacific an historic development? It is hard to tell at the outset, but it does indeed seem that history is being made.

159

The cooperative process is still in its infancy, and it is too early to predict its ultimate form and significance. Whatever arrangement eventually evolves will be unique to the Pacific. The diversity, culture, heritage, and traditions of the Pacific states constitute a different set of factors from the traditional relationship of nation-states in Europe or the confused and conflicting pattern of relationships elsewhere in the world. There is no guarantee that this positive trend will continue. In recognition of that fact, the United States, in conjunction with its friends and allies, will continue to carry out its security responsibilities in the area and will urge and assist others to do their part to maintain peace in the region.

Soviet intentions are less clear. Moscow's buildup of forces and its continued truculent behavior toward other states in the region clearly militate against any prospect for Soviet participation in this cooperative endeavor among free states in the Pacific Basin.

The possibilities for a thickening of multilateral economic relationships in the Pacific are only now becoming apparent. The process is still a delicate one, and, therefore, should not be burdened with excessive expectations. Expanded economic cooperation in the Pacific is most likely to occur among those economies which share a common interest in the enhancement and development of the free market system. This suggests that cooperation will be based on the strength of the private sector and will remain essentially economic in focus. It is also clear that, at the governmental level, for the foreseeable future, our bilateral political and economic relationships will remain paramount. Multilateral cooperation can supplement but not replace them. This suggests the great importance of strong, effective bilateral relationships in the security, political, and economic sectors.

Such relationships are the bedrock of our national interest, and a necessary precondition to broader multilateral cooperation. It is essential, therefore, that the nations of the Pacific continue to work together to create the environment of security, prosperity, and stability required to build our common future.

Part II: The Japanese View

Members of the Japanese Diet

Comment: The Honorable Soichiro Ito

U.S. Secretary of State George Shultz once observed that the Pacific region represents the future of mankind. In other words, the

160

gravity of world history is gradually shifting from the Atlantic to the Pacific. Therefore, the concept of cooperation within the Pacific region can offer a very important frame of reference for any discussion of Soviet strategy in Asia. And when we deal with the issues pertaining to Japanese defense policies and U.S.-Japan cooperation in defense matters, we need to consider them within the context of cooperation throughout the Pacific Basin.

Statistics indicate that the gravity of the world economy is shifting to the Pacific zone. Today the so-called Confucian economic zone of East Asia, where hard work is seen as a high virtue, shows a very rapid growth rate. The ASEAN countries have an average annual growth rate of 7 percent, Korea and Taiwan 8 to 9 percent, and Japan holds at about 4 to 4.5 percent. Japan, though, in recent years has had the highest economic growth rate among the advanced industrialized nations. Trade is also expanding in the Pacific region. The United States now conducts more trade with the Pacific region than with West Europe. Today the Pacific Basin countries account for 60 percent of total world Gross National Product (GNP), and over 50 percent of total world population. So, there is much momentum.

Pacific Basin Community

There has arisen the so-called "Pacific Basin Community" concept which is aimed at promoting further economic cooperation in a more organized and systematic manner. In Japan, under the Ohira administration in 1980, the first meeting was held on Pacific area cooperation. Recently in the United States, more emphasis has been placed on Pacific regional cooperation. Under Ambassador-at-Large Richard Fairbanks, a new high-level committee has been established in the United States to focus attention on Pacific Basin economic cooperation. Similarly, Japan has created within the Ministry of International Trade and Industry (MITI) a committee to study the Pacific region. Further, within Japan's Ministry of Foreign Affairs, another committee has been established for liaison on proposals to increase cooperation within the Pacific region.

Representing as they do 31 percent of world GNP, Japan and the United States are working hard at strengthening cooperation among the nations of the Pacific area. Of course the idea of political cooperation in the region has much to do with economic cooperation involving both governmental and private sector dimensions.

But it is not a very realistic approach to confine the concept of Pacific regional cooperation merely to economic matters. The Pacific region contains many diverse countries, some of which are liberal democratic while others authoritarian, and still others are communist and totalitarian. So, practically, in the short term it is almost impossible to work out an organization of cooperation to encompass Pacific area countries with different political systems.

Also, this area includes zones of conflict and crisis. In order to create a loosely tied system of economic cooperation out of this complex political reality, a long-term perspective is indispensible that can encompass not only economic but also both political and military factors. Such a grand-scale strategy, which is to be shared by both Japan and the United States, has to be further studied as we look toward the next century.

As to the proposed concept of a Pacific Basin Community, it has not been realistic to conceive of a community that can encompass all the countries of this basin. One possibility, then, would be to develop further an existing local community, such as the Association of South East Asian States (ASEAN). Also, in East Asia, another system of international cooperation may be conceivable, including South Korea, Taiwan, Hong Kong, Singapore, or those countries that are to be invited into the Organization for Economic Cooperation and Development (OECD) in the future. Together with Japan, these nations could form sort of a horizontal system of economic cooperation, perhaps called the East Asian Economic Community. Another possibility is to work out some other system of regional cooperation to cover the countries of the South Pacific and the Latin American nations bordering the Pacific.

Already institutionalized is the participation of the United States, Japan, Australia, and the European Community nations in the ministerial meeting composed of the foreign ministers of the ASEAN countries. It seems that such existing institutions can further develop into an expanded regional system of cooperation. But the essential concept of a Pacific Basin Community should aim at something larger than the one that encompasses regional groupings still operating alone. In other words, even if it is a loosely tied organization, some kind of larger scale system of cooperation has to be established in the Pacific Basin.

Regional Challenges

But a precondition to this is the safety and peace of the area. In this connection, two zones of special attention, the Korean peninsula and Indochina, have to be studied further. It seems that part of the Cold War atmosphere on the Korean peninsula has started to thaw. Between China and Korea there has been an exchange of sporting events, and their trade relations have increased. North Korea has recently approved joint venture business arrangements with foreign countries. North Korea seems to have learned a lot from the economic modernization measures being

162

taken by China. Even South Korea and North Korea will perhaps agree soon to some meaningful economic exchanges. Thus, there are signs toward unprecedented degrees of rapprochement between North and South Korea, even though North Korea has not recognized the government of South Korea. But in this context, one should take notice of the continuing stationing in South Korea of the U.S. forces. Also there is a kind of mutually complementary relationship between the Japanese and Chinese diplomatic approaches to North Korea. On the other hand, the situation in Indochina is much more complex. Vietnam is on the verge of an economic breakdown because of the heavy expenses involved in maintaining its troops in Cambodia. Perhaps the Japanese strategy toward Indochina should be based on long-term economic assistance that may induce the withdrawal of the Vietnamese forces from Cambodia.

Another strategic task for both Japan and the United States is to watch the future evolution of China with its one billion population. China is trying to move from agricultural modernization toward industrialization. Some coastal areas of China may in the future constitute a gateway to the Pacific economic cooperation system. Japan, the United States, and the European Economic Community countries have to adopt a long-term perspective toward economic cooperation with China. Of course it is more desirable to see China become a politically moderate country than to see a militant China that has failed in its economic modernization. If China is to succeed in its economic modernization, the political outcome would be much more favorable. So, at this point it is essential to continue watching carefully the evolution of China. But of course it is not possible to precisely predict what will be the future development of China.

Lastly, the most serious challenge to the concept of Pacific cooperation comes from the Soviet Union. It cannot be denied that the Soviet Union has a claim to be a Pacific nation based on geopolitical factors. The Soviet Union today, however, is not very interested in the concept of Pacific regional cooperation, except for its own economic relations with Mongolia, North Korea, and Vietnam. Soviet trade with the other nations of this region is very limited. As a Pacific state, the Soviet Union is more interested in reinforcing its military presence in the Far East area. And the Soviet Pacific Fleet has registered an impressive buildup for the past decade, to include gaining bases in Vietnam at Cam Ranh Bay and Danang.

What is the central objective of the Soviet military buildup in the Far East? First of all it is to challenge the American military presence in the Pacific and even eventually to surpass the American military capabilities in the area. Secondly, and more directly, the Soviet Union intends to beleaguer the Japanese archipelago militarily and then be able to interdict the sealanes linking the

Persian Gulf countries and the Northeast Asia countries. This ability can be used to obtain political leverage against Japan. So, without security of the sealanes in the Pacific Ocean, it is very difficult to conceive of a new age of Pacific area cooperation.

In order for Japan, the United States, and the other free nations of the Pacific region to create a very dynamic prosperity for the Pacific countries, it is first necessary to secure stability and peace in this entire area. Together with the United States, Japan has to work to stabilize the military balance in this area. Thus, increasingly important is the present program of upgrading Japanese defense capabilities together with the United States through close consultation. It will be an indispensable investment for Japan to secure peace and prosperity throughout the Pacific Basin area for the twenty-first century.

The Soviet Union seems to be aware that the huge Soviet military presence in the Pacific does not serve very well the Soviet interest in expanding Soviet influence in this area. Rather, the Soviet military presence works to increase the caution and worry about the USSR on the part of the Pacific countries. So, in this connection, it is necessary to try to persuade the Soviet Union that it would be better to collaborate with Japan and other free nations to develop Siberia. But, of course, due to the Marxist-Leninist worldview held by the Soviet Union, it is unlikely it will accept proposals on true cooperation.

Since the Pacific region seems to represent the future of mankind, Japan and the United States need to work closely together with the other nations of the region to open up the new age of the Pacific Ocean. Since the end of World War II, the Japanese people have tended to deny whatever is associated with military matters. But Japanese political opinion has somewhat changed, is more realistic, and increasingly recognizes the need for a greater military effort to help promote peace and security for Japan and the whole Pacific area.

Comment: The Honorable Eiichi Nakao

Every state through its own efforts must provide for the safety and defense of its territory and its people by its own efforts. Lack of adequate self-defense by any state may become an invitation to neighbors to undertake aggression. While a military alliance may be part of the defense of any state, each state remains responsible for maintaining adequate military strength for its own defense. Adequate military strength must be the mainstay of the defense of any state.

Lamentably, the present military strength of Japan is not adequate to meet the security threats facing the nation. Of

164

particular concern are the security threats posed in recent years by the rapidly increasing strength of the Soviet Union in East Asia. The Soviet Union is a neighbor of Japan and at present is holding islands close to Hokkaido, legitimately belonging to Japan. The increased number of SS-20 missiles in Siberia which are now targeted on various points in East Asia, including Japan, is a matter of grave concern to the security of Japan and of all East Asia. Another serious matter is the increased threat to the sealanes which are the lifelines of Japan. Japan is not making an adequate response to the security threats created by the aggressive moves of the Soviet Union.

Japan's Security

It is well known that when Yasuhiro Nakasone became Prime Minister of Japan, he had high hopes of improving Japan's defense capabilities at a more rapid rate than was being done. Despite Prime Minister Nakasone's hopes and intentions when he assumed office, the rate at which Japan is improving its defense remains slow and insufficient to provide defense capabilities adequate for the international situation in East Asia and for the security of Japan. In this matter, we reiterate the point that each state basically must be responsible for its own defense, and that a national military alliance should be only part of any country's defense system. It is understandable that the U.S. Congress and the Reagan administration are disappointed in the slow pace at which Japan is improving its defense capabilities.

There are four principal reasons why Japan is so slow in building up adequate defense capabilities for its own protection. First, there is the pacifism which developed in Japan after the nation's defeat in World War II. This pacifism remains strong, especially among people who lived through the war. It affects most aspects of Japanese life. Politically, pacifism is a base on which most political parties build some aspects of their political power.

Second, the mass media of Japan, both television and press, have failed adequately to inform the Japanese people of the seriousness of the international situation in East Asia. In particular, the mass media have not made clear the extent and the seriousness of the Soviet military buildup, not only in East Asia but in all parts of the world. The present nature and broad scope of Soviet military power has not been well presented to the Japanese people. The public has insufficient information on the increasingly serious threat to Japan's security posed by the USSR. One aspect of this has been pacifism, which also prevails among members of the mass media.

Budgetary Considerations

Third, there are the political and financial guidelines for the government's defense budget and the motivations of various political parties in the national Diet. This is a complicated and complex matter which can only be summarized here. Contrary to popular belief, the "less-than-one-percent-of-GNP" formula for the defense budget is not a legal restriction. It is simply an administrative guideline which was adopted in the early postwar years by a Japanese cabinet to quiet some of the attacks of the opposition party and the mass media on the defense budget and defense in general. As the years have passed by, the mass media have tried to make this "less-than-one-percent-of-GNP" a binding restriction on defense spending. The present Nakasone cabinet is having difficulties about this matter.

For defense expenditures, it is clear that the government should budget what is necessary for Japan to have adequate defenses without any reference to what percentage of the GNP the defense budget may be. The defense budget must be sufficient to provide for the adequate defense of Japan in relation to the security situation at any given time. The defense budget should not be limited by any set percentages of the GNP.

In recent years, some of the opposition parties have adopted realistic attitudes concerning the defense of Japan as the increased military threats posed by the USSR have become clear. However, the motivations and the position toward defense of the largest opposition party, the Japan Socialist Party (JSP), should be considered carefully.

The JSP has always opposed the Self-Defense Force, considering it unconstitutional. JSP leaders have made it very clear that if the JSP ever came to power, the Self-Defense Force would be disbanded. The JSP policy, as set forth by the party's national convention in Tokyo in February 1984, is that the Self-Defense Force is unconstitutional, and was only established by questionable legal procedure. This is an example of "brain-twisting." Japan's socialists believe that the money presently being spent on defense should be spent on social welfare and educational problems. As the largest opposition party in the Diet, the socialists have been able to make use of the deep feelings of pacifism found throughout Japan to increase their popular support.

The last major program to mention in connection with Japan's slow defense buildup is the problem of the government's large budget deficit. While Japan's budget deficit seems small when compared with the U.S. deficit, Japan's budget deficit has become a major factor in determining the appropriations for defense. For the fiscal year beginning April 1, 1984, the defense budget was increased a little over 6 percent, compared with the previous year.

166

All other items were either cut or frozen at previous levels in order to reduce the government's defense dependence on deficit financing.

In view of the difficulties outlined here so briefly, one can anticipate that the buildup of Japan's ability to defend its own territory and to secure the sealanes within 1,000 miles of Japan will continue at a slow pace. Pressure from the outside, especially from the United States, urging Japan to improve its defense capabilities, will be necessary. In this situation, it is necessary for the United States to know and to understand the major factors which deter or delay Japan's buildup of its defense forces. There must be an assessment of what is actually possible and an assessment of the conditions which actually prevail in Japan. In closing, it is mandatory that Japan assume responsibility for its own defense and for the defense of the sealanes which are so vital and necessary for the survival of Japan. It can be hoped that someday Japan will be fully responsible for its own defense. Until that time arrives, it will be necessary to contend with the major factors outlined above.

Comment: The Honorable Eiichi Nagasue

Since the Democratic Socialist Party (DSP) of Japan is an opposition political party, many Americans seem to think that the DSP is not a friend of the United States as is the governing Liberal Democratic Party (LDP). Such Americans tend to think that any opposition party in Japan, including the DSP, stands for abolition of the treaty between Japan and the United States, calls for neutrality without arms, and is not really a good friend of the United States. But Americans who believe this are misinformed.

The DSP is, of course, a member of the Socialist International. As such, the DSP is a friend of such Social Democrats as Willi Brandt and Helmut Schmidt of West Germany, Olof Palme of Sweden, and Felipe Gonzales of Spain. The DSP generally views the world as these people do. This is not to say that all of these people share every aspect of the same international view, but there is a common view that nations should not become allied with the Soviet Union. This is an important commonality among these leaders. The DSP basically shares this view, and it thinks of world peace and stability from that point of view.

DSP Support for Adequate Defense

Serving as the chairman of the DSP's Defense Committee, and thus being responsible for the defense policy of the DSP, this commentator can state that the DSP believes that the safety of Japan is based on the deterrence of the Soviet threat. The DSP thus believes that Japan's Self-Defense Forces are legal. It feels that these forces should be reinforced and strengthened. Also, the DSP says that the Self-Defense Forces should not be armed with nuclear weapons. The party believes that the security treaty with the United States is an important requirement of Japan's defense. U.S. cooperation is welcome and important in the deployment of conventional forces. The DSP feels that the security treaty with America is important for the stability and peace not only of Japan but of Asia. This is the basic defense approach of the DSP.

From the late 1950s and the early 1960s we have seen many democratic socialist political parties operating in Asia, most of which have belonged to the Socialist International, or at least had observer status. An Asian Socialist International was created, having its headquarters in Rangoon, Burma. Members included parties in India, Nepal, Sri Lanka, Burma, Malaysia, Singapore, Indonesia, and Japan. But today the only democratic socialist parties in Asia affiliated with the Socialist International are in Japan and Malaysia. Singapore's Socialist Party was attacked by leftist parties in Europe and withdrew from the Socialist International six years ago. Two other Asian parties that are not members of the Socialist International are the Uniform Socialist Party in South Korea, and the Japan Socialist Party. The Japan Socialist Party does not share the defense policy of the DSP nor that of the Socialist International.

Soviet Strategy

It is appropriate to take into account Marxist-Leninist ideology in examining Soviet strategy in Asia. Marxism-Leninism has been questioned by many in Japan, not so much from the point of view of its strategy but from the point of its doctrine, or its theoretical component. As Vietnam invaded Cambodia and as the Soviet Union became hostile toward China, it was demonstrated that Marxism-Leninism and communism do not stand for the truth. These conflicts have made Japanese realize that Marxism-Leninism and communism are really another form of advancing national interests. It is hoped that all Asians realize this.

Marxism-Leninism talks about the historical inevitability of creating a new society, but what is happening is that the Soviet Union is using Marxism-Leninism as a tool for advancing its own national interests. That is abundantly clear today.

Another reality is that the Soviet Union has large armed forces in Asia, thus showing that the truths of communism can only be advanced with the help of armed Soviet strength. This has also become very clear. The fact that the People's Republic of China (PRC) has chosen to go along increasingly with the free countries

168

and not with the Soviet Union also attests to the dubious character of the truths of Marxism-Leninism.

For the last 150 years, Japan has suffered from the expansionism of the Soviet Union. Today, of course, the four small islands north of Hokkaido have been illegally occupied by the Soviet Union. In Japan we believe that these islands are an innate part of Japanese territory, but they were lost to the Soviet Union at the end of World War II. Expansionism remains the main policy of the Soviet Union, just as it was earlier in Czarist Russia. There has been no change in policy between Czarist Russia and the Soviet Union.

One notes that the countries of Southeast Asia do not share common borders with the USSR, and they have not been the targets of direct Soviet intervention or invasion. However, the Soviet Union has given overt assistance to Vietnam, which has been used to try to occupy Kampuchea as well as Laos. Since Vietnamese troops moved into these two countries, the USSR now has a stronghold in Southeast Asia. The Association of South East Asian Nations (ASEAN) was originally formed, it seems, to cope with the threat posed by the PRC. However, it now appears that the PRC has moved from being in a very confused state to a stabilized growth pattern. The DSP believes that communism is wrong, but the ASEAN leaders cannot ignore the strength that communism has given to the PRC. Friends of the DSP in India and Malaysia have confided that as long as they see successes in China they cannot throw communism "out the window." In any case, ASEAN was not designed to be a military alliance but rather a clearinghouse.

After the withdrawal from Indochina by the United States in 1975, and after the move of Vietnam to take over the entire Indochina peninsula, the ASEAN states prepared to strengthen themselves, and it appears they did so very well. The ASEAN countries seek neutrality, peace, and freedom. The PRC, which used to support the anti-government forces in the ASEAN countries, stopped that assistance and began to support ASEAN. So therefore, ASEAN maintains a high degree of vigilance concerning the Soviet Union. One of the leaders of Thailand says that the Soviet Union sends $3 million a day to Vietnam to support Vietnamese troops in Laos and the Vietnamese invasion of Kampuchea. This Soviet money is not at all invested in the economic vitalization of Vietnam, which remains a poor nation.

The fact that the Soviet Union is directly using its forces in Afghanistan and the fact that the Soviet Union has used Vietnam as a proxy to expand its influence in Indochina have made all of the ASEAN countries very cautious. When a Soviet aircraft carrier was first deployed in the Soviet Asian port of Vladivostok, whether or not it would enter into the Bay of Thailand was of major concern to the ASEAN leaders. This fact demonstrates the sensitivity of the ASEAN leaders concerning the Soviet Union. The tremendous Soviet naval forces based at Cam Ranh Bay in Vietnam are of great concern to these ASEAN leaders.

In Asia the Soviet Union has also promoted so-called peace movements, and it has made proposals that the whole ASEAN area be made a nuclear-free zone. Soviet strategy employed in Asia covers the continental as well as the oceanic area of the Far Eastern theater of war. The USSR can employ theater weapons over a wide range. Thus, the arms control negotiations on strategic nuclear weapons between the United States and the USSR must be made on a global basis to have any meaning. The creation of a non-nuclear zone in one region would only transfer the risk to other regions. Furthermore, U.S.-USSR arms talks encompassing all nuclear weapons in the world are the only meaningful approach.

Since Japan has been the only country to experience a nuclear bomb, and because other Pacific nations have suffered from nuclear tests, this argument of creating a non-nuclear zone has a psychological appeal. But a nuclear-free zone is no guarantee that no one would violate the exclusivity of the zone. In the absence of such a guarantee, or verification, it would only be unilateral military theory. Thus, we should not support this concept of a nuclear free zone unless it is supported by verification.

In Europe there is the North Atlantic Treaty Organization and the Warsaw Treaty Pact. But in Asia, we do not have collective security arrangements such as those we see in Europe. Japan only has the bilateral agreements with the United States. The PRC is the only nuclear country in Asia besides the USSR. Given this situation, we do not see an advantage for Asia that Europe has in negotiating arms reduction or arms control. In Asia it is a one-sided situation involving Soviet military strength.

On January 19, 1983, the Central Committee of the Communist Party of the Soviet Union sent a letter to the DSP in Japan. The letter said that if Japan holds to the three unilaterally declared non-nuclear principles, then the Soviet Union is prepared to give a certain guarantee. But the Soviet Union did not make clear what this guarantee would be. Thus the DSP said it could not accept the proposal. If that Soviet guarantee had meant the withdrawal of SS-20s deployed in Asia, or removal of BACKFIRE bombers, then maybe there would have been something to negotiate. But in the absence of such concrete proposals, the DSP saw the letter as only a form of the Soviet threat.

One aspect which we must not neglect when we talk about the Soviet situation in Southeast Asia is that the region is very large and that its peoples are diverse. The area's large and multiracial society is also poor, thus creating an excellent opportunity for Soviet intervention and attempts to create civil wars.

The situation is similar in many countries in the South Pacific. For example five years ago the Solomon Islands became

170

independent, but the Labor Party there is affiliated with the World Federation of Trade Unions (WFTU) which is an organization created by the USSR. The USSR has made gestures toward the Labor Party in Western Samoa. With the support of the DSP, the Labor Party in Western Samoa has affiliated with the International Confederation of Free Trade Unions (ICFTU) which has its headquarters in Singapore. The ICFTU and the Asia Regional Organization (ARO), with the close involvement of Japan's Confederation of Labor, are working hard to check this Soviet labor-oriented strategy. Parliamentarianism in ASEAN countries is not fully developed. The ASEAN countries have labor unions, but they are limited in their strength. This situation makes it easy for the Soviet Union to intervene. Labor unions may seem divorced from Soviet strategy, but this is not so. It is necessary to fight against this aspect of Soviet strategy in Asia as well.

Comment: The Honorable Masao Horie

The entire population of Japan needs to accept and fully understand the facts about the massive buildup of Soviet military power in Asia. With this understanding, and with the consensus of the entire population of Japan, the nation's security and the peace of the world would be advanced. All Japanese need to be fully concerned with the qualitative and quantitative aspects of the Soviet military buildup in Asia and the world, and to focus special attention on those aspects of this buildup which directly affect Japan.

Soviet Military Buildup Against Japan

For instance, which Soviet military capabilities are being enhanced to include landing fields in the Northern Territories that can be used for the dispatch of aircraft to attack Hokkaido? What kind of psychological and cultural measures are being taken by the Soviet Union toward Japan? What kind of Soviet naval buildup is underway in Vietnam, including the deployment of BACKFIRE bombers? And what about the relationship between the Soviet Union and North Korea, which will certainly be very crucial from now on?

Politicians trying to build up Japan's defense capabilities have been worried about the sluggish improvement of these capabilities. Public attitudes in Japan are a major problem. In joint polls conducted by <u>Yomiuri Shimbun</u> and Gallup, it was shown that there is quite a difference in perception of defense needs, and views concerning the Soviet Union, among people in Japan, the United

States, Great Britain, France, and West Germany. Perhaps this is due to differences in geopolitical conditions, the anti-nuclear movements, and various policies and postures taken by leaders. But the Japanese people are rather ignorant about the Soviet threat. It is clear both in the Liberal Democratic Party (LDP) and in the opposition parties. While we may be reluctant to admit it, inescapable is the fact that this ignorance about the Soviet threat is indeed widespread throughout our society. A great many Japanese are regularly misled by Soviet propaganda which says that to follow U.S. policies will lead to more danger to Japan.

The problem is how to approach those people who do not realize the reality and the seriousness of the Soviet threat. It is most crucial and urgent in Japan to persuade the people through adequate public information programs about the nature of this threat and about the need for defense. We need efforts to cope with the problem of biased coverage by the mass media on this issue. Various symposia, lecture meetings, and materials are available on the issues, but of central concern is the substance of such public information efforts. First of all, after taking into account the need to secure defense secrets, we must provide the Japanese public with very realistic pictures and accurate descriptions of various aspects of the Soviet threat.

For example, concerning the issue of the sought-after return to Japan of the Northern Territories, we should perhaps show pictures of the Soviet progress in building up bases on these islands. If we can present realistic pictures to the Japanese public, then we should do it. We should do similarly with regard to the Soviet SS-20 missiles which threaten Japan. We should use the most up-to-date graphic techniques in order to be as convincing as possible.

In the most clear and simple manner possible, we need to inform the Japanese people about such matters as Soviet propaganda, the ruthlessness of the Soviet leaders in oppressing dissidents in the Soviet Union, the history of aggression by the Soviet Union, and the present and potential strategic role of Japan. We have to devise various means of public relations in order to tell the Japanese people about the non-military as well as the military aspects of the Soviet threat so that they will clearly understand. The non-military aspects of this threat are just as important as the military.

Comment: The Honorable Kazuo Tanikawa

Having previously served as Japan's Minister of State for Defense and as Director General of the Japanese Defense Agency, this commentator knows that the matter of national security is a very complicated issue. Thus the so-called "defense intellectuals" in

172

Japan need to be better known and receive a serious hearing. Other advanced industrial nations have visible and influential defense intellectuals, but those in Japan have not been given enough opportunities to speak up.

Need for U.S.-Japan Cooperation

The Japanese people need to learn about the massive Soviet military buildup underway in Asia. The major question facing Japan and the United States is how to bring the Soviet Union to the negotiating table. The dialogue with the Soviet Union should be resumed by all means. But first one indispensable condition must be met. That is that Japan and the United States must establish a position of strength. If we succeed in building up our position of strength, then we may be able to bring the Soviet Union to the negotiating table in the future. It is because the USSR has a social and political system that is totally opposed to that of Japan and the United States that negotiations with the Soviet leaders should be undertaken only from a position of strength.

The USSR certainly has a great many domestic problems, especially a faltering economy. But there appears to be no end to Moscow's drive to attain superiority over the United States and the Free World in every category of military activity. A major strength of the Soviet system is its firm, long-term objectives that always are persistent. The Soviet leaders bide their time, and exploit opportunities. This approach makes their system very strong.

Hopefully Japanese defense intellectuals in the future can collaborate more closely with their counterparts in the United States to learn more about the truly global and multifaceted Soviet threat, and what can be done about it. In four decades of the postwar era, no country has benefited more than Japan from the free enterprise system. In Japan, three issues -- politics, economics, and security -- can no longer be treated separately. It is obvious today that all of these issues need to be examined simultaneously in an integrated fashion. Hopefully concerned Japanese can come together and promptly build in Japan the consensus concerning what needs to be done in terms of defense for the Japanese and the Free World.

CONTRIBUTORS

John T. Berbrich. Special Assistant for National Estimates, Defense Intelligence Agency, Washington, D.C.

James R. Blaker. Deputy Assistant Secretary of Defense for Policy Analysis; former Personal Representative of the Secretary of Defense to the Mutual and Balanced Force Reduction (MBFR) talks in Vienna, Austria.

Ray S. Cline. Chairman, United States Global Strategy Council, Washington, D.C.; Professor of International Relations, Georgetown University, Washington, D.C.; former Director, Bureau of Intelligence and Research, U.S. Department of State; former Deputy Director for Intelligence, Central Intelligence Agency.

Stephen P. Cohen. Professor of Political Science and Director of the South Asian Security Project, University of Illinois at Urbana-Champaign.

Paul Dibb. Senior Research Fellow, Strategic and Defence Studies Centre, Australian National University; former Assistant Secretary, Strategic Policy Branch, Australian Department of Defence; former Deputy Director, Joint Intelligence Organization, Australia. Specialist on Soviet foreign policy.

Shinkichi Eto. Professor, Aoyama Gakuin University, Japan. Specialist in international relations.

Richard M. Fairbanks, III. Ambassador-at-Large, U.S. Department of State (focusing special attention on the Pacific Basin Community); previously Special Negotiator for the Middle East Peace Process.

S.R. Foley, Jr. Admiral, U.S.N.; Commander-in-Chief, U.S. Pacific Fleet.

174

Sumit Ganguly. Graduate student in the Department of Political Science at the University of Illinois at Urbana-Champaign.

Masao Horie. Member, Upper House, Japanese Diet; Liberal Democratic Party (LDP); Director, House Special Committee on Foreign Affairs and National Security; General (Ret.); previously Vice Chief of Staff, Japan Ground Self-Defense Force.

Soichiro Ito. Member, House of Representatives, Japanese Diet; Liberal Democratic Party (LDP); Director LDP Ad Hoc Committee on Military Bases; previously Minister of State for Defense.

Roger E. Kanet. Professor and Head, Political Science Department, University of Illinois at Urbana-Champaign; Sovietologist specializing in Soviet foreign policy.

Kim Yu-Nam. Director, Center for American and Soviet Studies; Professor of Political Science, Dankook University, Republic of Korea.

William R. Kintner. Professor of Political Science, University of Pennsylvania; previously U.S. Ambassador to Thailand; Specialist on Soviet global strategy.

Kenichi Kitamura. Admiral (Ret.); Advisor, Ishikawajima-Harima Heavy Industries Co., Ltd.; previously Chief of Staff, Maritime Self-Defense Force.

James Arnold Miller. Executive Director, United States Global Strategy Council, Washington, D.C.; Chairman, Interaction Systems Incorporated, Vienna, Virginia; Editor, <u>Alert Letter on the Availability of Raw Materials</u>; former counterintelligence officer, U.S. Air Force.

Osamu Miyoshi. Executive Director, World Strategy Forum of Japan, Tokyo; Professor of International Relations, Kyoto Sangyo University; previously Deputy Chief Editorial Writer, later Editorial Advisor, <u>Mainichi Shimbun</u>.

Eiichi Nagasue. Member, House of Representatives, Japanese Diet; Democratic Socialist Party (DSP); DSP Chief Negotiator for Parliamentary Affairs; Chief, DSP Defense Committee.

Eiichi Nakao. Liberal Democratic Party (LDP); previously Chairman, Committee on Foreign Affairs, House of Representatives, Japanese Diet.

175

William Schneider, Jr. President, International Planning Services, Inc.; former Under Secretary of State for Security Assistance, Science, and Technology; previously Associate Director for National Security and International Affairs, Office of Management and Budget, the White House; previously Senior Staff Member, the Hudson Institute, New York.

Hayao Shimizu. Professor, Tokyo University of Foreign Studies; Specialist in Soviet political history.

Kazuo Tanikawa. Former Minister of State for Defense; former Director General of the Japanese Defense Agency; previously Member, House of Representatives, Japanese Diet; Liberal Democratic Party (LDP); former Vice-Secretary General of LDP.

Takehiro Togo. Counselor, European and Oceanic Affairs Bureau, Ministry of Foreign Affairs, Japan; previously Counselor, Japanese Embassy, Washington, D.C., and Japanese Embassy, Moscow; Sovietologist.

INDEX

ABM Treaty. See Anti-Ballistic Missile Treaty
Absenteeism, 21
Acquiescence through intimidation, 15
Aden (S. Yemen), 39, 150
Aerial-refueling tanker, 35-36
Aeroflot (Soviet airline), 127
Afghanistan, 15, 24, 25, 27, 29, 30, 38, 40, 43, 64, 73, 78, 87, 90, 98, 108, 109, 131, 132, 133, 134, 136, 137, 139, 143, 144-145, 152, 153, 168
  Communist party, 131, 145
  mujaheddin, 139
Africa, 23, 27-28, 30, 143. See also Southern Africa; individual countries
Aircraft carriers, 36, 41, 43, 53, 58, 102, 107, 115, 168
Air defense units, 35, 37
Air line of communication, 14, 16
Air Self-Defense Force (ASDF) (Japan), 58, 77, 80, 81
Air-to-air missiles, 35
Alaska, 8
Alcoholism, 21
Aleksandr Nikoleyev (Soviet amphibious ship), 102
ALFA submarine, 41
Algeria, 23
Alice Springs (Australia), 115

Alliance Party (Fiji), 122
Allied-Japanese Peace Treaty (1951), 72
Amin, Hafizullah, 25, 144
Amphibious ships, 37
  joint exercise (1984), 43, 102
Amur River, 95
Andropov, Yuri, 21, 45, 61, 99
Anglo-Iraqi treaty (1955), 148
Angola, 5, 24, 25, 30, 108, 127
Antarctica, 117, 121
Anti-Ballistic Missile (ABM) Treaty (1972), 40
Anti-communism, 14
Anti-imperialist struggle, 2, 5
Anti-Sovietism, 71
Anti-submarine warfare (ASW), 37, 38, 39, 53, 56, 57, 58, 102
Anti-surface warfare, 36, 37, 41
Anti-tank helicopters, 80
An-12 CUB military air transport, 29
An-22 COCK military air transport, 29
ANZUS (Australia, New Zealand, United States) treaty, 58, 117, 118, 119-120, 122, 126, 127, 128
Aoji Chemical Plant (N. Korea), 90
Arab-Israeli conflict
  1967, 148
  1973, 30
Arbatov, Georgii, 65
Argentina, 123, 124
Armee Nationale Sihanoukiste, 109
Arms control, 13-14, 18, 19, 39-40, 61, 169
Arms race, 3

ARO. See Asia Regional
  Organization
ASDF. See Air Self-Defense
  Force
ASEAN. See Association of
  South East Asian
  Nations
Asia, 20, 23, 143, 160
  communist, 5-6, 8, 18, 20,
  46, 67, 102
  developing countries in,
  46, 47
  economic dynamism, 14,
  21, 49, 63, 101, 155
  non-communist, 6, 8, 9,
  14, 46, 63, 67
  population growth, 17
  See also individual
  countries
Asia-African Conference, 23
Asian Collective Security
  System (1970s), 23-24,
  71, 143
"Asian NATO," 120
Asian Socialist International,
  167
Asia Regional Organization
  (ARO), 170
Association of South East
  Asian Nations (ASEAN),
  16, 45, 46, 47-48, 49,
  54, 59, 67-68, 101, 113,
  119, 123, 157, 158, 160,
  161, 168, 169, 170. See
  also under China,
  People's Republic of;
  Japan
ASW. See Anti-submarine
  warfare
Atlantic Ocean, 113
Australia, 6, 58, 72, 113, 114,
  115-116, 117, 118, 119,
  120, 121, 122, 123, 124,
  126, 127, 128
  and ASEAN, 158
  Communist Party of, 120
  peacetime order of battle,

116
  Socialist Party of, 120
Austria, 64
Autarky, 11

Ba'ath party (Iraq), 148
BACKFIRE bombers, 15, 35,
  37, 41, 58, 169, 170
BADGER bombers, 15, 35,
  37, 38, 43, 102
Baghdad Pact, 148
Baikal, Lake, 26, 49
Baikal-Amur Mainline (BAM)
  railway project, 49, 75,
  85
Ball, Desmond, 114, 115
Baluchistan, 108, 135, 136
BAM. See Baikal-Amur
  Mainline railway project
Bangladesh, 24, 30, 131
Bashi Channel, 80
Bauxite, 157
BEAR bomber, 35, 39
BEAR-D reconnaissance
  aircraft, 29, 37, 38, 107
BEAR-F ASW aircraft, 37, 38
B-52 bomber (U.S.), 115
Bhutto, Zulfikar Ali, 135
Bilateral treaties, 24
BLACKJACK bomber, 35
Black market. See Second
  economy
Black Sea, 36
Blagoveshchensk (Soviet
  Union), 95
"Blue Belt of Defense"
  strategy, 28-29, 42
Bolsheviks, 2, 11, 95
Bonin. See Ogasawara
  Islands
Bougainville (Papua New
  Guinea), 123
Bourgeoisie, 5
Boxer Rebellion (1900), 95
Brandt, Willi, 166
Brazil, 124
Brezhnev, Leonid, 2, 3, 4, 5,

7, 15, 19, 24, 49, 64, 87, 98, 99
Brunei, 45, 82
Buchanan (U.S. destroyer), 82
Buffer zone, 64
Burma, 8. 167

CAAC. See Civil Aviation Administration of China
Cambodia. See Kampuchea
Cam Ranh Bay (Vietnam), 8, 15, 19, 28, 37, 38, 39, 43, 64, 67, 73, 102, 107, 113, 116, 162, 169
Canada, 119, 123, 157, 158
CANDID. See Il-76 CANDID military air transport
Capitalism, 5
Capitalist states, 1, 2, 3, 4, 46
Caribbean, 14
Carter, Jimmy, 19
CCP. See Chinese Communist Party
CENTO. See Central Treaty Organization
Central America, 14
Central Treaty Organization (CENTO), 131, 147
Ceylon. See Sri Lanka
C-5A GALAXY transport (U.S.), 29
Chang Tai-lei, 96
Chemical agents, 15, 40, 109
Chernenko, Konstantin, 86-87
China, People's Republic of (PRC), 5, 6-7, 46, 63, 68, 120, 132, 167
army, 106
and ASEAN, 102, 103, 110, 168
constitution (1975), 98
economy, 8, 47, 71, 100, 162
literacy, 6
and Middle East, 143

military power, 8, 59, 155
navy, 107
nuclear power, 26, 97, 169
population, 6, 162
religions, 6
socialism in, 97, 98
and Soviet Union, 7, 8, 9, 18-19, 24, 26, 27, 28, 47, 51-52, 54, 57, 64-65, 78, 88, 91, 95-96, 98-100, 101-102, 103, 104, 105-106, 108, 109, 110, 132, 133. See also Sino-Soviet split
and Third World, 7
See also Chinese Communist Party; under India; Japan; Kampuchea; North Korea; Pakistan; South Korea; United States; Vietnam
China/Taiwan, 6, 67, 80, 99, 155, 157, 158, 160, 161
Chinese Communist Party (CCP), 96, 98
Chinese Revolution (1911), 95
Chinhae (S. Korea), 79
"Choke point" strategy, 43, 51
Chongjin Thermal Power Station (N. Korea), 90
Chou En-lai, 7, 98
Chromium, 51
CINCPAC. See Commander-in-Chief, U.S. Pacific Command
Civil Aviation Administration of China (CAAC), 88
Clark Air Base (Philippines), 107
Class struggle, 3, 4
CMEA. See Council for Mutual Economic Assistance
Coal, 49
Cobalt, 51
Cockburn Sound (Australia), 115
Cold War, 63
Collective security pacts, 23-24, 25-26, 29, 30
and military access, 28, 29, 38, 39, 45, 55, 89
subsystems, 27-28, 29

180

Colorado, 115
Columbo Conference, 107
COMECON. See Communist
    Council for Mutual
    Economic Assistance
Comintern, 96
Commander-in-Chief, U.S.
    Pacific Command
    (CINCPAC), 81
Communism, 4, 5, 132, 144,
    167, 168
Communist Council for
    Mutual Economic
    Assistance
    (COMECON), 25
Communist parties, 24, 38,
    96, 120, 131. See also
    individual names
Communist Party of the
    Soviet Union (CPSU), 1,
    3, 5, 8, 28, 75, 96
    Central Committee, 46,
    74, 169
    Central Committee
    International
    Department, 71
    Congresses, 2, 5, 46, 86
    Politburo, 75
Communist Saur Revolution
    (1978) (Afghanistan),
    144
CONDOR military air
    transport, 29
Confucian economic zone of
    East Asia, 160
Consultation clauses, 25
Contact clauses, 25
Cook Islands, 126
Copper, 49
Cordon sanitaire, 101
Correlation of forces, 1, 9,
    19-20, 75
Cossacks, 95
Cotton, 49
Council for Mutual Economic
    Assistance (CMEA, 67,
    104

CPI. See India, Communist Party
    of
CPSU. See Communist Party of
    the Soviet Union
Crowe, William J., Jr., 80-81
Cruise missiles, 33-34, 35, 75
Cruisers, 36, 37, 106
Cuba, 24, 25, 30, 107, 108
Cultural assimilation, 69
Cultural Revolution (PRC), 98
Cutler (Me.), 114

Dahlak (Ethiopia), 39
Damanskii (Chenpao) island, 97
Danang (Vietnam), 28, 67, 73, 107,
    162
Darwin (Australia), 115
Davis Cub Eastern Zone rounds
    (PRC), 90
Defense, U.S. Department of, 27
Defense of Japan, 1982 (JDA), 77
Defense White Paper (1984)
    (Japan), 80
DELTA submarines, 36, 41, 73, 115
Demilitarized Zone (DMZ), 91
Democratic socialist parties
    (Asian), 167
Democratic Socialist Party (DSP)
    (Japan), 74, 166-167, 168,
    169, 170
Deng Xiaoping, 8, 86, 102
"Deng Xiaoping Trail," 105
Denmark, 119
Destroyers, 36, 37, 107
    Japanese, 77
    U.S., 82
Detente, 3-4, 5, 7, 12, 13, 16, 46
Deterrence, 4
Dhofar rebellion (Oman), 150
Dien Bien Puh (Vietnam), battle of
    (1954), 103
Diesel-powered submarines, 37
Dmitry Mendeleev (Soviet
    hydrographic ship), 125
DMZ. See Demilitarized Zone
Dong, Pham Van, 104
DSP. See Democratic Socialist

181

Party
Dulles, John Foster, 72
Durand, Mortimer, 136
Durand Line, 136, 138

East Europe, 12, 15, 23, 24, 25
East-West relations, 49, 61
Economic and Social Commission for Asia and the Pacific (ESCAP), 122
Egypt, 24, 30, 143, 148
Electronic intelligence ships, 126
El Salvador, 14
ESCAP. See Economic and Social Commission for Asia and the Pacific
Ethiopia, 24, 25, 27, 30, 39, 42
Etorofu (island), 78, 79
Eurasian strategy, 23, 24, 27, 28, 30
Europe, 17, 24, 48, 62, 64, 156. See also East Europe; West Europe
European Community, 158, 162
Exmouth (Australia), 115

FA-18 fighters (Australia), 116
Fairbanks, Richard M., III, 160
FENCER fighter aircraft, 35
Fiji, 18, 122, 125, 127, 128
Finland, 64
FISHBED fighter aircraft, 35
Fishing fleet, 124-125, 126, 127
FITTER-C fighter aircraft, 37
FLANKER fighter aircraft, 35
FLOGGER fighter aircraft, 35

F-111 fighter bombers (Australia), 116
Foodstuffs, 123, 124, 127, 157
Ford, Gerald, 19
Foreign capital, 21, 47
FORGER vertical take-off aircraft, 36
Forward deployments, 42
Foster, Richard B., 26
Four modernizations program (PRC), 8, 47, 100
France, 13, 62, 80, 103, 124, 148, 171
  nuclear testing, 119
  Pacific colonies, 122
  in Soviet view, 2, 3
French Polynesia, 122, 127
Frigates, 77, 102, 106
FROGFOOT ground-attack aircraft, 34
Fry, Gregory E., 126
F-16 fighters (U.S.), 73, 75, 79
Fuel-air explosives, 15
FULCRUM fighter aircraft, 35

Gallup poll, 170
Gandhi, Indira, 137
Gang of Four, 98
Germany, 62. See also West Germany
Gibraltar, 43
Gilgit (Pakistan), 132
GNP (gross national product). See under Japan; Pacific Basin; Soviet Union; United States
Gonzales, Felipe, 166
Gorbachev, Mikhail, 1, 8, 99
Gorshkov, S.B., 52, 53, 54
Great Britain, 13, 43, 58, 72, 80, 119, 131, 136, 148, 149, 151, 171
  in Soviet view, 2, 3
Great Leap Forward (PRC), 97
Grenada, 14
Gromyko, Andrei, 72, 75
Gross national product (GNP). See under

Japan; Pacific Basin;
Soviet Union; United
States
Ground Self-Defense Force
(GSDF) (Japan), 77, 80,
81
Grumman E-2C aircraft
(Japan), 80
GSDF. See Ground Self-
Defense Force
Guam, 80, 117
Gunboats, 106

Habomai (island), 78
Hainan (island), 106
Haiphong (Vietnam), 102
Hanks, Robert J., 53
HARPOON stand-off missile,
116
Hasselkorn, Avigdor, 26, 27
HAWK anti-aircraft artillery
groups (Japan), 77
Hegemony, 99, 110
Helicopters, 34, 37, 80
HELIX helicopter, 37
Heng Samrin, 104, 109
HIND helicopters, 34
Hindu Kush, 138
Hitler, Adolf, 62
Ho Chi Minh, 103
Ho Chi Minh City (Vietnam),
107
Hokkaido, 42, 56, 71, 72, 77,
78, 79, 81, 164, 170
fishermen, 75
Hokkaido University Slavic
Research Center, 78
Holland, 96
Hong Kong, 43, 88, 157, 161
Honne stance (Japan), 82
Honshu, 72, 73, 79
Horie, Masao, 170
HORMONE helicopter, 37
Hormuz, Strait of, 146
Hu Na, 99
Hungary, 123
Hussein, Saddam, 149

Hu Yaobang, 86, 88, 98
Hydrographic research, 122

ICBMs. See Intercontinental
ballistic missiles
ICFTU. See International
Confederation of Free Trade
Unions
Il-76 CANDID military air
transport, 29, 35-36
Imperialism, 5, 8, 15, 42
India, 24, 30, 45, 46, 47, 64, 96,
131, 133, 134, 137-138, 146
air force, 131, 132, 135
army, 132, 137
Communist Party of (CPI), 131
Congress Party, 131
democratic socialist party, 167,
168
and Far East Soviet collective
security system, 27, 29
and Great Britain, 131, 136
Janata government, 134
navy, 132
and Pakistan, 134-135, 136,
137, 138, 139. See also
India-Pakistan war
and PRC, 131
and U.S., 47, 131
India-Bangladesh Treaty of
Friendship and Cooperation
(1974), 24
Indian Ocean, 26, 27, 33, 39, 42,
67, 74, 101, 102, 107, 110,
114, 115, 122, 133, 134, 146
India-Pakistan war (1965, 1971),
30, 132, 136
Indochina, 8, 29, 55, 63, 67, 113,
161, 162, 168
Indochinese Communist Party, 104
Indonesia, 6, 8, 43, 82, 101, 103,
110, 123, 157, 167
Indonesian archipelago, 101
Indus River, 138
INF. See Intermediate-Range
Nuclear Force
Information policy, 16, 171

Intercontinental ballistic
missiles (ICBMs), 18,
33, 40, 115, 126
launchers, 33
Intermediate-range missiles.
See SS-20
intermediate-range
missiles
Intermediate-Range Nuclear
Force (INF), 13, 61
International Confederation
of Free Trade Unions
(ICFTU), 170
Iran, 38, 64, 108, 133, 144,
146, 147, 150, 153
shah, 150, 151
Iran-Iraq war, 146
Iraq, 24, 27, 29, 38, 146, 148-
149
communists, 148, 149
Islamic fundamentalism, 151,
153
Israel, 30, 38
Ito, Soichiro, 159
IVAN. See ROGOV-class
amphibious ships
Ivan IV (tsar of Russia), 95
Iwakuni (Japan), 79
Izvestia (Moscow), 5, 119

"JANZUS" treaty, 120
Japan, 6, 87, 91, 114, 117,
120
air defense. See Air Self-
Defense Force
army See Ground Self-
Defense Force
and ASEAN, 68, 82-83,
158
coast guard. See
Maritime Safety
Agency
Confederation of labor,
170
defense budget, 74, 80,
81, 83, 165-166
defense strategy, 57-58,

59, 74, 77-83, 160, 163-
164, 166, 167, 170, 171, 172.
See also Self-Defense Force;
"Three non-nuclear
principles"
economy, 3, 71, 74, 158, 160,
172
Foreign Affairs, Ministry of,
160
GNP, 80, 160, 165
mass media, 164, 165
Ministry of International Trade
and Industry (MITI), 160
navy. See Maritime Self-
Defense Force
Northern Territories (Soviet-
occupied), 19, 35, 49, 66, 72,
73, 75, 78-79, 81, 108, 164,
168, 170, 171
pacifism, 164
and Persian Gulf area, 145-146,
152
political parties, 74, 96, 165,
166, 167, 171
and PRC, 47, 52, 54, 71
and Soviet Union, 8, 9, 15, 18,
20, 22, 24, 25, 35, 41, 42, 43,
45, 46, 48-49, 55, 56, 57, 59,
62, 63, 64, 65-66, 71-75, 78,
79, 82, 83, 91, 95-96, 108,
162, 163, 164, 166-167, 168,
169, 170-171, 172
straits, 72, 75, 79. See also
specific names
textbook history of World War
II, 83
and U.S., 43, 44, 54, 56, 57, 58,
59, 63, 72, 75, 79-80, 81-82,
83, 119, 156, 157, 160, 163,
166, 167, 169, 172
See also Pacific Basin
Japan, Sea of, 8, 37, 52, 55, 56, 79,
117
Japan Defense Agency (JDA),
77
Japanese Communist Party
(1922), 96

184

Japan Socialist Party (JSP), 74, 165, 167
Japan-U.S. Security Treaty, 63, 65, 66, 166, 167
JDA. See Japan Defense Agency
Jim Creek (Wash.), 114
JSP. See Japan Socialist party
"Juche" ideology (N. Korea), 86
Just war, 4

Kabul (Afghanistan), 133
Kallisto (Soviet hydrographic ship), 122, 125
Kamchatka peninsula, 52, 78
Kampuchea, 5, 8, 24, 28, 29, 30, 40, 45, 67, 68, 98, 101, 103, 104-105, 106, 108, 109, 155, 162, 168
and PRC, 105
Kampuchean United Front for National Salvation, 104
Kanak Liberation (Melanesia), 122, 123
Kapitsa, Mikhail, 82
KARA-class cruiser, 37
Karakoram (mountains), 133
Kashmir, 137
Kenilorea, Peter, 122
Kerguelen Island, 121
Khabarovsk region (Soviet Union), 73
Khmer People's National Liberation Front (KPNLF), 109
Khmer Rouge, 104, 105, 109
Khomeini, Ruhollah (ayatollah), 150
Khrushchev, Nikita, 3, 5, 20, 96, 97, 143
KIEV-class aircraft carrier, 36
KILO-class submarines, 37
Kimchaek Steel Refinery

Complex (N. Korea), 90
Kim Chong-il 66, 86, 87, 89
Kim Il-Sung, 66, 86, 88, 89, 90, 91
Kimura, Hiroshi, 78
Kiribatim, 125
Kirov (cruiser), 36
Kola peninsula, 73
Kompong Som (Kampuchea), 67, 107
Korean Airlines Flight 007 shooting (1983), 66, 90
Korean peninsula, 57, 66, 72, 79, 85, 91, 155, 161
Korean war, 6
KPNLF. See Khmer People's National Liberation Front
KRESTA II cruisers, 106
KRIVAK destroyer, 107
Kunaev, D., 75
Kunashir (island), 78
Kurdish rebels, 149
Kurile Islands, 15, 55, 72, 73, 78
Kushiro (Hokkaido), 71
Kuwait, 144, 151
KYNDA-class cruiser, 36
Kyushu, 79

Labor unions, 170
Lange, David, 82
Lang Son (Vietnam), 106
Lao People's Democratic Republic (1976), 104
Laos, 5, 8, 40, 67, 68, 101, 104, 105, 109, 155, 168
Latin America, 161
LDP. See Liberal Democratic Party
Lebanon, 38
Lenin, V.I., 1, 2, 4, 96
Lenin anniversary address (1975), 5
Leninism, 1, 2
Liberal Democratic Party (LDP) (Japan), 171
Libya, 122, 127
Line Islands, 126
Look-down/shoot-down

system, 35
Lumber, 49, 157

Mackinder, Halford John, 11, 29
McLaurin, Robert L., 146
McNamara, Robert, 131
Mahan, Alfred Thayer, 11
Maine, 114
Malacca, Strait of, 42, 107, 108
Malaysia, 6, 45, 48, 58, 102, 108, 167, 168
Mamaloni, Solomon, 121
Manchuria, 95
Manganese, 51
"Mao's Group," 24
Mao Zedong, 6, 7, 86, 96, 97, 98
Mara, Kamisese, 122
Marine transportation routes, 67, 73
Maritime Safety Agency (Japan), 80
Maritime Self-Defense Force (MSDF) (Japan), 43, 44, 57, 58, 77, 80, 81
Marxist-Leninist parties, 5, 6, 69
Marxist-Leninist theory, 2, 11, 96-97, 145, 163, 167-168
Mauritius, 127
MBFR. See Mutual and Balanced Force Reductions
Meat. See Foodstuffs
Mediterranean Sea, 27
Melanesia, 122
Menon, Rajan, 71
Menon, V.K. Krishna, 132
Merchant Marine, 125
Mexico, 157
Middle East, 27, 55, 74, 117
and Soviet policy, 3, 24, 143-144, 147-149
Middle Eastern War. See

Arab-Israeli conflict
MIDWAY-class aircraft carriers (U.S.), 41
MiG-23 fighters, 73, 79
MIKE-class nuclear attack submarines, 37, 128
Miki, Takeo, 80
Military overflight privileges, 39
Mineral resources, 28, 49, 51, 134
Minsk (aircraft carrier), 36, 43, 102, 107
Misawa (Honshu), 73, 75, 79
MITI. See Japan, Ministry of International Trade and Industry
Mongolia, 5, 8, 24, 25, 26, 34, 46, 47, 64, 96, 162
Mongolian control, 62
Mongolian People's Party, 96
Moscow Radio, 24
Motorized rifle divisions, 15, 34
Motorized tank divisions, 34
Movement for the Liberation of Angola (MPLA), 30
Mozambique, 15, 24, 107, 127
MPLA. See Popular Movement for the Liberation of Angola
MSDF. See Maritime Self-Defense Force
Mutton, 124
Mutual and Balanced Force Reductions (MBFR), 18

Nagasue, Eiichi, 166
Najin (N. Korea), 64, 87
Nakao, Eiichi, 163
Nakasone, Yasuhiro, 56, 74, 75, 80, 82-83, 164, 165
Nansha. See Spratly Islands
NANUCHKA guided missile patrol craft, 37
Napoleon (emperor of the French), 62
Nasser, Gamal Abdul, 148
National Command Authorities (NCA),

U.S., 115
National Defense
Program Outline
(NDPO) (Japan), 77
National Liberation wars,
4, 109
NATO. See North Atlantic
Treaty Organization
Natural gas, 49, 134
NCA. See National
Command Authorities
NDPO. See National Defense
Program Outline
Nehru, Jawaharlal, 132
Nemuro Strait, 72
Nepal, 131, 167
Neutral countries, 64
New Caledonia, 122, 127
New Zealand, 58, 82, 113,
114, 116-117, 118, 119,
120, 121, 122,, 123,
124, 125, 126, 127, 128
and ASEAN, 158
Communist Party of, 120
Labor government, 118
Socialist Unity Party, 120
N-42 anti-aircraft gun, 77
Nicaragua, 14
Nickel, 122
NIKE-J missiles, 77, 80
Nixon, Richard M., 3, 5, 7, 98
Non-aligned countries, 47,
107
Non-ferrous metals, 49
"Nordpolitik," 90
North Atlantic Treaty
Organization (NATO),
13, 26, 62, 169
Northern Fleet, 15
Northern Territories. See
under Japan
North Korea, 5, 8, 35, 45, 46,
47, 57, 66, 85-90, 91,
92, 162, 170
defense share of GNP, 89
economy, 161
foreign debt, 90

and PRC, 64, 85, 86, 87,
88, 91, 92, 161-162
Seven-Year Development
Plan (1978-1984), 90
and South Korea, 85, 87,
88, 91, 92, 162
and U.S., 89, 91
North West Cape (Aus-
tralia), 114, 115, 118,
119
North West Frontier, 136
North Yemen, 24, 27, 149
Norway, 119
Nuclear first strike
capability, 26
Nuclear-free zone, 119, 169
Nuclear Non-Proliferation
Treaty (1968), 39
Nuclear powered ballistic
missile submarines
(SSBN), 26, 27, 28, 36,
37, 40, 53, 56, 73, 115
Nuclear powered guided missile
cruiser, 36
Nuclear war, 4, 7, 114
Nurrungar (Australia), 115
118, 119

OBERON-class submarine
(Australia), 116
Oceania, 113, 114, 116, 117, 118,
119, 120-121, 122-123, 125,
126, 127, 128, 161
OECD. See Organization for
Economic Cooperation and
Development
Ogaden, 30
Ogasawara Islands, 58
Ohira, Masayoshi, 160
Oil, 3, 27, 38, 49, 51, 108, 143, 144,
145, 146, 149, 151, 157,
Ikean II global exercises, 73
Okhotsk, Sea of, 8, 56, 73
Okinawa, 73
Olympic Games (Seoul) (1988), 90
Oman, 150
"One-state socialism" (PRC),

97
Organization for Economic Cooperation and Development (OECD), 161
OSCAR submarines, 41
Ottoman Turkish Empire, 62-63
Outer Mongolia, 95
Overland invasion routes, 14, 49

Pacific Basin, 155-156, 158-159, 160-163
  GNP, 160
  population, 160
  See also Asia; individual countries
Pacific Basin Community proposal, 161
Pacific Fleet, 15, 18, 19, 36, 37, 39, 42, 52, 64, 73, 79, 106, 107, 114, 115, 155, 162
  naval infantry, 37
Pacific Ocean, 33, 42, 49, 55, 63, 67, 80, 101, 107, 110, 114, 116, 156
"Pacific Pact," 120
Pakistan, 24, 30, 64, 108, 109, 131, 132, 133, 136, 138-139, 144, 153
  Communist Party of, 131
  military, 135, 136, 138, 139
  nuclear program, 134, 135
  and PRC, 132
  and U.S., 131, 137
  See also under India
Palme, Olof, 166
Pan American World Airways, 99
Panjsher Valley (Afghanistan), 38
Papua New Guinea, 117, 118, 122, 123, 127, 155
Pathet Lao, 104
PATRIOT missile system

(Japan), 80
Patrol craft, 37
PDPA. See People's Democratic Party of Afghanistan
"Peace Constitution" (Japan), 74
Peaceful coexistence, 1-2, 3, 4, 5, 8, 64, 97
Peking National University, 96
People's Democratic Party of Afghanistan (PDPA), 145. See also Afghanistan, Communist party
People's Liberation Army (PRC), 106
Persian Gulf, 27, 33, 38, 42, 74, 117, 133, 134, 145-147, 148, 149-153, 163
Perth (Australia), 115, 116
Petropavlovsk (Soviet Union), 52, 73
Philippines, 6, 8, 39, 45, 48, 49, 55, 57, 58, 62, 67, 73, 80, 82, 101, 102, 117, 119, 123
Phnom Penh (Kampuchea) 28, 104
Pine Gap (Australia), 115, 118, 119
Poland, 62, 132
POLARIS missiles (U.S.), 26
Pol Pot, 101, 104, 105, 109
Popular Movement for the Liberation of Angola (MPLA), 30
Port Augusta (Australia), 115
Port Pirie (Australia), 115
POSEIDON submarine (U.S.), 114
Post-revolutionary society, 20
Power projection, 42, 43
Powles, Guy, 120
Pravda (Moscow), 4, 5, 7, 8, 20, 104
PRC. See China, People's Republic of
Professor Bogorov (Soviet hydrographic ship), 125
Proletariat, 5

Propaganda, 63, 82, 171
P-3C ORION anti-submarine
    patrol planes
    Australian, 116, 128
    Japanese, 80
Pyongyang Generator Plant
    (N. Korea), 90

Qasim, Abdul Karim, 148

Radar, phased-array, 40
Radford-Collins Agreement,
    117
Rajasthan (India), 135, 136
Rangoon (Burma), 167
Rapid Deployment Force
    (U.S.), 151
Reagan, Ronald, 99
Ream (Kampuchea), 67
Red Army, 96
Red Sea, 42
Revolution, 4, 5, 20
ROGOV-class amphibious
    ships, 37, 43
Rubber, 48
Rumania, 24, 25
Rumoi (Hokkaido), 72
Russianization, 64, 65, 68
Russian Revolution (1917),
    95, 96
Russo-Japanese war (1905),
    44

SA-5 missiles, 38
Saigon. See Ho Chi Minh
    City
Sakhalin Island, 72, 79, 126
Sallal, Abdullah, 149
SALT. See Strategic Arms
    Limitation Talks
Sann, Son, 109
SARC. See South Asian
    Regional Council
Sasebo (Japan), 79
Satellite surveillance
    systems (U.S.), 115
Saudi Arabia, 144, 149, 150-

    151
SAVAK (Iranian internal security
    force), 150
Schmidt, Helmut, 166
Scientific Research Institute
    (Sakhalin), 125-126
SDF. See Self-Defense Force
Sealane interdiction, 52, 53, 55,
    56, 57, 79, 102, 162
Sea lines of communication, 14,
    16, 19, 42, 53, 55-56, 102,
    107, 116-117
Sea Power of the State, The
    (Gorshkov), 53
SEATO. See South East Asia
    Treaty Organization
Second economy, 21
Self-Defense Force (SDF)
    (Japan), 77, 78, 81, 165, 167
Semijonov, Gregori Mikhailovich,
    95-96
Shen Tu, 88
Shikotan (island), 78
Ship construction, 52
Shultz, George, 158, 159
Siberia, 8, 22, 49, 75, 85, 95,
    115, 163
Sibir Khan (state), 95
SIERRA-class nuclear attack
    submarines, 37, 128
Sihanouk, Norodom (prince of
    Cambodia), 109
Sind (Pakistan) 135, 136
Singapore, 6, 43, 45, 48, 58, 108,
    161, 170
    Socialist Party, 167
Sino-Japanese rapprochement, 71
Sino-Soviet split (1960), 6, 8, 24,
    26, 45, 63, 96-98, 101
Sino-Vietnam war (1979), 29
SLBMs. See Submarine-launched
    ballistic missiles
Social conflict, 2, 5
Social Democrats (European), 166
Socialism, 2, 3, 5, 8, 11, 65, 97,
    118
Socialist International, 166, 167

Socialist Unity Party. See
    under New Zealand
Socialist world order, 26
Solomon Islands, 121, 122,
    127, 128, 169
    Labor Party, 170
Somalia, 24, 30, 143
South Africa, 43
South Asian Regional Council
    (SARC), 134
South China Sea, 29, 39, 43,
    55, 63, 67, 102, 105,
    106, 107, 117
South East Asia Treaty
    Organization (SEATO),
    131, 147
Southern Africa, 15, 28
South Korea, 6, 8, 35, 57, 58,
    62, 66, 79, 88, 90, 114,
    161
    economy, 158, 160
    industry, 90
    and PRC, 88, 90, 93-
    94(n14), 161
    Uniform Socialist Party,
    167
    See also under North
    Korea; United States
South Pacific Forum, 122,
    128
South Seas Eskadra, 107
South Yemen, 24, 25, 27, 38-
    39, 42, 108, 149-150
Sovetskaya Gavan (Soviet
    Union), 73
Soviet-Afghan Treaty of
    Friendship, Good-
    Neighborliness, and
    Cooperation (1978),
    25
Soviet-Cuba Mutual Cooper-
    ation Treaty (1972), 25
Soviet-Egypt Treaty of
    Friendship and Cooper-
    ation (1971), 24, 30
Soviet-India Peace, Friend-
    ship, and Cooperation

Treaty (1971), 24, 132
Sovietization, 134
Soviet-Japan Treaty of Good-
    Neighborliness and
    Cooperation proposal,
    25, 70(n6), 74, 76(n4)
Soviet military air transport
    (VTA), 29
Soviet Military Power (U.S. Dept.
    of Defense), 27, 29
Soviet-Mongolian Mutual Assis-
    tance Treaty, 25
Soviet Union
    air forces, 8, 15, 19, 26, 28,
    29, 34-36, 37, 39, 41, 45,
    56, 57, 73, 79
    as Asian nation, 23, 30, 62,
    140(n10)
    Central Asia, 47
    eastern, 17-18, 26, 33
    economic aid from, 3, 47,
    85, 89, 90, 92, 102, 131,
    149
    economy, 21, 22, 90, 108, 172
    Far Eastern Maritime District,
    85, 113
    Far Eastern military districts,
    18, 34, 35
    Far Eastern Theater, 8, 27, 169
    five-year plans, 20
    geopolitics, 1-2, 4, 11-16, 17,
    42, 66, 86
    GNP, 20
    ground forces, 18, 19, 26, 34,
    51, 57, 64, 73, 155
    industry, 21
    and internal reform, 21
    international relations, 1, 2, 3,
    4. See also Capitalist states;
    Collective security pacts;
    Detente; Peaceful
    coexistence
    life expectancy in, 20-21
    military assistance from, 3, 28,
    29, 30, 38-39, 47, 68, 85, 89,
    92, 131-132, 148, 149, 150
    and military force, 1, 22, 29, 40,

51, 54-57, 117
military power, 8, 11, 12,
  15, 17, 21-22, 23, 26,
  33-37, 40, 42, 45, 52,
  61-62, 69, 72-73, 74,
  77-78, 102, 108, 159,
  162, 163, 167, 169, 170-
  171, 172
navy, 8, 15, 18, 19, 26,
  28-29, 36-37, 38, 39,
  41, 42, 43, 45, 52-54,
  55, 56-57, 64, 73, 78,
  79, 85, 102, 106, 107,
  114, 115, 117, 125, 126,
  127-128, 155, 162, 168-
  169, 170
non-military strategy, 20,
  22, 45-49, 61, 62,
  63, 102, 147, 163, 171.
  See also Soviet Union,
  and political influence;
  Soviet Union, trade
nuclear power, 4, 15, 18,
  26, 28-29, 33-34, 53,
  62, 169
oceanographic research,
  125-126
as Pacific nation, 23, 162
and political influence,
  63-69, 74, 75, 102, 118,
  120-123, 127, 143, 148,
  153, 170
population, 23
security, 4, 63, 113, 147
Southern Theater, 27
trade, 18, 46-49, 65, 99,
  123-125, 126-127, 131,
  162
Western Theater, 27
world view, 2, 4, 5, 17, 19
See also Asia; Communist
  Party of the Soviet
  Union; individual
  countries; under China,
  People's Republic of;
  Japan; United States
Soviet-Vietnam Treaty of

Friendship and
  Cooperation (1978), 104,
  106
SOVREMENNYY destroyer, 36
Soya Strait, 55, 56, 72, 79
Spain, 166
Spender, P.C., 72
Spratly Islands, 105, 106
Sri Lanka, 131, 167
SSBNs. See Nuclear powered
  ballistic missile sub-
  marines
SS-4 missiles, 34
SS-5 missiles, 34
SS-11 missiles, 115
SS-18 missiles, 115
SS-20 intermediate-
  range missiles, 15, 18,
  26, 34, 45, 56, 65, 155
  deployment, 61, 62, 74, 78, 164,
  169, 171
  launchers, 34
  reentry vehicles, 34
SS-21 missiles, 38
SS-N-18 missiles, 36
SS-N-20 missiles, 36
SS-NX-23 missiles, 36
SS-NX-24 missiles, 33
SS-NX-25 missiles, 33, 40
Stalin, Joseph, 1, 2, 4, 6,
  71, 96
Stanford Research Inter-
  national, 26
Sternberg, Ungern von, 96
Strategic Arms Limitation
  Talks (SALT)
  I (1972), 39, 40
  II, 13, 40
Strategic Studies Center
  (Stanford Research
  International), 26
Subic Bay (Philippines),
  39, 107
Submarine-launched ballistic
  missiles (SLBMs), 40, 126
Submarines, 36, 37, 38, 39-40, 41,
  52, 53, 56, 73, 102, 107,

115, 117, 126, 128
Australian, 116
Japanese, 77, 80
U.S., 114, 115
Subsonic missiles, 34
Suez, 43
Sugar, 157
Summits (U.S. and Soviet
Union), 4,19
Sun Tzu, 51, 52
Supersonic aircraft, 35
Supersonic anti-ship
missiles, 36
Surface ships, 36-37, 38,
41
Surface-to-air-missiles,
38, 80
Surface-to-surface
missiles, 38
Suslov, Mikhail, 5
Suzuki, Zenko, 79, 80
Sweden, 64, 166
Syria, 24, 27, 38, 148

Tactical air power, 15
Taiwan. See China/Taiwan
Tanaka, Kahuei, 49
Tanikawa, Kazuo, 171
Tank-landing ship, 107
Tanks, 34
Taraki, Nur Mohammad, 144
TASS (Soviet news agency),
74
Tatemae stance (Japan), 82
Technology, 12, 14, 21, 22,
41, 42, 46, 47
Soviet vs. U.S., 100
Telemetry encryption, 40
Thailand, 6, 29, 45, 48, 58,
103, 105, 107, 108, 109,
168
Communist Party of, 105
Thailand, Bay of, 168
Third World, 7, 13, 15, 42,
143, 152
Thompson, W. Scott, 146
"Three non-nuclear

principles" (Japan), 74,
75, 81-82, 167, 169
Threshold Test Ban Treaty,
40
Tin, 157
Togo, Heihachiro, 44
TOMAHAWK Cruise missiles
(U.S.), 34, 75
Tonga, 118, 121, 126, 127, 128
Tonkin, Gulf of, 43, 102
Toxin weapons, 40
Trans-Siberian railway, 114
TRIDENT submarines (U.S.), 114,
115
Tripartite talks. See North Korea,
and South Korea
Truman, Harry, 71
T-72, 34
Tsugaru Strait, 72, 79
Tsushima Strait, 29, 56, 57,
72, 79
Tudeh Communist party (Iran),
38, 150
Tuna, 125
Tu-95 BEAR long-range recon-
naissance aircraft, 29, 107
Turkey, 64
Turnkey project (Philippines), 48
Tu-16 BADGER medium bombers,
102
TYPHOON submarines, 36, 41

UDALOY destroyer, 37
Underground nuclear tests, 40
United Nations, 105, 109, 122, 145
United States
air force, 79
and ASEAN, 157, 158
and Asian countries, 6, 9, 14,
16, 42, 43, 48, 58, 59, 63,
68, 87, 103, 156-158, 160
and Caribbean, 14
and Central America, 14
and China/Taiwan, 99
containment policy, 12
and European trade, 156
GNP, 156, 160

Indian Ocean forces, 26,
67, 114
and Middle East, 143,
145-146, 147, 148, 150,
151, 152, 153,
navy, 27, 41, 44, 56, 58,
79
nuclear power, 4, 26, 27,
28, 34, 62
Pacific Ocean forces and
bases, 26, 39, 44, 56,
57, 58, 67, 73, 74, 75,
79, 107, 113, 114-115,
116, 117, 118, 119
and PRC, 7, 52, 54, 78,
97, 98, 99, 100
Sixth and Seventh Fleets,
27
and South Korea, 85, 87,
89, 157, 162
and Soviet Union, 13, 26,
27, 28, 41, 51, 52, 55,
78, 91, 108, 120, 124,
144, 162, 169, 170-171.
See also Arms control;
Detente
in Soviet view, 2, 3, 4,
71, 87
trade, 156-157, 160
See also under India;
Japan; North Korea;
Pakistan
Ural mountains, 62, 95
Uruguay, 123
U.S. First Marine Aircraft
Wing, 79
Ussuri River border con-
flicts (1969), 26, 97

Vanuatu, 121, 122, 127, 128
Verification, 40, 169
Vertical short take-off and
landing (V/STOL), 36,
107
Very Low Frequency (VLF)
facilities, 114, 115
VICTOR III submarines, 37,

41
Vietnam, 4, 5, 8, 24, 27,
28, 29, 30, 42, 45, 46,
47, 51, 52, 54, 64, 67,
68, 89, 90, 98,101, 102,
103, 104, 106-109, 114,
133, 155, 162, 168, 170
agriculture, 108
Chinese in, 63
and Laos, 104, 168
navy, 102
and PRC, 29, 52, 54, 68, 103,
105, 106
See also Cam Ranh Bay;
Danang; Kampuchea; Sino-
Vietnam war
Vietnam-Cambodia Treaty of
Peace, Friendship, and
Cooperation (1979), 24,
104
Vietnam war (1965-1975), 6,
103, 168
Vitiaz (Soviet hydrographic
ship), 125
Vladivostock (Soviet Union),
19, 52, 64, 73, 79, 113,
114, 125, 168
Vladivostock-Vostochnyy-
Nakhodka naval complex,
85
VLF. See Very Low Frequency
facilities
V/STOL. See Vertical short
take-off and landing
VTA. See Soviet military air
transport

Wakhan corridor, 133
War capability, 52-53, 54-57
Warm-water ports, 137, 146
Warsaw Pact, 24-25, 27, 31
(nn2, 3), 43, 169
Washington, 114
Western Samoa, 118, 126, 128
Labor Party, 170
West Europe, 3, 12, 13, 68, 120,
152, 153

West Germany, 13, 80, 148, 166, 171

WFTU. See World Federation of Trade Unions

Whampoa (PRC), 107

White Army, 96

White Russians, 95

Whyalla (Australia), 115

Wool, 123, 124, 127, 157

Woomera (Australia), 115

Workers University of the Far East (Moscow), 96

World Conference of Communist Parties (1969), 24

World Federation of Trade Unions (WFTU), 170

World resources, 2, 51, 121, 147

World War II, 71, 83

Xinjiang Province (PRC), 96, 97, 132

Yalta Conference (1945), 72

Yang Tezhi, 105

YANKEE submarines, 36, 39-40

Yellow Sea, 57

Yermak (Cossack), 95

Yevtushenko, Yevgeny, 18

Yomiuri Shimbun (Tokyo), 170

Yulin (PRC), 107

Yumen (PRC), 97

Zhanjiang (PRC), 107

Zhao Ziyang, 86, 102

Zia ul-Haq, Mohammad, 134, 135